Reconstruction in the Cane Fields

The Sugar Harvest in Louisiana, by A. R. Waud.
Harper's Weekly, October 30, 1875

Reconstruction

in the

Cane Fields

§§

From Slavery to Free Labor
in Louisiana's Sugar Parishes
1862–1880

JOHN C. RODRIGUE

LOUISIANA STATE UNIVERSITY PRESS
Baton Rouge

12 11 10 09 08 07 06 05 04 03
6 5 4 3 2

Designer: Melanie O'Quinn Samaha
Typeface: ACaslon
Typesetter: Crane Composition, Inc.
Printer and binder: Thomson-Shore, Inc.

Library of Congress Cataloging-in-Publication Data:
Rodrigue, John C.
    Reconstruction in the cane fields : from slavery to free labor in Louisiana's sugar parishes,
1862–1880 / John C. Rodrigue.
        p. cm.
Enlargement of author's thesis (doctoral)—Emory University.
Includes bibliographical references (p.) and index.
    ISBN 0-8071-2656-X (alk. paper) — ISBN 0-8071-2728-0 (pbk.: alk. paper)
    1. Sugar workers—Louisiana—History. 2. Plantation workers—Louisiana—History.
3. Slavery—Louisiana—History. 4. Slaves—Emancipation—Louisiana—History. 5. Sugarcane
industry—Louisiana—History. I. Title.
    HD8039.S85 U67 2001
    331.7'63361'09763—dc21

00-011767

to my parents

CONTENTS

§§

ILLUSTRATIONS

§ఫ

ACKNOWLEDGMENTS

It is a pleasure to acknowledge the assistance I have received in bringing this project to fruition. Financial support from the Department of History, the Graduate School of Arts and Sciences, and the Graduate Student Council of Emory University; the Frederick Douglass Institute for African and African-American Studies at the University of Rochester; and the Andrew W. Mellon Foundation all facilitated completion of the doctoral dissertation upon which this book is based. Supplemental research and writing were supported in part by a summer stipend from Louisiana State University's Council on Research in the Office of Research and Economic Development and by a Research Fellowship for Non-Tenured Faculty from LSU's College of Arts and Sciences, which provided a semester's leave to undertake final revisions on the manuscript.

I thank the professional staffs and student assistants of the various archives I had the pleasure to visit for their help and for permission to quote from and reproduce materials in their care. I am indebted as well to the staffs of the interlibrary loan offices of Emory University, the University of Rochester, the University of Maryland, and Louisiana State University.

The following scholars, colleagues, and friends have read all or parts of the manuscript, or have offered advice on matters large and small: Ira Berlin, Robert Calhoon, Paul A. Cimbala, Peter A. Coclanis, William J. Cooper Jr., Stanley L. Engerman, Karen E. Fields, Michael W. Fitzgerald, Elizabeth Fox-Genovese, Eugene D. Genovese, Steven Hahn, Rick Halpern, John A. Heitmann, Larry E. Hudson Jr., Joseph E. Inikori, Randall M. Miller, Robert L. Paquette, Paul F. Paskoff, Joseph P. Reidy, Charles Royster, Rebecca J. Scott, Charles J. Shindo, Clarence Walker, and Michael Wayne. I wish to extend special thanks to Louis Ferleger, an unstinting supporter who read several drafts of the manuscript, and to my colleague Gaines M. Foster, who also read more than one draft and who offered invaluable advice on how to condense the manuscript. In Gaines's case, I wish I had been able to reciprocate.

Parts of this study were presented at meetings of the Southern Historical Association, the Louisiana Historical Association, the Agricultural History Society, and the St. George Tucker Society. I thank fellow participants, commentators, and audiences for their questions and suggestions. Certain sections of this book have previously appeared in the *Journal of Southern History*, *Agricultural History*, and *The Freedmen's Bureau and Reconstruction: Reconsiderations*, edited by Paul A. Cimbala and Randall M. Miller. My thanks go to the two journals and to Fordham University Press for permission to reprint material herein.

Before joining LSU's history department, I had the privilege of serving an apprenticeship at the Freedmen and Southern Society Project at the University of Maryland, College Park. I express my deepest appreciation to my former colleagues Susan E. O'Donovan, Leslie S. Rowland, and especially Steven F. Miller, who, in addition to reading various parts of this study and offering much helpful advice, allowed me the opportunity to work with them and to learn a great deal from them about the historian's craft.

Nancy Barr and Mark Schantz, Martha and Steve Goodson, Mary-Margaret Johnston-Miller and James Miller, Mart Stewart, Kay Kimball, and John Merriman all provided essential moral support during my graduate school days and since. Dave Betten has assisted me in innumerable ways over the years, including putting me up during my research trip to Washington, D.C. Dave, along with Jim Thorpe, also helped to keep me sane in ways that perhaps only fellow natives of New Jersey can appreciate.

I count my blessings for having been given the opportunity to become a member of LSU's history department, where a reasonable teaching load (in these days of "accountability"), a collegial environment, and colleagues who are serious about their work—but not about themselves—afford a situation conducive to the life of the mind and help me remember why I wanted to become a historian in the first place.

My experiences with LSU Press have left me skeptical of everything I had heard about the adversarial relationship that authors are supposed to have with their publishers. My editor Maureen G. Hewitt steadfastly championed this project. Sylvia D. Frank, my unofficial editor, has, in the face of unrelenting authorial obstinateness, nonetheless managed to make this a much better book. Gerry Anders and Sara Anderson made the process of copy editing the manuscript a pleasure. I also wish to thank two readers of the manuscript who suggested revisions that were as challenging as they were beneficial. I trust they will not be too chagrined to be associated with this book, even anonymously.

Mr. Edward J. Gay III of Covington, Louisiana, graciously made available to me a photograph of his ancestor. Robert F. Pace designed the map.

James L. Roark, my dissertation adviser, mentor, and friend, has consistently proven over the years that all the good things I had heard about him when I was contemplating graduate study at Emory were actually gross understatements. As a scholar, teacher, and humanist, Jim has been a model whom I am not embarrassed to say I have tried to emulate. I doubt, however, that I would have responded with the same forbearance that Jim showed me to a student who turned in an almost two-hundred-page dissertation chapter.

To my family I owe my greatest debt. My sisters Ann-Marie, Jackie, and Terry, however distant in space, have been an invaluable source of love and support. The dedication of this book does not begin to express my gratitude to my parents, Maureen and John Rodrigue, for everything they have done.

Finally, I thank Sylvia for turning my life upside down.

༄༅

ABBREVIATIONS

AFP   Alexander Franklin Pugh

AFPP   Alexander Franklin Pugh Papers

Agt   Agent

AH   *Agricultural History*

AC   Assistant Commissioner

ASAC   Assistant Subassistant Commissioner

BRFAL   Records of the Bureau of Refugees, Freedmen, and Abandoned Lands, Record Group 105, National Archives, Washington, D.C. All BRFAL documents are from the Office of the Assistant Commissioner for Louisiana or from Subordinate Field Offices.

DP   *New Orleans Daily Picayune*

EJG   Edward J. Gay

EJGP   Edward J. Gay and Family Papers, LSU

Freedom 1 Ira Berlin et al., eds. *Freedom: A Documentary History of Emancipation, 1861–1867.* Ser. 1, Vol. 1, *The Destruction of Slavery.* Cambridge, U.K., 1985

Freedom 3 Ira Berlin et al., eds. *Freedom: A Documentary History of Emancipation, 1861–1867.* Ser. 1, Vol. 3, *The Wartime Genesis of Free Labor: The Lower South.* Cambridge, U.K., 1990

FSSP   Freedmen and Southern Society Project, University of Maryland, College Park. Alpha-numeric designations accompanying FSSP citations refer to the project's system for filing copies of National Archives documents, consulted at the FSSP.

HMD   House Miscellaneous Document

HR   House Report

JSH   *Journal of Southern History*

LHQ   *Louisiana Historical Quarterly*

LH   *Louisiana History*

LS   Letters Sent

LSU   Louisiana and Lower Mississippi Valley Collections, Hill Memorial Library, Louisiana State University, Baton Rouge

NILSB   *New Iberia Louisiana Sugar-Bowl*

NSU   Allen J. Ellender Archives, Allen J. Ellender Memorial Library, Nicholls State University, Thibodaux, Louisiana

RASP   *Records of Ante-Bellum Southern Plantations: From the Revolution through the Civil War.* Kenneth M. Stampp, gen. ed. *Ser. G: Selections from the Barker Texas History Center, University of Texas, Austin.* Part 1: *Texas and Louisiana Collections* (Frederick, Md., 1987); *Ser. I: Selections from Louisiana State University, Baton Rouge.* Part 1: *Louisiana Sugar Plantations* (Frederick, Md., 1989)

Rep(s). Report(s)

SAC   Subassistant Commissioner

SHC   Manuscripts Department, Southern Historical Collection, Wilson Library, University of North Carolina, Chapel Hill

UT   George W. Littlefield Southern History Collections, The Center for American History, University of Texas, Austin. Includes the Natchez Trace Collection and the Southern History Archival Collections.

WJMP   William J. Minor and Family Papers, LSU

Reconstruction in the Cane Fields

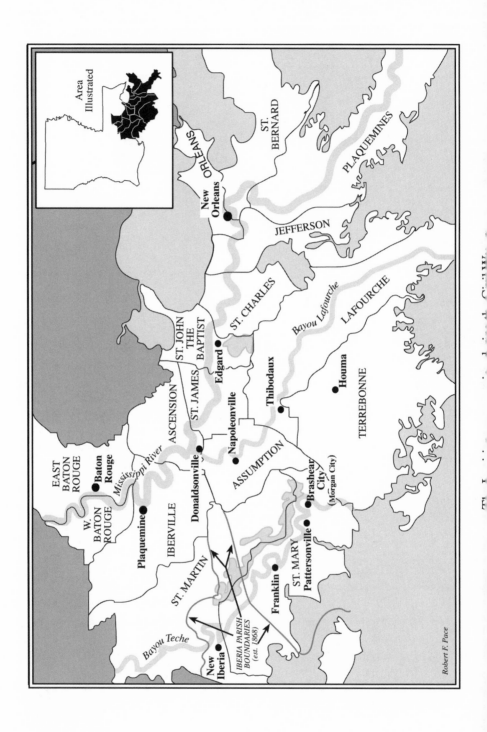

Robert F. Pace

§♭

INTRODUCTION

The destruction of slavery justifiably occupies a central place in American annals. Even as it seemed to mock the ideals upon which the United States was founded, slavery profoundly influenced the nation's economic, social, and political development. Because the peculiar institution lay at the very core of American life, its demise raised intractable problems concerning the future course of the nation. Not only did the abolition of slavery compel Americans to question the meaning of freedom, it forced the United States to do nothing less than re-create itself.

The present study looks at this process of re-creation by exploring emancipation and its consequences in one enclave of the American South—the cane sugar region of southern Louisiana—during and after the Civil War. Taking into account the distinct environmental and geographic factors that imposed inescapable limits on the process of sugar production in the region, this book examines the relations between planters and freedmen in slavery's aftermath. It argues that the particular demands of sugar production accorded freedmen considerable leverage in the conflict that attended the creation of a new labor system. The exigencies of sugar cultivation in Louisiana, combined with the centralized plantation regimen that survived emancipation, left planters vulnerable to the freedmen's concerted efforts to gain control of their working lives. Freedmen did not dictate terms to planters, but the distinguishing features of sugar production in Louisiana enabled freedmen to bargain from a position of strength in the struggle over free labor.

Among the unique characteristics of sugar production were the need for large capital investment and high concentrations of land and labor. Sugar production also involved a series of tasks throughout the agricultural year that had to be accomplished on time lest the crop be jeopardized. Sugar plantations therefore operated most effectively under a centralized system wherein laborers worked in gangs under the supervision of white managers or overseers, who ensured the coordination of the workers' activities. After the Civil War, in contrast to the various forms of sharecropping and tenancy that prevailed in the cotton South, wage labor and this centralized regimen predominated in the sugar region. Although the daily routine on postbellum sugar plantations resembled that of the slave regime, a seismic shift had nonetheless occurred in the way planters and workers related to one another. At least in theory, the planters no longer owned their workers but had to deal with them on equal terms. Because most planters disbursed pay monthly, the contest over wages emerged as the main point of contention between them and the freedmen. Disputes over pay, however, were but one aspect of the larger struggle that accompanied the reorganization of plantation routine. Planters and freedmen also skirmished over the hours and conditions of labor, access to the plantation's economic resources (land, animals, and implements), rations, and housing. Familiar with the process of sugar production, and aware of how easily they could disrupt plantation operations, freedmen converted their skills and knowledge into powerful leverage in disputes with their employers.

The freedmen's ability to gain favorable terms on wages and other matters had profound repercussions. Not only did it lead them to tolerate work routines that resembled those of the slave regime, it also impelled them to accept wage labor rather than to push for such alternative arrangements as sharecropping. Wage labor was not imposed by omnipotent planters against the will of powerless former slaves, and its triumph did not signal the freedmen's acquiescence to the dictates of their former owners. Instead, freedmen in the sugar region embraced wage labor once they had mastered the rudimentary workings of the free labor market. Although they won many of the battles over the new labor system, they ultimately lost the broader struggle for economic independence. Their loss, however, became clear only with the benefit of hindsight; it could hardly have been anticipated by a people whose primary frame of reference in constructing free labor was that of enslavement. Freedmen thus unknowingly participated in the process by which they became relegated to dependency within the plantation system.

This study lies within three overlapping historiographical traditions. First, it builds upon the now familiar literature that places slaves and freedmen at the center of the story of emancipation and the creation of a new labor system. Because most such works focus on the cotton South and the origins of sharecropping, they emphasize the freedmen's resistance to wage labor and work patterns reminiscent of the antebellum era. I engage this literature, however, by showing how freedmen of the sugar country repudiated neither wage labor nor their old work routines. Instead, they refashioned northern free-labor ideology to comport with their own experiences of life and labor on sugar plantations and with the communitarian ethos that had afforded them psychological and spiritual sustenance under slavery. Familiar with the dictates of sugar cultivation, they conceded the need for a centralized plantation routine. But their fighting over wages, working conditions, freedom of movement, disposition of family labor, and access to the plantation's resources shows they envisioned a free-labor system that ensured both a measure of personal autonomy and a sense of collective self-determination within the plantation's operating system. Freedmen did not see wage labor as inherently repressive, or as "wage slavery." Instead, they regarded it as but one among a host of factors that, considered together, enabled them to reconcile their desire for independence with the dictates of sugar production.[1]

This book also builds upon the many local or community studies that examine the reorganization of southern plantation society after slavery. These studies are well known to scholars of the nineteenth-century South, but again, most focus on developments in the cotton belt. The South, however, was no monolith, and raising cotton was not like raising cane. My study thus adds to the existing literature by showing how the sugar plantation's centralized regimen actually facilitated the

---

1. The most systematic treatment of the slaves' role in the destruction of slavery is found in *Freedom* 1. There is a vast literature on former slaves' resistance to wage labor and gang labor after emancipation, and on the subsequent rise of sharecropping. Some important works include Thavolia Glymph and John J. Kushma, eds., *Essays on the Postbellum Southern Economy* (College Station, Tex., 1985); Gerald David Jaynes, *Branches without Roots: Genesis of the Black Working Class in the American South, 1862–1882* (New York, 1986); Jay R. Mandle, *The Roots of Black Poverty: The Southern Plantation Economy after the Civil War* (Durham, N.C., 1978); and Roger L. Ransom and Richard Sutch, *One Kind of Freedom: The Economic Consequences of Emancipation* (Cambridge, U.K., 1977). For treatment of these themes in particular southern communities, see the works cited in note 2.

freedmen's efforts to shape many aspects of free labor to their advantage. Nevertheless, this emphasis on the distinctiveness of sugar should not be construed as an endorsement of crop determinism, the view that certain crops inevitably spawn particular labor systems. To be sure, the exigencies of sugar cultivation imposed limits on the kinds of labor arrangements that might have replaced slavery in southern Louisiana, but they did not predetermine the postwar labor settlement. While eschewing determinism, I argue that the free-labor system that emerged in the sugar region was at least partly shaped by the objective realities of sugar production as well as by the pressures that planters historically faced in southern Louisiana. An examination of the transition to free labor in the sugar country thus offers a fresh perspective on the familiar problem of the recasting of the postbellum southern plantation.[2]

Finally, this work considers the question of whether continuity or discontinuity best describes the transition from the Old South to the New South. The theme of discontinuity received its classic treatment in C. Vann Woodward's *Origins of the New South, 1877–1913,* and virtually all scholars who have written on the New South since have had to contend, in one way or another, with Woodward's thesis. This debate, of course, has always been one of degrees rather than of absolutes. Still, historians continue to dispute the newness of the New South in general and of the New South plantation in particular. This book engages the discontinuity question by showing that apparent similarities can mask deeper changes in social relations. Comparing work routines on a sugar plantation before and after the Civil War reveals a host of striking parallels. Moreover, although many sugar planters lost their estates during the war years, a fair number retained their property. Thus, in considering how the former slaves worked, as well as for whom, one might conclude that continuity characterizes the transition from the Old South to the New in Louisiana's sugar country.[3]

In fact, just the opposite is the case. The abolition of slavery precipitated a funda-

2. Some important local studies include Jonathan M. Bryant, *How Curious a Land: Conflict and Change in Greene County, Georgia, 1850–1885* (Chapel Hill, N.C., 1996); Randolph B. Campbell, *A Southern Community in Crisis: Harrison County, Texas, 1850–1880* (Austin, Tex., 1983); Ronald L. F. Davis, *Good and Faithful Labor: From Slavery to Sharecropping in the Natchez District, 1860–1890* (Westport, Conn., 1982); Joseph P. Reidy, *From Slavery to Agrarian Capitalism in the Cotton Plantation South: Central Georgia, 1800–1880* (Chapel Hill, N.C., 1992); Julie Saville, *The Work of Reconstruction: From Slave to Wage Laborer in South Carolina, 1860–1870* (Cambridge, U.K., 1994); Michael Wayne, *The Reshaping of Plantation Society: The Natchez District, 1860–1880* (Baton Rouge, 1983); and Jonathan M. Wiener, *Social Origins of the New South: Alabama, 1860–1885* (Baton Rouge, 1978).

3. In addition to the works cited in note 2, see Dwight B. Billings Jr., *Planters and the Making of a "New South": Class, Politics, and Development in North Carolina, 1865–1900* (Chapel Hill, N.C., 1979); Barbara Jeanne Fields, *Slavery and Freedom on the Middle Ground: Maryland during*

mental transformation in relations between capital and labor. Planters no longer owned their workers and therefore had to purchase the labor power of their employees, who were now free to move as they chose and to sell their services to the highest bidder. The rise of a functioning labor market, in conjunction with the exigencies of sugar production, thus enabled freedmen in the sugar region to gain advantageous terms on wages and other matters. Despite their own efforts—legal and otherwise—to thwart the workings of the labor market, planters bemoaned the labor problem from the freeing of the slaves until well into the twentieth century. If daily work routines during and after slavery were hauntingly similar, and if some freedmen remained on their old estates for years after emancipation and continued to work for their former masters, planters and freedmen engaged one another within a radically altered legal and political framework. Planters who had once held legal title to the bodies and the labor power of their workers now negotiated with them as putative equals while purchasing their services on the market. Black laborers continued to work the cane, but they did so within a very different social and political landscape.

This new landscape owed much to the emergence of black politics during Reconstruction. Indeed, I further contribute to the literature on emancipation by demonstrating the inexorable link between politics and the daily contest over labor both during and after Reconstruction. Although black political power shaped labor arrangements throughout the South after the war, Radical Reconstruction had especially profound consequences in the sugar region, where a coordinated, centralized plantation regimen both launched and then sustained the freedmen's political mobilization, which was itself a collective endeavor. The freedmen's working in gangs—much as they had as slaves—fueled their political struggle, while at the same time political power bolstered their efforts to reorganize daily labor in accordance with their own aspirations. Not only did freedmen capitalize on the rights of citizenship in order to reshape their working lives; as long as Reconstruction lasted in Louisiana, planters could not call upon the state militia to impose control over labor. Thus, while the demands of sugar production and the development of a labor market contributed integrally to the former slaves' success in shaping free labor, so too did the freedmen's ascendancy to membership in the polity.[4]

---

the Nineteenth Century (New Haven, Conn., 1985); Walter J. Fraser Jr. and Winfred B. Moore Jr., eds., *From the Old South to the New: Essays on the Transitional South* (Westport, Conn., 1981); Harold D. Woodman, *New South—New Law: The Legal Foundations of Credit and Labor Relations in the Postbellum Agricultural South* (Baton Rouge, 1995); Gavin Wright, *Old South, New South: Revolutions in the Southern Economy since the Civil War* (New York, 1986).

4. One important work on the link between politics and labor relations in the cotton South is Michael W. Fitzgerald, *The Union League Movement in the Deep South: Politics and Agricultural Change during Reconstruction* (Baton Rouge, 1989).

The importance of politics to the labor struggle is further highlighted by the overthrow of Reconstruction in Louisiana in 1877. Although independent black politics continued in the sugar region after that date, and although black men continued to vote and to hold office, they did so within a very different political context. The end of Reconstruction tipped the scales in favor of planters, who could now call upon the coercive power of the state in moments of crisis. This new political climate did not completely negate the advances that freedmen had derived from the exigencies of sugar production and from the labor market, which continued to function, but planters now enjoyed a decided advantage. This eventuality, while not immediately apparent, became so with the tragic events of 1887.

In attempting to explain the origins of free labor in the sugar region, I am obligated to offer a working definition of that amorphous term *free labor*. As understood in the mid-nineteenth-century North, free labor did not simply refer to nonslave labor. Instead, it had specific, positive connotations. Free-labor ideology encompassed a host of ideas and values that reverberated throughout antebellum northern society and reflected the aspirations of its citizens. In essence, northern advocates of free labor championed personal autonomy and freedom as well as the right of the individual to sole possession of his or her own body and his or her own labor. They also professed the sanctity of voluntary contracts, espoused the inviolability of private property, and celebrated the marketplace and the unlimited upward social mobility it provided. Free labor's proponents affirmed the dignity of labor and insisted that manual labor ennobled rather than degraded the individual. They also presupposed a consensus of interests between capital and labor. The realities of even northern antebellum society, of course, often did not match these ideals, and free-labor ideology proved especially inadequate for the unique regimen of the sugar plantation. Consequently, the development of a free-labor system in the sugar region was beset by the problem of how to reconcile the ideals of free-labor ideology with the needs of plantation-based sugar production.[5]

In trying to harmonize free labor with sugar production, both planters and freedmen formulated their own contrasting versions of free labor. Freedmen, as noted, strove for a measure of autonomy within the realm of sugar production. In addition to offering a new interpretation of that striving for autonomy, the present study devotes greater attention than has often been the case to the planters' perspective, assessing how the constraints under which they operated influenced

---

5. Eric Foner, *Free Soil, Free Labor, Free Men: The Ideology of the Republican Party before the Civil War*, with a new introductory essay (1970; reprint, New York, 1995), 11–39. See also Jonathan A. Glickstein, *Concepts of Free Labor in Antebellum America* (New Haven, Conn., 1991), and James D. Schmidt, *Free to Work: Labor Law, Emancipation, and Reconstruction, 1815–1880* (Athens, Ga., 1998), chaps. 1 and 2.

their thinking on free labor. Although most planters eventually reconciled themselves to the abolition of slavery, they insisted that sugar was a "forced" crop in Louisiana and that, consequently, the demands of its production had to take precedence over what mid-nineteenth-century northerners defined as free labor. Planters thus considered strict labor control essential to their operations. But because, in the minds of planters, free laborers—not to mention free black people—would never voluntarily submit to the level of discipline that sugar production required, planters contended that the state had to regulate the labor system. The respective notions of free labor that planters and freedmen espoused were incompatible and led to conflict that manifested itself in familiar ways and at predictable times in the annual cycle of sugar production. In order to understand this conflict adequately, it is necessary to give equal weight to both sides of the story.

Even as planters faced the challenge of making sugar with free workers, they confronted other changes that profoundly affected their fortunes. Since Louisiana's subtropical environment produced inferior grades of sugar, which required further processing in refineries, planters could not compete, even under ideal circumstances, against foreign sugars without a protective tariff. The years following the Civil War were not the best of times for Louisiana planters. The physical destruction wrought by the war, the lack of credit in the South, and the labor problem all conspired to stymie the return to antebellum production levels until the 1890s. The dramatic increase in sugar consumption in the United States during the same years, moreover, compounded the problems of Louisiana planters, whose influence over the domestic sugar market declined accordingly. Equally striking changes altered the international sugar market. Due largely to the rise of the European beet sugar industry, world sugar production *doubled* between 1860 and 1880. Louisiana planters thus operated from a position of weakness within a rapidly changing sugar market at the very moment that they confronted the problem of labor readjustment.

I have attempted to situate my analysis within these shifting economic realities, and to assess how economic considerations impinged upon the thoughts and actions of both planters and freedmen in the creation of the new labor system. That being said, however, it is important to note that this work is not a traditional economic history. It makes no claims to have generated fresh economic data or to have broken new ground in economic theory. The questions that concern economic historians of southern emancipation are of secondary rather than primary importance here. Instead, *Reconstruction in the Cane Fields* is essentially a social history, one that tells the story of the relations between contending social classes within a specific agricultural context.

In telling that story and thereby documenting the creation of a new labor system, this book includes both chronological and thematic chapters. The first chapter offers a historical overview of the Louisiana sugar industry, explications of sugar production and plantation routine, and an interpretation of southern Louisiana as a slave society. The next three chapters employ a chronological approach in outlining the origins and development of free labor during the 1860s. Chapter 2 examines the wartime genesis of the monthly wage-labor system. Chapter 3, which focuses on the period of presidential Reconstruction, traces the emergence of a full-fledged labor market while also considering the question of why alternatives to wage labor did not take root in the sugar region. Chapter 4 discusses the beginnings of Radical Reconstruction in southern Louisiana and explores the impact of black political mobilization upon the freedmen's working lives.

Chapters 5, 6, and 7 employ a topical approach in order to explore particular facets of the new labor system from the late 1860s to the early 1880s. Chapter 5 offers a new angle on the question of planter persistence (the degree to which antebellum planters held onto their estates after the war) by linking it to that of the modernization of the sugar industry. Chapter 6 examines the labor market's maturation in the sugar region by assessing labor turnover and mobility. Chapter 7 investigates conflicts over wages and the method of payment while exploring the question of how freedmen spent their earnings. Chapter 8 returns to the issue of the connection between political power and labor, focusing upon white Louisianians' attack on the Reconstruction state during the mid-1870s and assessing the implications of Redemption in Louisiana for labor relations in the sugar region. The Epilogue then moves forward several years to examine the November 1887 strike by sugar workers that culminated in the infamous Thibodaux Massacre. Not only did the strike's denouement reveal the potential for violence between planters and workers that had always remained just below the surface, it also highlighted the planters' ability to call upon the power of the state in dealing with labor after Redemption.

Because the subject of this study is the relation between planters and freedmen, issues of considerable importance in recent historiography on the American South are dealt with only insofar as they affect the main account. Just as the master-slave relationship stood at the core of antebellum southern society, the struggle between former slaveholder and former slave became the central point of conflict in the postbellum South. How was labor to be reorganized following slavery's demise? Who was to wield decision-making power on the plantation? How were former slaves to secure the fruits of their own labor? These emerged as the pivotal issues in all postemancipation societies; what follows is the story of how they were resolved in the sugar parishes of southern Louisiana.

ॐ1ॐ

LOUISIANA SUGAR—AMERICAN SLAVERY

The anxieties attending the cultivation of sugar are great and so much depends upon the judicious employment of labour, it is scarcely possible to exaggerate the importance of experience in directing it, and of the power to insist on its application.

—William Howard Russell, *My Diary North and South*

The Old South comprised many diverse localities, each in its own way unique, but none matched southern Louisiana in its distinctiveness. A legacy of French and Spanish imperial ambitions engulfed by the Anglo-American world, and a bastion of Roman Catholicism encircled by evangelical Protestantism, southern Louisiana was—as it is to this day—a place unto itself. Its ante- and postbellum uniqueness, however, also owed to Queen Sugar's reign in the land where cotton was king. Southern Louisiana was a slave society, but that was only half the truth: it was also a sugar society. The demands of sugar production and the historical development of slavery in the American South together—rather than either one alone—gave the region its identity. Combining features of New World sugar production and American slavery, Louisiana sugar plantations were a *tertium quid.*

Southern Louisiana's peculiarity as a sugar society within the slave South is the central theme of the sugar region's history between the close of the eighteenth century and the Civil War. From its beginnings in 1795 and rapid growth in the following decades, sugar cultivation altered the area's social, political, economic, and physical landscape. Slavery was not unknown in Louisiana before sugar's introduction, but sugar transformed southern Louisiana from a society with slaves into a slave society. Sugar production defined the plantation system and gave rise to a distinctive slaveholding elite as well as to large, complex slave communities. Louisiana sugar plantations shared much with antebellum cotton plantations, but the worlds of cotton and sugar differed in as many ways before the Civil War as they would after it.

Before the war, sugar plantations dominated the region of southeastern Louisiana encompassing the parishes of Ascension, Assumption, Iberville, Jefferson, Lafourche, Orleans, Plaquemines, St. Bernard, St. Charles, St. James, St. John the Baptist, St. Mary, Terrebonne, and West Baton Rouge. Although a singular entity, the sugar region was thought of as three distinct localities: the Mississippi "coast" (land along the river from Baton Rouge to the Gulf of Mexico), the Lafourche district, and Bayou Teche. Many smaller bayous throughout the area also hosted plantations. Over centuries, levees had formed along the waterways, from which the delta's alluvial bottoms sloped gently to the vast swampland. The fecund strips of land between levee and swamp made up a small proportion of the region's total area, but they spawned the sugar plantations and the way of life that attended them.[1]

The nineteenth-century Louisiana sugar industry faced exigencies universal to sugar production as well as environmental constraints particular to southern Louisiana. Since conditions for its cultivation were not ideal, sugarcane was considered a forced crop. A tropical product, it requires a mild climate, moderate and well-distributed rainfall, and a growing season of about eighteen months. In Louisiana, rain is plentiful but seldom evenly distributed. Because south Louisiana lies in the subtropics, frost becomes a possibility by late fall. Louisiana planters, compelled to harvest the cane before winter, faced a growing season of only ten months. The 1817 introduction of ribbon cane—which matured rapidly and was more resistant to frost—alleviated planters' environmental concerns somewhat, but it did not solve their central dilemma. Sugar may have been well suited to the area's environment—that is, within a social order committed to commodity production and slave labor—yet there would always remain what one scholar has called a "lack of complete harmony between land and product."[2]

[handwritten margin note: sugar wasn't necessarily easy to grow in the South]

1. J. Carlyle Sitterson, *Sugar Country: The Cane Sugar Industry in the South, 1753–1950* (Lexington, Ky., 1953), 76. On the history of Louisiana sugar plantations from the perspective of a cultural geographer, see John B. Rehder, *Delta Sugar: Louisiana's Vanishing Plantation Landscape* (Baltimore, 1999).

2. Sitterson, *Sugar Country*, 13. On the relationship between environment, labor, and the larger social order generally, see Mart A. Stewart, *"What Nature Suffers to Groe": Life, Labor, and Landscape on the Georgia Coast, 1680–1920* (Athens, Ga., 1996), 1–20.

This lack of harmony was partly reconciled by Jean Etienne de Boré, the legendary "Savior of Louisiana," in 1795. Born in the Illinois country in 1741, educated in France, and formerly a member of the King's Household Guard, Boré acquired a plantation near New Orleans in 1781. Nearly bankrupt as an indigo planter, he turned to sugar production in the mid-1790s and, using techniques imported by slave and free-black refugees from Haiti, produced Louisiana's first commercial crop of granulated sugar. Boré's success gave rise to a new era in Louisiana, which before then had been more a remote colonial outpost than a thriving plantation society. Settlers had cultivated sugarcane as early as the 1750s, but they had not been able to get the cane juice to granulate and so used it instead for molasses. While Louisiana planters had long relied upon the labor of enslaved Africans by the late eighteenth century, Boré's demonstration that sugar could be produced profitably led the way for southern Louisiana to become a plantation-based slave society.[3]

The sugar region's destiny unfolded several years later with the Louisiana Purchase in 1803. Soon afterward, Americans flocked to the new territory, many bringing slaves. In 1812 Louisiana entered the Union as a slave state. The slave population of the sugar parishes (excluding New Orleans) mushroomed from just under 10,000 in 1810 to more than 42,000 by 1830, while the white population doubled from 11,500 to just over 24,000 during the same years. Both slave and white populations of the sugar region again more than doubled between 1830 and 1860, by which time slaves outnumbered whites 88,439 to 60,356. Although Louisiana had a small white majority in 1860, the sugar parishes were home to a substantial black majority.[4]

However overpowering, the Anglo and African tidal wave could not wash

3. On Boré, see Charles Gayarré, "A Louisiana Sugar Plantation of the Old Régime," *Harper's New Monthly Magazine* 74 (March 1887): 606–21. On the development of slavery and plantation agriculture in Louisiana during the eighteenth century, see Ira Berlin, *Many Thousands Gone: The First Two Centuries of Slavery in North America* (Cambridge, Mass., 1998), chaps. 4, 8, and 12; Gwendolyn Midlo Hall, *Africans in Colonial Louisiana: The Development of Afro-Creole Culture in the Eighteenth Century* (Baton Rouge, 1992); Thomas N. Ingersoll, *Mammon and Manon in Early New Orleans: The First Slave Society in the Deep South, 1718–1819* (Knoxville, Tenn., 1999); James Thomas McGowan, "Creation of a Slave Society: Louisiana Plantations in the Eighteenth Century" (Ph.D. diss., University of Rochester, 1976); and Daniel H. Usner Jr., *Indians, Settlers, and Slaves in a Frontier Exchange Economy: The Lower Mississippi Valley before 1783* (Chapel Hill, N.C., 1992).

4. U.S. Bureau of the Census, *Statistical View of the United States . . . ; Being a Compendium of the Seventh Census . . .* (Washington, D.C., 1854); *Eighth Census of the United States*, 4 vols. (Washington, D.C., 1864–1866); *Ninth Census of the United States*, 3 vols. (Washington, D.C., 1872).

away the foundations of Louisiana's cultural landscape. The French language, the Roman Catholic Church, the civil code, and the somewhat more tolerant racial attitudes, mixed with a dash of Iberian flavor from the period of Spanish rule (1763–1803), created a culture unique to North America. Joining descendants of French settlers and enslaved Africans were a number of other ethnic groups, including the free people of color. Sugar added to this ethnocultural mélange. The combination of sugar and the ethnically diverse population has traditionally spiced life in southern Louisiana, which constitutes the northern reaches of Latin America as much as it does the southern reaches of the United States.

Nonetheless, the French connection was not indomitable. With the Anglo migration, the established population was forced to confront a culture predicated upon British political and legal traditions, evangelical Protestantism, cotton culture, and rigid notions of race. The French cultural foundation remained intact, but after Louisiana became a state the Anglos soon achieved political and economic ascendancy. Such immigrants to southern Louisiana as the Palfreys of the Teche and the Pughs of the Lafourche exemplified nineteenth-century American nabobs who established themselves within the dominant planter elite.[5]

American migration coincided with sugar's geographic expansion and increased production. While some newcomers immediately engaged in growing sugarcane, others at first planted cotton. Southern Louisiana's soil often proved inadequate to cotton cultivation, however, and periodic falls in price convinced planters that sugar would be more profitable. By the mid-1830s, sugar dominated the area south of Baton Rouge; almost 700 farms and plantations made sugar, and production surpassed 100,000 hogsheads (wooden casks in which raw sugar was shipped; they weighed about 1,100 pounds when full). The industry's growth accelerated in the 1840s—a true boom period. After 1841, annual production failed to reach 100,000 hogsheads only once before the Civil War. By 1849, 1,536 farms and plantations—the greatest number in any single year of the slave era—produced almost 250,000 hogsheads. After 1850 the industry underwent consolidation. In 1859, 1,308 sugar establishments—228 fewer than a decade earlier—produced 221,840 hogsheads. The record 1861 crop, which yielded almost 460,000 hogsheads, was the last crop before the federal invasion of southern Louisiana and the last one made exclusively with slave labor. Much of this harvest was sitting on the wharves when federal forces occupied New Orleans in May 1862.[6]

5. Sarah Russell, "Ethnicity, Commerce, and Community on Lower Louisiana's Plantation Frontier, 1803–1828," *LH* 40 (fall 1999): 389–405.

6. Sitterson, *Sugar Country*, 28–30; Ulrich Bonnell Phillips, *American Negro Slavery: A Survey of the Supply, Employment, and Control of Negro Labor As Determined by the Plantation Regime* (1918; reprint with a new foreword by Eugene D. Genovese, Baton Rouge, 1966), 166–8;

* * *

The exigencies of sugar cultivation and the geography of southern Louisiana defined annual routine on antebellum sugar plantations. A central fact of plantation life was the overlapping crop seasons; planters saved about one-fifth of their harvested cane for planting. The year's labors began in mid-January with spring planting, which had to be completed by early March since slaves had many other duties to perform and because cane needed time to mature by fall. Slaves did not plant an entire crop each year. A perennial, sugarcane yields multiple harvests. Louisiana planters usually expected three harvests from a single planting. Thus they spoke of "plant" cane, "first rattoons" (second year), and "second rattoons" (third year).[7]

With planting done, slaves—men and women—cultivated the crop over the next four months. They hoed the young stalks carefully, since poorly hoed cane quickly became choked with weeds or grass. Such work occupied the slaves until late June, when the cane crop was "laid by," since it no longer required cultivation, and planters set their slaves to other tasks. They cleared ditches and canals, repaired plantation roads, maintained levees, and attended to other crops, especially corn. Because the sugar mill required vast amounts of wood for processing the harvest, slaves devoted much time to gathering and cutting it in Louisiana's bounteous cypress swamps. Late summer and early fall were devoted to readying the mill and completing any undone chores. Always seeking to increase their improved acreage, planters saw to the clearing and draining of unimproved land—work so disagreeable that they often hired unskilled white laborers rather than jeopardize the health of valuable slaves.[8]

Few planters could expect to complete the myriad tasks of a sugar plantation during the crop season. Thus, they depended upon their slaves to perform certain duties on their own time for compensation; this "slaves' economy" also served as a concession by planters for the arduous nature of sugar cultivation. Beyond their daily assigned tasks, slaves collected or chopped wood; repaired levees, roads, and ditches; and worked extra hours at harvest. In return, planters permitted slaves to

---

Champomier, *Statement of the Sugar Crop Made in Louisiana . . . 1861–62.* On the sugar industry's early period in southern Louisiana, see Sarah Russell, "Cultural Conflicts or Common Interests: The Making of the Sugar Planter Class in Louisiana, 1795–1853" (Ph.D. diss., University of Maryland, 2000).

7. The description of plantation routine in this section follows Walter Prichard, "Routine on a Louisiana Sugar Plantation under the Slavery Regime," *Mississippi Valley Historical Review* 14 (September 1927): 168–78, and Sitterson, *Sugar Country,* 112–32.

8. J. Carlyle Sitterson, "Hired Labor on Sugar Plantations of the Ante-Bellum South," *JSH* 14 (May 1948): 192–205.

grow vegetables on their garden plots, to raise chickens or hogs, and to collect Spanish moss—all of which they sold to the planter or in nearby towns. Slaves were sometimes paid cash for their goods or labor, but more often they received credit on the plantation books, with which they purchased both necessities and certain luxury items. Slaves conducted their activities under their owners' watchful eyes, but the slaves' economy gave them experience in quasi-market behavior as well as a sense of independence that served them well after emancipation.[9]

Even with the slaves' cooperation, plantations rarely ran without a hitch. The prevailing conditions were usually something close to controlled chaos. Planters were often beset by any number of contingencies during the crop season, including frost in winter, floods in spring, and either torrential thunderstorms or weeks of drought in summer, not to mention infestations of parasitic insects or the ravages of predatory animals, especially rats. Even more unpredictable was the Mississippi River itself, which could offer little warning before embarking upon its destructive course. Rarely did a year go by that planters did not suffer one or more of these environmental calamities.

Assuming the crops survived until mid-October, they would then be ready for commencement of the sugar harvest, commonly known as the "rolling season." Here a planter's instinct, experience, and even daring came into play, for the longer sugarcane ripens, the higher its juice's saccharine content, resulting in more and higher-quality sugar. By delaying the rolling season, however, a planter increased the chances of exposing the cane to frost, which could destroy it. Once the planter gave the word, slaves spent about two weeks cutting and storing plant cane for next year's crop. By late October, the entire community eagerly anticipated the cutting of cane for the mill. After the local priest's traditional blessing of the crop, slaves— organized in gangs and wielding razor-sharp knives—took to the fields, where they commenced the back-breaking, repetitive task of severing the cane from its roots, stripping its leaves from the stalk, and cutting away its unripened joints. Cane cutters, male and female, worked to the pace of the slave in the first or "lead row," a prized position occupied by the fastest cutter. Other gangs, often composed of children and the elderly, gathered up and loaded the stalks onto horse-drawn carts for transport to the mill. Once the mill had started, synchronization between it and field operations was critical, for while the mill needed a steady supply of cane, the juice in the stalks spoiled within about two days if unprocessed. Planters had to ensure that field and mill work were in harmony.[10]

9. Roderick A. McDonald, *The Economy and Material Culture of Slaves: Goods and Chattels on the Sugar Plantations of Jamaica and Louisiana* (Baton Rouge, 1993), chaps. 2 and 4.

10. On holding the lead row, see Solomon Northup, *Twelve Years a Slave*, ed. Sue Eakin and Joseph Logsdon (1853; reprint, Baton Rouge, 1968), 159n.

At the sugar mill, slaves placed the cane on a conveyor belt that carried it to the mill proper, which usually consisted of a set of three rollers. Other slaves fed the cane into the rollers, which crushed it to extract the juice. From here, the juice was purified by being boiled in a series of between three and five kettles. As the liquid heated, impurities floated to the top and were ladled off by slaves. Each kettle was smaller than the previous one and the heat under it more intense, so more impurities were removed. This process required precise coordination. Heated kettles could lie empty for only a few moments, and the juice could not remain in the kettle too long after the impurities were removed. Therefore, the sugar maker— usually a white man but sometimes a free man of color—had to know exactly when to pass the juice to the next kettle.[11]

With the impurities gone, granulation, or the "strike," took place. This was the critical moment. Determining when the syrup had reached a consistency sufficient to granulate required every bit of the sugar maker's skill and experience. When ready, the syrup was poured into large, shallow vats and stirred. Crystals soon appeared, and successive layers of syrup were then poured over the first. With granulation completed, slaves transferred the raw sugar into hogsheads, from which molasses, a by-product, drained. At this stage, the product was not white sugar but rather brown sugar, which planters shipped to refiners in New Orleans, St. Louis, or northern cities for further processing.

While the rolling season continued relentlessly for two months, contingencies interfered with almost every harvest. The mill periodically had to be shut down for either repairs or delays in the cane supply. Rain also interrupted cane cutting, as planters did not want the unpaved roads to become rutted by heavy, cane-laden carts. Moreover, rarely did a rolling season not see a hard freeze. If a freeze seemed likely, the planter stopped the mill and sent his slaves to the fields to "windrow" standing cane. Windrowing entailed cutting the cane, setting it down in the furrows, and covering it with the leaves and the tops of the stalks. Planters debated windrowing's effectiveness in protecting cane, but most subscribed to it.[12]

Although the community viewed it as a festive occasion, the rolling season tested both master and slave. In addition to cutting cane by day, slaves also took rotating night shifts, known as "watches," at the mill. The heat, fire, boiling juice, and long hours all combined to make sugar mill work as dangerous as it was arduous. The rolling season stretched slaves, who were usually sleep-deprived, to the limits of physical endurance. Consequently, it was an article of faith among planters

11. This description of sugar making follows Sitterson, *Sugar Country*, 133–56.

12. W. F. Weeks to M. Weeks, Dec. 6, 1858, and W. F. Weeks to Charley, Jan. 28, 1859, David Weeks and Family Papers, LSU; Oct. 21, 1861, Plant. Diary 33, WJMP; Sitterson, *Sugar Country*, 124–5.

that slavery was essential to their operations, since free workers would not submit to such conditions. "[I]t may be conceded," remarked a visitor to the sugar region in 1861, "that nothing but 'involuntary servitude' could go through the toil and suffering required to produce sugar."[13]

The slaves' working lives and material conditions, however deplorable to modern sensibilities, are best viewed within their historical context. The lot of most European peasants, and of many urban wage earners in the North and in Europe at mid–nineteenth century, was probably only marginally better than that of slaves. Southern proslavery theorists made great political capital of industrialization's horrors, yet even some critics of slavery believed that American and European wage laborers endured conditions worse than those of southern slaves. The permanency of their legal status set slaves apart from all other rural or urban workers. But the slaves' working conditions must be gauged by the standards of the mid–nineteenth century, not those of today, and they must be divorced, as far as possible, from the issue of the slaves' legal status.[14]

Likewise, the demands on the planter, if qualitatively different from those placed on slaves, were also exacting. He tried to see that operations ran smoothly, which they often did not. Even as the planter worried about things within his control, he also fretted over matters that were beyond it—in particular, nature. But of all the factors that affected sugar making, labor was most crucial. Slothful work could jeopardize a crop; a single recalcitrant hand could spell disaster. One overseer informed his employer during the 1858 rolling season that a slave had run away. "If he is . . . not sent back," the overseer insisted, "it will have a very bad effect on the other hands." Since planters could not tolerate such behavior, violence was a constant threat. Put to work as a driver in the sugar mill, the slave Solomon Northup was handed a whip and ordered to use it on any idle slave lest he feel the lash himself.[15]

The threat of corporal punishment was a powerful inducement to slaves on sugar plantations. Yet violence alone does not explain how a handful of white men kept scores of slaves, who were armed with deadly knives, diligently at work. Ob-

13. William Howard Russell, *My Diary North and South,* ed. Eugene Berwanger (Philadelphia, 1987), 177.

14. A good overview of industrialization and its effects on the northern and European wage-earning classes is Eric Hobsbawm, *The Age of Capital, 1848–1875* (London, 1975; reprint, New York, 1996). On southern critics of industrial capitalism, see Richard Hofstadter, "John C. Calhoun: The Marx of the Master Class," in *The American Political Tradition and the Men Who Made It* (1948; reprint, New York, 1974), 86–117, and Eugene D. Genovese, *The World the Slaveholders Made: Two Essays in Interpretation* (New York, 1969), pt. 2.

15. W. W. White to J. Moore, Dec. 15, 1858, Weeks Papers, LSU; Northup, *Twelve Years a Slave,* 148.

servers noted the enthusiasm with which slaves worked during the rolling season. That resistance or revolt might result in permanent separation from one's family probably kept most slaves in line. Similarly, resistance that threatened a planter's solvency also imperiled the slave community's survival. Such inducements to labor were reinforced by planters' conscious efforts to foster the sense of conviviality that surrounded the rolling season. Some planters distributed token gifts and small amounts of money, while others allowed their slaves to hold a "ball" at the sugar mill if a few hours' breathing-space allowed. And slaves knew that after the harvest they would enjoy the Christmas holiday of about a week. Such beneficence, to be sure, strengthened the planter's authority, but it also underscored his obligation to his slaves and thus affirmed their humanity.[16]

But perhaps the answer to why slaves worked so hard lies deeper still. Slaves undoubtedly viewed the rolling season as a festive occasion that provided a change from the routine drudgery of everyday life. The nineteenth-century sugar plantation was often likened to a factory, but in truth industrial notions of time and clock discipline were alien to it. Instead, slaves adhered to essentially preindustrial work rhythms: periods of monotonous, mind-numbing work were followed by incredible bursts of energy and enthusiasm that were dictated by the seasons and the requirements of the crop. Moreover, it is not inconceivable that slaves could take pride in their work and devote themselves to the success of the plantation while repudiating their enslavement. Throwing their energies into making a successful crop did not entail psychological submission. Slaves may not have been having a good time, as some observers believed. But for reasons of their own they worked diligently and dutifully. Discussing why slaves worked best during the rolling season, Frederick Law Olmsted observed that they had "a degree of freedom, and of social pleasure, and a variety of occupation which brings a recreation of the mind, and to a certain degree gives them strength for, and pleasure in, their labor."[17]

The organization of labor on sugar plantations comported with the needs of sugar production. Atop the pyramid stood the planter. On especially large plantations,

16. For examples, see Jan. 1, 1857, Magnolia Plant. Journal 2, Henry Clay Warmoth Papers, SHC (microfilm); W. F. Weeks to M. Weeks, Feb. 27, 1859, Weeks Papers, LSU; Dec. 20, 1861, Plant. Diary 33, WJMP; Dec. 30–1, 1861, Jan. 6, 1862, Priscilla "Miltie" Munnikhuysen Bond Diary (typescript), LSU; B. A. Botkin, *Lay My Burden Down: A Folk History of Slavery* (Chicago, 1945), 127.

17. Frederick Law Olmsted, *A Journey in the Seaboard Slave States, with Remarks on Their Economy* (1856; reprint, New York, 1968), 668. For a contrasting view of time and clock discipline in the antebellum South, see Mark M. Smith, *Mastered by the Clock: Time, Slavery, and Freedom in the American South* (Chapel Hill, N.C., 1997).

or where a planter owned more than one estate, a resident manager was hired. The planter or manager directed operations through the overseer, who commanded slaves through black drivers. These, in turn, directed the various gangs. Slaves were customarily divided into gangs on the basis of sex, age, and ability. During planting and cultivation, plow gangs performed the difficult work of breaking up the land and thus were composed of the stronger men. Hoe gangs—whose work was slightly less difficult but equally unrelenting—included men and women. Children and elderly slaves did not escape their share of labor—they gathered corn, picked peas, and engaged in various light tasks. Other projects were divided by sex, and although black women were sometimes spared the most physically demanding tasks, this practice was abandoned as needed in order to get the work done on time. Levee maintenance, perhaps the most thankless work on a sugar plantation, was the domain of men, but all hands were set to repairing "crevasses," or breaks in the levee. Few slaves were spared during the rolling season. On one plantation in 1861, only 16 of 149 adult slaves, a notably small proportion of just over 10 percent, performed no work. Almost everyone had a task on a sugar plantation.[18]

Because sugar production was one of the most technologically advanced enterprises in the antebellum South, it required much skilled labor. The more intelligent and dependable slaves who worked at the sugar mill occupied unusual positions within the plantation hierarchy. Their knowledge and skill could make the difference between success and failure. If it proved nothing else, employing slaves at the mill belied claims that the antebellum South's lack of industrial development owed to the incompatibility of slave labor with industrial pursuits. In addition, planters often employed white and free-black skilled laborers to maintain the complex mill equipment, as well as a sugar maker to oversee operations.[19]

Despite their use of technologically advanced equipment, planters evinced ambivalence about applying science to sugar production. Although anxious to improve the efficiency of their operations, they were also wary of the risks that necessarily accompanied scientific advances. With one foot in agriculture and the other in industry, planters relied upon both intuition and science. They were not always averse to technological improvement of sugar production, yet as members of an agrarian elite that often expressed misgivings toward progress, planters gave

18. Week of Nov. 25, 1861, Magnolia Plant. Journal 3, Warmoth Papers, SHC; Russell, *My Diary,* 179–80; V. Alton Moody, "Slavery on Louisiana Sugar Plantations," *LHQ* 7 (April 1924): 234–7; Prichard, "Routine on a Sugar Plantation," 172; Sitterson, *Sugar Country,* 63.

19. For a discussion between planters on the hiring of sugar makers, see E. S. Prescott to "Dear Father," Sept. 27, 1858, and W. Lourd to J. Moore, Sept. 30, 1859, and Sept. 9, 1861, Weeks Papers, LSU.

considerable weight to the notion of doing things as their predecessors had done. Sugar making entailed enough risk, many of them believed; the last thing they needed was to jeopardize their solvency further by gambling on some newfangled technique. As a group, planters tended to adhere to what already worked and hesitated to embark upon risky endeavors, no matter how great the potential return. This suspicion was not the product of stubbornness. Rather, making sugar the old-fashioned way made good, practical business sense.[20]

Concerned with making profits, however, planters could hardly afford to ignore technological innovations. Recognizing that their long-term future demanded scientific solutions to certain problems, especially at the sugar mill, planters slowly adopted those modifications to traditional sugar production that appeared to promise success. The most widespread advance involved shifting from mule-powered to steam-powered mills. Steam provided greater and more evenly distributed power to the rollers, increasing the proportion of cane juice extracted from the stalks. Steam mills first appeared in Louisiana during the 1820s, and their use spread during the next decade. By the early 1840s they outnumbered animal-powered mills; by 1861, 1,027 of 1,291 sugar establishments in Louisiana used steam.[21]

Conversely, using steam power to convert cane juice into sugar, by means of the multiple-effect evaporator process, met with less enthusiasm during the antebellum era. Developed by Norbert Rillieux, a free-black creole, during the 1830s, this process would eventually prove to be the most important technological advance in the history of sugar making. It entailed evaporating cane juice in a series of enclosed, linked containers, or pans, under a vacuum. Steam and vapor from the first pan was used to heat the next, and so on. Rillieux's process allowed for boiling cane juice more efficiently and at lower temperatures than was the case with open kettles, and it produced a higher grade of sugar. Nonetheless, despite the demonstrable success of the method by the mid-1840s, planters remained suspicious of it, perhaps because several had tried it when it was still in its developmental stages and had failed miserably—exactly the kind of disaster planters did

---

20. John A. Heitmann, *The Modernization of the Louisiana Sugar Industry, 1830–1910* (Baton Rouge, 1987), chaps. 1 and 2; Sitterson, *Sugar Country*, 146–54. For a view that emphasizes planters as profit maximizers who sought technological development, see Richard J. Follett, "The Sugar Masters: Slavery, Economic Development, and Modernization on Louisiana Sugar Plantations, 1820–1860" (Ph.D. diss., Louisiana State University, 1997). For an interpretation that stresses Lower South planters' ambivalence toward science and technology during the eighteenth century, see Joyce E. Chaplin, *An Anxious Pursuit: Agricultural Innovation and Modernity in the Lower South, 1730–1815* (Chapel Hill, N.C., 1993).

21. Sitterson, *Sugar Country*, 138; Heitmann, *Modernization*, 11–2.

not forget. Moreover, the multiple-effect process required a capital investment beyond most planters' means. Thus few were willing to abandon the old method. Not until well after the Civil War did Louisiana planters finally abandon open kettles for vacuum pans.[22]

Planters achieved varying degrees of success with other innovations. Some laid railroad tracks to transport cane to the mill. Various filtering or clarifying agents improved the quality of sugar but were expensive and sometimes difficult to work with. A number of planters switched from wood- to coal-burning furnaces. Others adopted a furnace method developed in 1854 that burned bagasse—trash from crushed cane stalks. The polariscope, invented in 1846 and widely adopted thereafter, allowed for measuring the chemical composition of sugar during granulation, removing much guesswork from that process.[23]

Though often suspicious of science, Louisiana planters approached technological advances with a pragmatic attitude. They were not so much rural conservatives mired in the old ways as short-term profit maximizers wary of taking the risks necessary for change and long-term development. Yet whatever planters thought about science and technology, one feature of sugar making they considered inviolate was using enslaved labor to plant, cultivate, and harvest the cane.

Though always a labor-intensive undertaking, cultivating sugarcane did not require complex equipment. For centuries, farmers in the Old World and New grew small cane crops to make molasses or syrup. Large-scale sugar production, however, necessitated a substantial investment in land, labor, and equipment, pricing it beyond the reach of all but the wealthiest of planters. This defining feature of sugar production held true in Louisiana, where the 525 elite planters (owners of fifty or more slaves) in 1860 boasted an average of 110 slaves, 730 acres of improved land, and $14,500 worth of farm equipment.[24]

This planter elite made up a small fraction of the sugar region's slaveholders, who were themselves a minority of the adult white male population (twenty years of age or older) in 1860. Of 14,393 adult white males in the sugar region (excluding

22. Sitterson, *Sugar Country*, 146–50; Heitmann, *Modernization*, 14–24; Louis Ferleger, "Productivity Change in the Post-Bellum Louisiana Sugar Industry," in *Time Series Analysis*, ed. O. D. Anderson and M. R. Perryman (New York, 1981), 147–61.

23. Sitterson, *Sugar Country*, 150–3; Heitmann, *Modernization*, chaps. 1 and 2.

24. Joseph Karl Menn, *The Large Slaveholders of Louisiana—1860* (New Orleans, 1964), 23–32, 38–43. The figures in this section have been calculated from the agricultural schedules and the aggregate data of the 1860 federal census, Menn's *Large Slaveholders*, and Champomier, *Statement, 1860–61*. Defining the "planter elite" as owners of fifty or more slaves takes into account the labor demands of sugar production, which were greater than those of cotton.

Orleans Parish), 4,177, or 29 percent, owned slaves; of these slaveholders, 525, or 12.6 percent, owned fifty or more slaves each (table 1). This planter elite, however, owned 66.5 percent of the region's slaves (table 2). Therefore, about one-eighth of the slaveholders owned two-thirds of the sugar parishes' slaves.[25]

The planter elite controlled landholding as thoroughly as it did slaveholding, collectively owning 68.2 percent of the sugar regions's improved acreage. Elite dominance was consistent with general landholding patterns in the region, where a small minority at the top owned the vast majority of productive land. For the sugar parishes as a whole, owners of 500 or more improved acres made up only 13.7 percent of all landholders but owned 63 percent of the improved land. Those who owned between 100 and 499 acres made up 22 percent of all landholders and owned 27.3 percent of the land, while those who owned less than 100 acres constituted 64.3 percent of all landholders but owned only 9.7 percent of the land (tables 3 and 4). Moreover, since landholders made up only about one-fifth of the sugar

TABLE 1

Distribution of Slaveholders by Size of Holding, 1860

| | NUMBER OF SLAVEHOLDERS | | | | |
| | 1–49 Slaves | | 50+ Slaves | | Total |
PARISH	N	%	N	%	N
Ascension	247	89.2	30	10.8	277
Assumption	433	90.5	45	9.5	478
Iberville	367	83.0	75	17.0	442
Jefferson	282	91.3	27	8.7	309
Lafourche	437	92.6	35	7.4	471
Plaquemines	200	86.6	31	13.4	231
St. Bernard	106	88.3	14	11.7	120
St. Charles	107	77.5	31	22.5	138
St. James	426	90.8	43	9.2	469
St. John the Baptist	331	93.2	24	6.8	355
St. Mary	343	79.4	89	20.6	432
Terrebonne	204	82.3	44	17.7	248
West Baton Rouge	170	82.1	37	17.9	207
Totals	3,652	87.4	525	12.6	4,177

Sources: U.S. Bureau of the Census, *Eighth Census of the United States* (Washington, D.C., 1864–1866); Karl Joseph Menn, *The Large Slaveholders of Louisiana—1860* (New Orleans, 1964).

25. The figure of adult white males is used to provide an estimate of the approximate number of households in the sugar region. Orleans Parish has been excluded from these calculations since it consisted mostly of the city of New Orleans.

TABLE 2

Distribution of Slaves by Size of Holding, 1860

| | NUMBER OF SLAVES | | | | |
| | 1–49 Slaves | | 50+ Slaves | | Total |
PARISH	N	%	N	%	N
Ascension	1,783	24.2	5,593	75.8	7,376
Assumption	3,529	43.6	4,567	56.4	8,096
Iberville	4,301	31.8	7,279	68.2	10,680
Jefferson	2,020	39.5	3,100	60.5	5,120
Lafourche	2,536	39.7	3,859	60.3	6,395
Plaquemines	1,442	26.8	3,943	73.2	5,385
St. Bernard	925	41.3	1,315	58.7	2,240
St. Charles	824	19.7	3,358	80.3	4,182
St. James	3,446	42.6	4,644	57.4	8,090
St. John the Baptist	2,530	55.1	2,064	44.9	4,594
St. Mary	3,522	27.0	9,535	73.0	13,057
Terrebonne	1,716	25.3	5,069	74.7	6,785
West Baton Rouge	1,606	30.1	3,734	69.9	5,340
Totals	29,280	33.5	58,060	66.5	87,340

Sources: U.S. Bureau of the Census, *Eighth Census of the United States* (Washington, D.C., 1864–1866); Karl Joseph Menn, *The Large Slaveholders of Louisiana—1860* (New Orleans, 1964).

region's adult white male population, the large landholders were quite a small elite, representing only 2.7 percent of all adult white males.[26]

The planter elite likewise dominated both the region's and the nation's sugar crop, producing 77.2 percent of the region's 1859 crop and 60.2 percent of all sugar made in the United States that year. (Sugar was also made in Texas, South Carolina, Georgia, Alabama, and Mississippi.) In the sugar parishes, then, a group of 525 planters—of an adult white male population of over 14,000—owned two-thirds of the slaves and more than two-thirds of the improved land and made over 75 percent of sugar in the sugar parishes on the eve of the Civil War.[27]

Statistics illustrate the structure of wealth in the sugar parishes, but individual holdings demonstrate the riches that antebellum planters accumulated. The largest

26. Defining membership in the planter elite on the basis of slaveholding has its drawbacks for measuring elite control of land, since owners of fifty or more slaves did not necessarily own 500 improved acres of land and vice versa. In fact, whereas 525 slaveholders owned fifty or more slaves in the sugar region in 1860, 390 landholders owned 500 or more improved acres. Nonetheless, there was considerable overlap between the two categories. Except in rare cases, large landholders also owned substantial numbers of slaves (if not necessarily fifty), while large slaveholders also owned substantial amounts of land (if not necessarily 500 improved acres.)

27. U.S. Bureau of the Census, *Eighth Census;* Menn, *Large Slaveholders.*

TABLE 3

Distribution of Landholders by Improved Acreage, 1860

| | NUMBER OF LANDHOLDERS | | | | | | |
| | 1–99 | | 100–499 | | 500+ | | Total |
PARISH	N	%	N	%	N	%	N
Ascension	186	79.2	23	9.7	26	11.1	235
Assumption	355	74.6	84	17.6	37	7.8	476
Iberville	147	53.1	82	29.6	48	17.3	277
Jefferson	36	45.0	23	28.8	21	26.2	80
Lafourche	212	75.5	38	13.5	31	11.0	281
Plaquemines	98	67.1	27	18.5	21	14.4	146
St. Bernard	116	81.1	12	8.4	15	10.5	143
St. Charles	34	43.6	17	21.8	27	34.6	78
St. James	106	56.4	47	25.0	35	18.6	188
St. John the Baptist	124	65.6	34	23.3	21	11.1	189
St. Mary	74	28.0	136	51.5	54	20.5	264
Terrebonne	246	76.2	55	17.0	22	6.8	323
West Baton Rouge	78	57.3	30	22.1	28	20.6	136
Totals	1,812	64.3	618	22.0	386	13.7	2,816

Source: U.S. Bureau of the Census, manuscript agricultural schedules, 1860 census.

slaveholder in Louisiana was sugar planter John Burnside, who owned 940 slaves on several contiguous estates along the Ascension–St. James Parish border. With real and personal property valued at $2.6 million in 1860, Burnside was the wealthiest man in Louisiana and among the wealthiest in the South. Burnside was not alone. Duncan F. Kenner of Ascension Parish owned 473 slaves, as did R. R. Barrow, proprietor of several plantations in Lafourche and Terrebonne Parishes. Other prominent sugar planters included William J. Minor—a Mississippi cotton planter who also owned 584 slaves on his three plantations in Terrebonne and Ascension—as well as members of the Pugh clan, who owned collectively more than a thousand slaves on some dozen plantations along Bayou Lafourche. Notable Bayou Teche families included the Weekses, Palfreys, and Patouts. These individuals and families exemplified southern Louisiana's small but distinct elite that constituted the nineteenth-century version of Big Sugar.[28]

Planters translated their material wealth into social influence and political power. As a distinct elite, they enjoyed a lifestyle that set them apart from the rest of southern Louisiana's white population. As masters of plantation households that constituted the basic units of production and reproduction in southern soci-

28. Menn, *Large Slaveholders,* 105–6, 113, and appendix B.

TABLE 4

Distribution of Land by Improved Acreage, 1860

| | NUMBER OF ACRES HELD | | | | | | |
| | 1–99 | | 100–499 | | 500+ | | Total |
	N	%	N	%	N	%	N
Ascension	4,050	9.3	5,103	11.7	34,501	79.0	43,654
Assumption	9,697	16.9	19,111	33.3	28,540	49.8	57,348
Iberville	4,885	7.8	19,217	30.9	38,189	61.3	62,291
Jefferson	1,809	7.4	4,595	18.8	17,975	73.7	24,379
Lafourche	5,261	12.8	9,142	22.2	26,808	65.1	41,211
Plaquemines	2,748	9.6	6,928	24.3	18,900	66.1	28,576
St. Bernard	2,417	14.3	2,722	16.1	11,750	69.6	16,889
St. Charles	1,562	5.3	3,861	13.2	23,930	81.5	29,353
St. James	2,931	6.5	11,205	24.8	30,910	68.7	45,013
St. John the Baptist	4,094	12.5	10,689	32.7	17,888	54.8	32,671
St. Mary	3,728	4.7	29,906	38.2	44,743	57.1	78,377
Terrebonne	5,132	13.2	14,944	38.5	18,740	48.3	38,816
West Baton Rouge	3,361	10.5	7,238	22.6	21,448	66.9	32,047
Totals	51,675	9.7	144,661	27.3	334,322	63.0	530,658

Source: U.S. Bureau of the Census, manuscript agricultural schedules, 1860 census.

ety, sugar planters shared much in common with their fellow planters in the rest of the Old South. The realities of sugar production, however, also distinguished them from other southern slaveholders.[29]

During the early nineteenth century, entry into the planter elite was open. Although sugar production demanded large capital investment, it was not uncommon for an enterprising individual to start small and with a little luck grow two or three successful sugar crops that would propel him into the budding upper echelon. As sugar cultivation spread during the 1830s and 1840s, however, the possibilities for working one's way up the social ladder decreased. By the early 1850s, with the best land concentrated in the hands of the few, it became virtually inconceivable to enter the elite's ranks without having first amassed the requisite capital in other pursuits.

29. On the world of the sugar-planter elite, see Sitterson, *Sugar Country,* 68–88. For contrasting viewpoints on the planter elite's role in the slave South, see Eugene D. Genovese, *The Political Economy of Slavery: Studies in the Economy and Society of the Slave South* (New York, 1965), and James Oakes, *The Ruling Race: A History of American Slaveholders* (New York, 1982). On the concept of the "household" as an analytical tool for interpreting the Old South, see Elizabeth Fox-Genovese, *Within the Plantation Household: Black and White Women of the Old South* (Chapel Hill, N.C., 1988), chap. 1.

Having attained financial security, the large planters began to assert their social and cultural dominance as early as the 1840s. Some constructed Big Houses that overlooked the Mississippi and Bayous Lafourche and Teche. During sugar's early period, plantation homes were relatively modest, but as the gentry became wealthier and more conscious of its status, its emphasis on ostentation grew. By the early 1850s, planters built lavish mansions that announced their wealth to all passersby. They also engaged in other activities that distinguished them from the rest of white society. As planter families intermarried, bonds of social class were reinforced by kinship. Sons were educated at schools in the North or Europe, and daughters attended finishing schools. Visitors heightened the conviviality of plantation society, as did numerous balls, dances, and other social events. Some planters spent thousands of dollars on European treasures, while others indulged their fancy for horse racing. A few engaged in private philanthropy. Only cotton planters of the Natchez District—to the north in Louisiana and Mississippi—or rice planters of the South Carolina and Georgia low country rivaled sugar planters as aspirants to the ideal of a southern aristocracy.[30]

At the same time, planters belonged to a democratic polity that celebrated the equality of all white men before the law. They could not afford to let their elitism slip into haughtiness lest it provoke their neighbors' resentment. Planters cultivated toward white people of lesser station a patriarchal attitude that fostered, ever so subtly, deference and respect for their authority. Any resentment that planters' status might have sparked was tempered by the knowledge that they could be called upon in times of trouble. "[I am] compeled for to address these lines to you," scribbled Lewis Doyle to his former employer, John Moore of St. Mary Parish. "[W]hen I worked on sechamore [plantation] I got in Delbt to Mr. Stansbury 25 Dolars and now He has sued for it." Doyle needed Moore's help. "[I] have got no Mony for I Did not earn any thing Last year What I earned on your plantation and please sir and pay it for me you sir is the only friend that I have got." If Moore settled the debt, his doing so would probably have kindled Doyle's gratitude; his refusal to help may have rankled.[31]

30. Sitterson, *Sugar Country,* 67–8. On the Natchez District, see Wayne, *Reshaping Plantation Society,* chap. 1; on the low country, see William Dusinberre, *Them Dark Days: Slavery in the American Rice Swamps* (New York, 1996).

31. L. Doyle to J. Moore, May 6, 1861, Weeks Papers, LSU. On relations between southern slaveholders and nonslaveholders, see Elizabeth Fox-Genovese and Eugene D. Genovese, "Yeoman Farmers in a Slaveholders' Democracy," in *Fruits of Merchant Capital: Slavery and Bourgeois Property in the Rise and Expansion of Capitalism* (New York, 1983), 249–64. The standard account of nonslaveholders in nineteenth-century Louisiana is Roger W. Shugg's *Origins of Class Struggle in Louisiana: A Social History of White Farmers and Laborers during Slavery and After, 1840–1875* (1939; reprint, Baton Rouge, 1968).

The sugar planters' outlook was further tempered by their proximity to New Orleans. A world-class commercial center and the Old South's largest city, it was home to a powerful class of bankers, merchants, factors, lawyers, and other professionals familiar with the ways of business. The gaze of its mercantile class extended beyond the nearby sugar plantations to the cotton of the Mississippi Valley and beyond, yet because New Orleans lay within the sugar region, its influence resonated throughout southern Louisiana in innumerable ways. Specifically, the inclusion of this major financial hub and metropolis in a region known for its lack of urban development imbued sugar planters with a stronger cosmopolitan outlook and commercial ethos than was the case among most other southern slaveholders. Many planters, especially those along the river, regularly visited the city to attend the theater or opera, consult with factors, and purchase slaves. Some even kept both city and country homes.

Public duty also beckoned sugar planters, who formed part of the coalition— along with Natchez District and Red River planters and the New Orleans business community—that ruled Louisiana. Because the apportionment provisions of Louisiana's antebellum constitutions tended to privilege the more developed southern parishes over the rest of the state, sugar planters wielded what critics complained was a disproportionate degree of political influence. Planters also controlled parochial offices and dominated membership of parish police juries. Several were elected governor, while others served in Congress. Not only did sugar planters grip the reins of power firmly, they also shaped public opinion on the issues of the day, especially that of slavery.[32]

The preferred political leaning of sugar planters was Whig. Indeed, southern Louisiana was a bastion of southern Whiggery. Whig strength among sugar planters owed mostly to the party's support for the protective duty on sugar, without which Louisiana planters believed they could not survive and which they defended with a zeal surpassed only by their defense of slavery itself. Even with the Whig Party's demise in the 1850s, Whig sentiment persisted, as many planters turned to the nativist Know-Nothing Party rather than join the Democrats. The emergence of slavery as the all-consuming issue in national politics in the 1850s compelled planters to redouble their efforts to preserve that institution even as their enthusiasm for southern independence remained tepid. Sugar planters supported the Confederate cause once secession became reality, but their ambivalent

32. On antebellum Louisiana politics, see Joseph G. Tregle Jr., *Louisiana in the Age of Jackson: A Clash of Cultures and Personalities* (Baton Rouge, 1998), and John Michael Sacher, "'A Perfect War': Politics and Parties in Louisiana, 1824–1861" (Ph.D. diss., Louisiana State University, 1999).

political loyalties would have important consequences during the Civil War and well after it.[33]

Sugar planters shared a commitment to slavery with other slaveholders. Slavery placed slaveholders, including sugar planters, at odds with the northern free-labor ideology. Slaveholders repudiated the notion that capitalists bore no responsibility for their workers and merely purchased labor power in a free and open market. Instead, they adhered to a paternalistic outlook, which held that they must provide for their slaves' general welfare. Of course, the reality of slavery departed widely from the paternalistic ideal. But slaveholders' failure to live up to their ideals did not thereby invalidate them. If plantation slavery was as much a way of life as a way to make money, then most slaveholders regarded humane treatment of their slaves as both Christian duty and sound business.[34]

To the degree that it existed, paternalism arose from the particular features of slavery in the American South. First, slaveholdings were small when compared with those of other New World slave societies, in particular the British and French West Indies, where individual holdings routinely numbered in the hundreds. Moreover, the degree to which slaveholders were absent from their estates for long periods, though notable in parts of the South, was negligible when measured against the tradition of absenteeism that had prevailed in the British Caribbean. Finally, abolition of the international slave trade in 1808 coupled slavery's future with natural reproduction of the slave population and compelled slaveholders to attend to their slaves' well-being. On the surface, it would seem that conditions in southern Louisiana were not conducive to paternalism. Some planters owned hundreds of slaves. Others possessed multiple estates and thus were absent much of the time. And sugar planters, though prohibited from the foreign slave trade, readily bought and sold slaves in a domestic trade and thus might have cared little for the welfare of individual slaves. Paternalism would seem to have stood little chance of being practiced in the sugar region.[35]

Nonetheless, sugar planters were not entirely devoid of paternalistic sensibilities. They may not have kept abreast of the details of their slaves' lives, but they

33. Sitterson, *Sugar Country*, 175–8; David O. Whitten, "Tariff and Profit in the Antebellum Louisiana Sugar Industry," *Business History Review* 44 (summer 1970): 226–33; Joseph G. Tregle, "Louisiana and the Tariff, 1816–1846," *LHQ* 25 (January 1942): 24–148.

34. On northern free-labor ideology, see Foner, *Free Soil;* Glickstein, *Concepts of Free Labor;* and Schmidt, *Free to Work,* chaps. 1 and 2. On paternalism, see Eugene D. Genovese, *Roll, Jordan, Roll: The World the Slaves Made* (New York, 1974), 3–7.

35. For an overview of other New World slave societies, see Robin Blackburn, *The Making of New World Slavery: From the Baroque to the Modern, 1492–1800* (London, 1997).

customarily wrote about individual slaves—field hands as well as domestic servants—in a manner that connoted familiarity. Planters who owned several estates
were rarely absent for extended periods. They frequently visited their various
plantations or routinely received reports from managers, overseers, or sons who
acted as surrogates. Few Louisiana planters behaved as true absentee landlords.
And although sugar planters availed themselves of the internal slave trade, it also
made sense economically and ideologically for them to enable their slaves to reproduce, representing as they did a valuable investment. Slaves on large plantations probably received better health care, by the standards of the day, than did
slaves on smaller estates. Indeed, aware of the conditions under which their slaves
lived and worked, sugar planters were likely more sensitive to their slaves' welfare
than were most other slaveholders.[36]

Even if the realities of slavery in the sugar region spawned a measure of paternalism, sugar making was a business from which planters had to derive a profit.
Sugar planters' search for profitability was complicated by the vagaries of the capitalist world market. The protective tariff ensured them a measure of security, but
they still engaged in a risky business, one in which the chance to strike it rich
equaled the prospects of failure. All southern slaveholders, to be sure, had to concern themselves with profitability, but cotton planters wielded a degree of control
over the international cotton market about which sugar planters could only dream.
This combination of risk and opportunity fostered an aggrandizing, profit-
oriented ethos among sugar planters, who, being involved in a semi-industrial
process, already exhibited a predisposition to think like northern capitalists. Paternalism was not entirely absent from their thinking, but they could not afford to ignore the bottom line. If their businesses did not turn a profit, ideological justifica-
tion of slavery was moot.

The profit incentive alone, however, does not indicate capitalism or a capitalist
society. Despite their desire to accumulate wealth, Louisiana sugar planters rejected the doctrines that labor power was a commodity and that those who purchased it bore no responsibility for those who sold it. Instead, the paternalistic
outlook bred of American slavery and the exigencies of making sugar within the
capitalist market formed the contours of the sugar planters' world view. While
slaveholders throughout the South evinced this tension between profitability and

36. On absenteeism, see J. Carlyle Sitterson, "The William J. Minor Plantations: A Study in
Ante-Bellum Absentee Ownership," *JSH* 9 (February 1943): 59–74, and "Lewis Thompson, A
Carolinian and His Louisiana Plantation, 1848–1888: A Study in Absentee Ownership," in
Essays in Southern History, ed. Fletcher Green (Chapel Hill, N.C., 1949), 16–27. On slaves' med-
ical care, see David O. Whitten, "Medical Care of Slaves: Louisiana Sugar Region and South
Carolina Rice District," *Southern Studies* 16 (summer 1977): 153–80.

paternalism, it was especially pronounced among the sugar region's planter elite. Sugar planters were profit maximizers who exploited labor ruthlessly, and they were paternalists for whom labor was not merely a commodity to be bought and sold.

The sugar planters' social position was inconceivable without slaves, whose labor generated the slaveholders' wealth and bestowed upon them their special place in southern society. Intrinsic to slaveholding was a constellation of values and assumptions about the status of the slaveholder, who could not trade his slaves for another form of property and retain the prestige that inhered in owning human beings. But slavery cannot be thought of in terms of what it did to slaveholders without considering what it did to slaves. Slavery denied slaves control over their own persons, and it enabled one group of people to live upon the fruits of another's labor. Even as it allowed for systematic plunder, slavery disguised its class character behind the veil of racial subordination. Slavery was a system of racial oppression, but it was also a means of exploiting labor. The class and racial dimensions of American slavery, although distinct, were inextricably intertwined. While only black people in the South were slaves, they were enslaved for their labor as well as the color of their skin.[37]

Labor—harsh, unrelenting, and backbreaking—consumed most of the slaves' waking hours, but it formed only part of their daily existence. Facing unspeakable oppression, they struggled to give meaning to their lives and to create communities from which they drew strength. At the center of the slaves' world—both in the sugar region and throughout the South—stood an abiding faith in Christianity and a unwavering devotion to their families. If nothing else, this struggle to find meaning and to build communities testified to the resiliency of the human spirit.[38]

Slaves also attempted to capitalize upon the paternalism of planters to create niches of autonomy. The reciprocal obligations between subordinate and superior inherent in paternalism became for slaves a means by which to establish traditional privileges that the master was bound to respect by custom if not by law. The

37. On the unique status that slaveholders derived from owning slaves as opposed to other forms of property, see Genovese, *Political Economy,* chap. 1; David Brion Davis, *The Problem of Slavery in the Age of Revolution, 1770–1823* (Ithaca, N.Y., 1975), 557–64; Elizabeth Fox-Genovese and Eugene D. Genovese, "Jurisprudence and Property Relations in Bourgeois and Slave Society," in *Fruits of Merchant Capital,* 337–87; and Mark Tushnet, *The American Law of Slavery: Considerations of Humanity and Interest* (Princeton, N.J., 1981), esp. 30–43.

38. On slave family life in antebellum Louisiana, see Ann Patton Malone, *Sweet Chariot: Slave Family and Household Structure in Nineteenth-Century Louisiana* (Chapel Hill, N.C., 1992).

process of negotiation between master and slave embraced such everyday matters as the pace of work, the severity of punishment, and the amount and quality of the slaves' provisions. By no means did slaves tell their masters how to run their affairs, but planters would hardly serve their own purposes by acting as tyrants. Only at the risk of disrupting plantation regimen did a slaveholder exercise authority arbitrarily or deny slaves their customary privileges. If, by accepting the basic tenets of paternalism, slaves undermined their ability to contest their enslavement, they nonetheless found in paternalism a strategy for physical and psychological survival.[39]

In the sugar region, however, there were distinct limits to paternalism and to the slaves' ability to use it for their own purposes. Planters' demonstrable preference for male slaves to perform the arduous work of sugar production profoundly affected the slave population's demographic profile and, consequently, slave family life. Among slaves of productive age (15 to 59) in the sugar parishes (excluding Orleans Parish) in 1860, men outnumbered women 32,028 to 23,662, or 57.5 percent to 42.5 percent. The sex ratio among this part of the slave population, then, was 1.4 males for every female—a dramatic imbalance among any population that has not experienced a cataclysmic event, such as war. Among particular age cohorts within certain parishes, the sexual imbalances were even more striking. In Jefferson, 61.6 percent of slaves 20 to 29 were men; in St. James, 63.7 percent of slaves 30 to 39 were men; and in Iberville, 68.4 percent of slaves 40 to 49 were men. Therefore, slave populations on many sugar plantations included a significant proportion of men of productive and reproductive age who had almost no prospects for marriage. Some planters were aware that skewed sex ratios would imperil the stability of their slaveholdings, and they tried to achieve better sexual balance among their slaves. But it was also clear that a number of planters purchased male slaves to run their plantations, evidently ignoring the fact that many of them would never find marriage partners.[40]

Despite the demographic challenges they confronted, slaves on sugar plantations secured as meaningful a family life as possible. Over time, the composition of slave households stabilized and increased in complexity; slaves established nuclear households as well as extended kin networks. Nonetheless, planters' behavior undermined the prospects of many of their male slaves to marry and establish their own families. Thus, paternalism in the sugar region did not override planters' determination to secure the labor needed to run their estates. Moreover, the apparent lack of familial attachment among many male slaves had important reper-

39. The slaves' manipulation of paternalism for their own purposes has received its foremost treatment in Genovese, *Roll, Jordan, Roll.*

40. U.S. Bureau of the Census, *Eighth Census;* Malone, *Sweet Chariot,* chaps. 3 and 5.

cussions after emancipation: the preponderance of single, unattached young men would contribute to what planters viewed as the unstable and transient character of their labor forces under free labor.

On January 26, 1861, a special convention in Baton Rouge overwhelmingly ratified an ordinance of secession. Louisiana became the sixth state—following South Carolina, Mississippi, Florida, Alabama, and Georgia—to sever its ties to the Union upon Abraham Lincoln's election as president the previous November. After forming a provisional government, the seceding states were eventually joined by Arkansas, Texas, North Carolina, Tennessee, and Virginia in forging the Confederate States of America, which now faced the struggle to win independence as a new nation. Secession enjoyed popular support in Louisiana and the other slave states. This support was not unanimous, however, as Unionist sentiment, or at least misgivings over secession, prevailed among many white southerners during winter and spring 1861. One such group was the sugar planters, among whom fire-eating had never been fashionable. Andrew McCollam, delegate to the secession convention from Terrebonne Parish, described his vote for secession as the "bitterest pill that I ever took." Nonetheless, whatever their feelings before secession, planters shuddered at the prospects of a federal victory in the war that must surely follow. They knew they had no choice but to support southern independence.[41]

In the months following secession, plantation matters remained largely undisturbed. Despite one planter's insistence, as Lincoln's inauguration approached, that "the Negroes have got it into their heads they are going to be free on the 4th of March," life went on much as it always had. If, once the fighting started, slaves began to ponder the potentially revolutionary dimensions of the conflict, they did not share such thoughts with their owners. Notwithstanding the rumored uneasiness among slaves that invariably circulated in times of turmoil, planters reported no disruption of work routine.[42]

The war made itself felt, however, in financial affairs. The federal naval block-

41. A. McCollam to E. McCollam, Jan. 27, 1861, Andrew McCollam Papers, SHC. See also Jan. 27, 1861, Plant. Diary (typescript), AFPP, *RASP,* ser. I; W. F. Weeks to Sir, Jan. 10, 1861, Weeks Papers, LSU. On the secession crisis in Louisiana, see Charles B. Dew, "The Long Lost Returns: The Candidates and Their Totals in Louisiana's Secession Election," *LH* 10 (fall 1969): 353–69, and "Who Won the Secession Elections in Louisiana?" *JSH* 36 (February 1970): 18–32; Mary Lilla McLure, "The Elections of 1860 in Louisiana," *LHQ* 9 (October 1926): 601–702; Charles P. Roland, "Louisiana and Secession," *LH* 19 (fall 1978): 389–99; Roger W. Shugg, "A Suppressed Co-operationist Protest against Secession," *LHQ* 19 (January 1936): 199–203; and Ralph Wooster, "The Louisiana Secession Convention," *LHQ* 34 (April 1951): 103–33.

42. Feb. 24, 1861, Plant. Diary (typescript), AFPP, *RASP,* ser. I.

ade of southern ports in spring 1861 crippled commerce in New Orleans and prevented marketing of a bumper sugar crop. Even before the blockade, the New
Orleans financial community was in chaos and trade throughout the Mississippi
Valley was erratic. As early as November 1860, sugar was selling, in the words of
one merchant, "at prices so irregular that it is impossible to quote." By fall 1861 the
situation was dire. "[O]ur white sugars . . . cannot now be sold," complained one
planter. The price of sugar was down, he noted, while other commodities were
"very scarce and very high." By the following spring, planters faced severe hardship.[43]

Equally unsettling to white residents of southern Louisiana in spring 1862 was
the amassing of federal troops at Ship Island, Mississippi, in preparation for an
imminent invasion. "Things look gloomy and we will have terrible fighting before
many weeks," one planter predicted in February. Few white southerners would
have been reassured by the response a few weeks later to a call for militia troops in
Plaquemines Parish, the area's first line of defense. "Patriotism is very low in this
parish," complained one resident. Flagging patriotism paled next to what lay
ahead, as war was about to hit home in ways that few had foreseen.[44]

43. Darby & Tremoulet to J. Moore, Nov. 14, 1860, Weeks Papers, LSU; Nov. 8, 1861,
Magnolia Plant. Journal 3, Warmoth Papers, SHC. See also R. A. Oliver to W. W. Pugh, Oct.
22, 1860, and W. L. Knox to W. W. Pugh, Dec. 17, 1861, Pugh Papers, *RASP,* ser. G; Milledge L.
Bonham, ed., "Financial and Economic Disturbances in New Orleans on the Eve of Secession,"
LHQ 13 (January 1930): 32–6; E. Merton Coulter, "Effects of Secession upon the Commerce of
the Mississippi Valley," *Mississippi Valley Historical Review* 3 (December 1916): 275–300.

44. Feb. 9, 1862, Lawrence Plant. Diary, Brashear and Lawrence Family Papers, SHC; Mar.
4, 1862, Magnolia Plant. Journal 3, Warmoth Papers, SHC.

§ 2 §

THE SWEETNESS OF FREEDOM

A man had as well be in purgatory, as attempt to work a sugar
plantation under existing circumstances.

—November 14, 1863, William J. Minor Plantation Diary

The world of master and slave in southern Louisiana was turned upside
down in late April 1862, when a U.S. naval fleet darted past Forts Jackson
and St. Philip, near the mouth of the Mississippi River. Rendered de-
fenseless, New Orleans soon capitulated to federal forces under General Benjamin F. Butler, commander of the newly formed Department of the Gulf.[1]

Butler's troops had come to preserve the Union, not to end slavery. Nonetheless, slaves on plantations along the Mississippi ascribed their own meaning to the
federal presence. Within days of watching Union gunboats pass, slaves began ab-
sconding to federal lines. In the weeks ahead, as word of the Yankees' arrival spread,
hundreds bolted for freedom, with one planter reporting a "perfect stampede" of
slaves in early July. Some hot-tempered slaveholders responded by impetuously
driving off those who remained behind. Repudiating his paternalistic obligations,
one planter told his slaves that "the Yankees are King now" and that they must "go
to their King for food and shelter." Such were slaveholders' embittered reactions
to their loss of mastery.[2]

1. Chester G. Hearn, *The Capture of New Orleans, 1862* (Baton Rouge, 1995); John D. Winters, *The Civil War in Louisiana* (Baton Rouge, 1963), 71–102.

2. Apr. 24, 30, May 7, 13–4, 19, 25–6, Magnolia Plant. Journal 3, Warmoth Papers, SHC; July
8, 1862, Plant. Diary (typescript), AFPP, *RASP,* ser. I; *Freedom* 1:210–1. On southern slaveholders'

At the same time that the slaves' flight to freedom enraged their owners, it forced federal policy makers to confront the issue of slavery. By early summer 1862, the federal government still had not adopted a consistent policy on fugitive slaves. But the unexpected arrival at Union camps of hundreds of slaves—in Louisiana and in other parts of the Confederacy under federal control—compelled it to do so. Congress passed in July 1862 the second Confiscation Act and the Militia Act, marking an important turning point in federal policy on slavery. By freeing slaves of disloyal slaveholders (those who had abandoned their plantations to aid the Confederacy or had driven off their slaves) and by authorizing employment of fugitive slaves to suppress the rebellion, mostly as military laborers, the acts removed much uncertainty surrounding the status of certain slaves but dodged the issue of slaves whose masters were ostensibly loyal. This omission proved especially troublesome in Louisiana, where many slaveholders remained on their plantations after federal occupation and swore the loyalty oath. The competing claims of slaves and loyal slaveholders vexed many a Union officer in the following months.[3]

The slaves' flight from the plantations during summer and early fall 1862 triggered conflict among slaves, slaveholders, and Union army officers. Planters relentlessly pursued what to them was their property. Many appealed to Butler to return their runaway slaves and even to provide provost guards on the plantations. An implacable foe of slavery, Butler would not turn his army into a slave patrol, but as a stickler for constitutional niceties, he realized that he lacked authority to

responses to their loss of mastery, see James L. Roark, *Masters without Slaves: Southern Planters in the Civil War and Reconstruction* (New York, 1977), 68–108. The central role played by slaves in the destruction of slavery is well established. See *Freedom* 1:1–56. Previous examinations of the sugar region during the Civil War include Robert F. Pace, "'It Was Bedlam Let Loose': The Louisiana Sugar Country and the Civil War," *LH* 39 (fall 1998): 389–409; Walter Prichard, "The Effects of the Civil War on the Louisiana Sugar Industry," *JSH* 5 (August 1939): 315–32; C. Peter Ripley, *Slaves and Freedmen in Civil War Louisiana* (Baton Rouge, 1976); Charles P. Roland, *Louisiana Sugar Plantations during the American Civil War* (1957; reprint with a new foreword by John David Smith, Baton Rouge, 1997), and "Difficulties of Civil War Sugar Planting in Louisiana," *LHQ* 38 (October 1955): 40–62; and Sitterson, *Sugar Country*, 205–27. On free labor's wartime origins in southern Louisiana, see *Freedom* 1:187–99; *Freedom* 3:346–77; and William F. Messner, *Freedmen and the Ideology of Free Labor: Louisiana, 1862–1865* (Lafayette, La., 1978).

3. In August 1861 Congress had enacted the first Confiscation Act, mandating seizure of all property, including slaves, used directly in support of the rebellion, but that measure applied to relatively few slaves. *Statutes at Large of the United States of America* (Washington, D.C., 1863) 12:319. For the second Confiscation Act and Militia Act, see 589–92 and 597–600 of the same volume, and *Freedom* 1:19–20. On the evolution of federal policy concerning fugitives, see Louis S. Gerteis, *From Contraband to Freedman: Federal Policy toward Southern Blacks, 1861–1865* (Westport, Conn., 1973).

attack slavery directly and was legally obligated to protect slave property of loyal citizens. Further, Butler realized that he needed planter cooperation to restore order in the countryside and establish a loyal government in Louisiana. He thus faced the unenviable task of reconciling the goals of slaves and slaveholders, while simultaneously reining in subordinates such as Generals John W. Phelps and Neal Dow, who acted upon their abolitionist sentiments by encouraging slaves to leave their masters and by issuing "free passes" to them.[4]

While planters and officers addressed the problem of runaway slaves, the 1862 growing season was slipping away. Hoping to reestablish order and to save the lucrative sugar crop, Butler entered into an agreement in October with loyal planters of St. Bernard and Plaquemines Parishes that inaugurated quasi-free labor. Born largely of expediency, the program imposed elements of free labor but prohibited its unfettered development. By recognizing the claims of loyal slaveholders while guaranteeing minimal rights for slaves, Butler's labor policy advanced the army's goals of restoring order and reviving the plantation economy.

Under Butler's guidelines, planters agreed to pay male laborers monthly wages of $10, less $3 for clothing (the standard pay of military laborers; women received an unspecified lesser amount), and to provide laborers and dependents with rations, housing, and medical care. In return, laborers would work for ten hours per day, twenty-six days per month. Slaves of planters who refused to sign the agreement were permitted to hire themselves to loyal planters. Butler prohibited corporal punishment but agreed to furnish military patrols to keep laborers on plantations. While evading the question of slavery's future, the agreement provided for manumission of any slave who suffered physical abuse from his or her owner. Thus Butler's policy, despite its limitations, not only established certain rights for laborers but also interposed federal authority between master and slave, significantly undermining slavery in the sugar region. Although the Emancipation Proclamation would exempt federally controlled parts of Louisiana from its provisions, slavery was doomed there so long as federal authority prevailed.[5]

4. For examples of planters' efforts to have fugitive slaves returned, see June 14, 1862, Magnolia Plant. Journal 3, Warmoth Papers, SHC, and July 9, 1862, Plant. Diary (typescript), AFPP, *RASP,* ser. I. Much has been written on Butler's controversial administration in New Orleans. For a recent analysis, see Chester G. Hearn, *When the Devil Came Down to Dixie: Ben Butler in New Orleans* (Baton Rouge, 1997). Phelps, a Vermont abolitionist, continually quarreled with Butler before eventually resigning his commission. Dow, a Maine abolitionist, began distributing free passes in August to slaves whose masters had driven them away. *Freedom* 1:194; Frank L. Byrne, "'A Terrible Machine': General Neal Dow's Military Government on the Gulf Coast," *Civil War History* 12 (March 1966): 5–22.

5. U.S. War Department, *The War of the Rebellion: Official Records of the Union and Confederate Armies,* 128 vols. (Washington, D.C., 1880–1901), 15:594–5; *Freedom* 3:383–5.

Although slaves were not party to the accord, their owners soon learned that their wishes could not be ignored if plantation operations were to resume. On Magnolia, the Plaquemines Parish estate of Effingham Lawrence, for instance, discipline slowly eroded during late summer and fall. Laborers came and went almost at will, and they slowed the pace of work. Fearing loss of the crop, Lawrence in September promised his slaves "a handsome present" if they worked well during the rolling season. Yet matters worsened for Lawrence. As rolling approached, the laborers became more assertive, reducing the hours of work or refusing to work at all. By October 19, plantation discipline had completely disintegrated. "Revolt & Insurrection among the negroes," Lawrence exclaimed. "They all went up to McManus's Plantation. Returned with flags & drums shouting Abe Lincoln and Freedom." Not until late November did laborers begin to cut cane for the sugar mill, and even then they demanded better provisions and threatened to leave. "Negroes grumbling about food etc. wont work they say on *pork & corn-bread*," Lawrence noted. "Must *have flour biscuit beef etc. or they will go else where.*"[6]

Nevertheless, once the rolling season began in earnest, Lawrence's laborers threw their full efforts into it, producing a crop of more than five hundred hogsheads, which compared well with antebellum levels. In so doing, they exhibited their understanding of the order that was to be. Aware of what sugar production required, the laborers exerted themselves so long as they received wages and exercised some control over their working lives. "Everything in the sugar house is working nicely and it is most gratifying to see the good conduct of the negroes," Lawrence noted in December. Because of Butler's agreement, the laborers no longer worked as they once had, yet in Lawrence's mind they were not free. The $2,500 he distributed among them in late January 1863 was not compensation but a present, he said, and he lectured them that "they were not free but my slaves and my property."[7]

Events on Magnolia previewed relations between planters and ex-slaves in coming years. Rejecting the authority of their masters, former slaves were determined to redefine plantation regimen. Yet they also voluntarily engaged in the work of sugar production once they believed that they were laboring not as slaves but as free people. Planters like Effingham Lawrence saw matters very differently. Neither party probably found the experiences of this first rolling season under free

6. The discussion of events on Lawrence's plantation is based on entries between August 1862 and January 1863 in Magnolia Plant. Journal 3, Warmoth Papers, SHC. Quotations are at Sept. 6, Oct. 19, and Nov. 24. For Magnolia's antebellum background, see J. Carlyle Sitterson, "Magnolia Plantation, 1852–1862: A Decade of a Louisiana Sugar Estate," *Mississippi Valley Historical Review* 25 (September 1938): 197–210.

7. Dec. 1, 1862, Jan. 25, 1863, Magnolia Plant. Journal 3, Warmoth Papers, SHC.

labor satisfying, but one thing was certain: laborers were slaves in name only, and only because officials like Butler had no choice but to temporize on their status.

Butler's labor program was limited geographically to Plaquemines and St. Bernard Parishes. By fall 1862 federal authority barely extended beyond the land adjacent to the Mississippi. Even as Butler drafted his original agreement, however, he prepared to bring the area surrounding Bayou Lafourche, west of New Orleans, under Union control. In late October U.S. troops under General Godfrey Weitzel invaded the Lafourche country. After bitter fighting, much of it on plantations and in unharvested cane fields, the federals occupied Thibodaux; by early November they controlled the entire Lafourche region. As the Union army proceeded down the bayou, news of its arrival inspired hundreds more slaves to flee plantations and seek sanctuary with those they hailed as liberators. After troops passed his plantations in late October, one planter reported "great excitement among the slaves." Over the next week discipline deteriorated. "Found our negroes completely demoralized, some gone and more preparing to go," he noted. "I fear we shall lose them all." [8]

Managing hundreds of fugitive slaves, or contraband, while conducting a military campaign posed immense logistical problems for Weitzel, who did not relish his role of liberator. "What shall I do about the negroes?" he asked Butler, who had already begun to address the situation. On November 9 Butler issued General Order 91, imposing his original labor agreement upon the Lafourche district and sequestering the estates of disloyal owners. A Sequestration Commission was created to administer confiscated property and to supervise plantation affairs in the district.[9]

Butler's action provoked a wide range of responses from Lafourche planters. A small minority abandoned their estates and took refuge in the Confederate interior. The Sequestration Commission rented their plantations to lessees, some of whom were northerners in search of opportunity. Northerners who had moved

8. Oct. 27–Nov. 3, 1862, Plant. Diary (typescript), AFPP, *RASP*, ser. I. On the federal invasion of the Lafourche country, see Winters, *Civil War in Louisiana*, 157–64; Barnes F. Lathrop, "The Lafourche District in 1862: Invasion," *LH* 2 (spring 1961): 175–201; and Stephen Scott Michot, "Society at War: Sectionalism, Secession, and Civil War in Louisiana's Lafourche Region" (Ph.D. diss., Mississippi State University, 1994), chap. 5.

9. James Parton, *General Butler in New Orleans: History of the Administration of the Department of the Gulf in the Year 1862* (New York, 1864), 580; Benjamin F. Butler, *Private and Official Correspondence of Gen. Benjamin F. Butler during the Period of the Civil War*, 5 vols. (Norwood, Mass., 1917), 2:439. For General Order 91, see U.S. War Department, *War of the Rebellion*, 15:592–5. Sequestration of property was in response to transactions that had taken place between disloyal planters whose plantations were liable to confiscation and speculators who were purchasing them. On the Sequestration Commission, see *Freedom* 3:352.

south also entered into business partnerships with planters who agreed to Butler's labor policy but lacked funds to make regular wage payments. Most Lafourche planters assented to paying wages, having no other choice, but others took drastic action. Coming only weeks after Lincoln's preliminary emancipation decree in September, General Order 91 seemed to presage slavery's end. Believing their slaves would soon be freed, many planters refused to cooperate with Butler. Instead, they drove away the slaves with a scorched-earth policy, hoping to throw the region into further chaos. If they could not make sugar with slave labor, they would not make it at all.

The results of the 1862 rolling season seem to confirm the success of planters' scorched-earth strategy. Louisiana produced 87,000 hogsheads in 1862, down from 460,000 the previous year. This loss would also appear to validate the planters' claim that sugar production required coerced labor. "The sugar crop as now cultivated is not one that can be left to the chances of a system, under which labor may leave the employer or may attempt a strike at the critical moment," a New Orleans journalist observed. "The capital necessary for it will not be laid out by any man, who does not feel that he can count upon the absolute control of his labor at certain seasons." In late 1862 and early 1863 few planters could count upon such control. Though the slaves' legal status remained unclear, recent events showed that the old plantation regimen belonged to the past. Even more disturbing was what such events portended. With the frustrations of the harvest fresh in their minds, planters faced a new crop season with the same laborers who had unequivocally repudiated their authority.[10]

On January 1, 1863, President Abraham Lincoln redeemed the pledge he had made the previous September by issuing the Emancipation Proclamation. Declaring the slaves in rebellious states to be free, the proclamation made abolishing slavery a Union war goal and transformed the war's meaning. At the same time, however, the proclamation specifically exempted from its provisions the sugar parishes and other parts of the Confederacy that had come under federal control and where steps toward creating loyal governments had begun. Under Butler's stewardship, elections had already taken place in Louisiana's First and Second Congressional Districts, which included the sugar region. Moreover, in addition to Lincoln's refusal, on grounds of constitutional scruples, to attack slavery in areas not in rebellion, he also hoped to win the support of loyal slaveholders for a Unionist government for Louisiana. Nonetheless, as the 1863 crop season progressed, slaves seized the opportunity to dismantle the slave regime further. Loyal

10. *DP,* Mar. 15, 1863.

planters, for their part, grasped at the proclamation's exemption in a desperate, rearguard attempt to preserve slavery. Army officers, in turn, mediated relations between would-be masters and quasi-free laborers.[11]

The Emancipation Proclamation left planters' long-term future in doubt, and their immediate prospects appeared no better. Stretches of unharvested cane standing in fields that should already have been prepared for planting offered incontrovertible evidence of their woes. Worse, planters operated in the midst of a complete breakdown in plantation discipline. Realizing that every moment lost in spring planting jeopardized the crop, they concocted schemes designed to induce their slaves to resume work. But the failure of such stratagems proved how irrevocably relations with their former slaves had changed.[12]

Desperate to regain control over their workers, planters appealed to military authorities in hopes of obtaining a labor policy that reflected their proslavery vision. In January 1863 a delegation met with General Nathaniel P. Banks, who had replaced Butler in December as departmental commander, for the purpose of expressing, as William J. Minor put it, "our necessities & what guarantees we wanted to enable us to undertake with safety to make a crop this year." A Massachusetts Republican and former speaker of U.S. House of Representatives, Banks was among the many northern politicians commissioned as Union officers in order to gain their constituents' support for the war. Lincoln had sent Banks to Louisiana to erase the bitterness created by the irascible Butler, but Banks was not about to cotton to slaveholders. Instead, he dismissed them as "full of theories, prejudices, opinions based on the old system" and urged them to "look to the new state of things, to the future & not to the past."[13]

11. James D. Richardson, ed., *A Compilation of the Messages and Papers of the Presidents*, 20 vols. (New York, 1897–1917), 8:3358–60. For one comprehensive examination of Lincoln's decision to issue the Emancipation Proclamation, see William C. Harris, *With Charity for All: Lincoln and the Restoration of the Union* (Lexington, Ky., 1997). Important works on Lincoln's wartime Reconstruction policy for Louisiana include LaWanda Cox, *Lincoln and Black Freedom: A Study in Presidential Leadership* (Columbia, S.C., 1981); Joseph G. Dawson III, *Army Generals and Reconstruction: Louisiana, 1862–1877* (Baton Rouge, 1982); Gerteis, *Contraband to Freedman*; Peyton McCrary, *Abraham Lincoln and Reconstruction: The Louisiana Experiment* (Princeton, N.J., 1978); Messner, *Freedmen and Ideology of Free Labor*; Joe Gray Taylor, *Louisiana Reconstructed, 1863–1877* (Baton Rouge, 1974); and Ted Tunnell, *Crucible of Reconstruction: War, Radicalism, and Race in Louisiana, 1862–1877* (Baton Rouge, 1984).

12. For examples of planters' efforts to recapture their slaves, see F. E. Sprague to AFP, Jan. 10, 1863; Mrs. G. Pugh to AFP, Jan. 10, 1863; Foley, Avery & Co. to AFP, Jan. 23, 1863; E. M. Pugh to AFP, Feb. 2, 1863, with enclosure from J. Pugh; E. Pugh to AFP, Feb. 15, 18, 25, and undated [Feb. or Mar.], 1863, all in Pugh Papers, *RASP*, ser. G.

13. Jan. 8, 20, 1863, Plant. Diary 35, WJMP. See also *Freedom* 3:408–10. Banks has been the

While his response left planters sorely disappointed, Banks was wary of alienating them. Indeed, knowing that he depended on their support in reconstructing
Louisiana, Banks implemented a labor policy of which planters might have approved had they been willing to accept anything besides slavery. In early February
the Sequestration Commission, acting under the authority of Banks's General
Order 12, established new labor guidelines. Like Butler's policy, Banks's program
reflected the army's desire for order and planters' need to control labor while rele-
gating laborers' aspirations to the background. Under military guard if necessary,
the "Slaves" would provide faithful labor and exhibit "perfect subordination," in
return for which planters would furnish necessities. The laborers' prescribed compensation fell far short of Butler's terms from the previous fall. Under a share-
wage arrangement, workers would collectively receive at year's end a mere one-
twentieth share of the proceeds of the crop, which they would then divide among
themselves. If both parties agreed, planters would pay laborers monthly wages,
but at rates of $2 for men and $1 for women. Like Butler, Banks had not deigned
to consult with laborers before issuing his regulations. The ex-slaves soon made
their dissatisfaction known.[14]

Even before laborers could articulate their displeasure with army labor policy,
however, planters expressed their own reservations about anything less than the
antebellum status quo. At a meeting in New Orleans in mid-February, one planter
proposed that a committee meet with Banks to determine whether his policy
would "secure the return of negroes . . . to the plantations to which they are *bound
as laborers.*" Around the same time, other planters called Banks's attention to the
contradiction of imposing free labor where slavery still existed. To do so, they argued, "would be an attempt to reconcile things which, in their nature, are utterly
incompatible. . . . [V]oluntary or free labor cannot be governed by the same rules
as forced or slave labor, without changing entirely the status of the slaves."
Unfortunately for planters, these overtures were ignored. The logic may have been
sound, but Banks was uninterested in debating political economy. His attention
centered instead on the economic and political reconstruction of Louisiana.
Needing slaveholders' support to achieve those ends, Banks was willing to lend a
sympathetic ear to their travails, but he was not about to confer the labor control
they deemed essential to running their estates.[15]

Unable to command labor, planters viewed their operations during the 1863
planting and cultivating seasons as disastrous. Laborers refused to exhibit the

subject of two biographies, including James G. Hollandsworth Jr., *Pretense of Glory: The Life of
General Nathaniel P. Banks* (Baton Rouge, 1998).

   14. *Freedom* 3:419–21, quotation 420; see also 414–5.

   15. *DP,* Feb. 20, 1863; *Freedom* 3:421–3.

"perfect subordination" called for in Banks's labor regulations, coming and going as they pleased despite military patrols, and neither working nor comporting themselves as they once had. "Negroes doing next to nothing & I can't make them do any better by talking to them," complained one planter. Isaac Erwin of Iberville Parish also decried the collapse of plantation discipline. "Negros took to day with out saying a word for Holliday," he noted in late May, "and say they are Free and have as much law in their favor as I have."[16]

Under such circumstances, planters believed only the lash could restore discipline, even though its use violated military orders. If laborers would not work, one planter instructed his overseers, physical punishment "must be resorted to & inflicted in a proper manner." Planters were demanding, a Union officer noted in June 1863, either that provost guards "*compel* the negroes to work" or that they themselves "be authorized, and sustained in using force." Yet if slaveholders were more intent on restoring the old order than adjusting to the new, they underestimated their workers' resolve to contest previous forms of domination. "The planters and overseers do not sufficiently appreciate . . . the change that has taken place," one provost marshal reported. Exhibiting "a spirit of independence," laborers would not endure "the same treatment, the same customs, and rules—the same language—that they have heretofore quietly submitted to." An elderly black man put the matter succinctly. "All I want for my people," he told a Union officer, "is to be rid for ever of Masterism!"[17]

Laborers rejected masterism, but they repudiated neither sugar production nor its plantation regimen. Instead, they evinced a readiness to perform the work of making sugar so long as planters did not think of and treat them as slaves. They expected to earn their keep, but they anticipated that their knowledge of sugar production would enable them to tailor the evolving labor system. Unlike their former owners, ex-slaves did not see free labor and sugar production as mutually exclusive. "On plantations managed by energetic men who desired free labor to succeed, the negroes worked well," a Union chaplain noted, "but where the former overseers had been retained who desired 'all *their* slaves to be sent back' the

16. Feb. 25, 1863, Plant. Diary 35, WJMP; May 27–June 8, June 15, 1863, Erwin Diary, LSU. See also Jan. 22, Feb. 26, 28, June 8, 25, 1863, List of Negroes Off [n.d.], and List of Negroes who have left Southdown & Hollywood up to Feb. 8, 1863, Plant. Diary 35, WJMP; Mar. 23, 1863, Plant. Account Book 7, McCollam Papers, SHC; Apr. 10, 1863, Plant. Diary, AFPP, *RASP,* ser. I; Apr. 20, 1863, Lawrence Plant. Diary, Brashear Papers, SHC; M. Dickinson to S. Gay, June 8, 1863, Andrew Hynes Gay and Family Papers, LSU; O. Lauve to G. Lauve, June 26, 1863, Gustave Lauve Letter, LSU; B. A. Johnson to AFP, Aug. 6, 1863, Pugh Papers, *RASP,* ser. G; Oct. 8, Nov. 6, 8, 1863, Plant. Diary, Palfrey Papers, *RASP,* ser. I.

17. Mar. 4, 1863, Plant. Diary 34, WJMP; *Freedom* 3:454–6 (quotation 455); A. J. H. Duganne, *Camps and Prisons: Twenty Months in the Department of the Gulf* (New York, 1865), 36.

Negroes were represented as unwilling to work well." Another federal officer similarly found laborers not only willing but eager to work when treated properly, adding that they "labor better and more faithfully under the present, than under the old regime." Indeed, by organizing themselves and electing leaders on abandoned estates, ex-slaves showed they were not averse to the hard work and discipline required to make sugar. Laborers operated one plantation, a Treasury Department agent observed, "without the assistance of any white man." They worked diligently, he indicated, and "larger returns will be found from the management of this place than any one I have seen managed by inexperienced Govm't agents or Soldiers."[18]

If most ex-slaves submitted to the arduous work of sugar production, they could also make life miserable for planters who gave them cause for disaffection. This was especially true during the rolling season, as events on William J. Minor's plantations during fall 1863 demonstrated. Given Minor's labor troubles up to that time, prospects for a successful harvest hardly seemed promising, but his rolling season was so chaotic that no observer familiar with antebellum routines would have recognized it. Slack work interrupted the cane supply and forced Minor repeatedly to shut down the sugar mill. Laborers would not work in inclement weather. Many refused to take night watches, especially on Saturday, and they objected to working on Sunday. The very old and young also caused trouble, as did women with infants in their care, whom Minor described as "the most lazy insolent & worthless."[19]

One point of contention between Minor his workers involved seed cane. Ordinarily, Minor would have saved a fifth of the crop to plant the next year, but because he was not assured a sufficient labor force for the coming season, he needed to decide whether to put aside seed cane or grind his entire crop. The laborers had no doubt about what Minor should do. Working under an arrangement in which they would receive a one-twentieth share of the proceeds, they wanted to grind the whole crop, take their wages, and leave. By holding back seed cane, however, Minor would be asking his laborers to forfeit part of their 1863 earnings to finance his 1864 crop. Not surprisingly, his decision to save seed cane sparked resistance. After the laborers windrowed seed cane for three days, Minor estimated they had completed only one day's worth of work. "Three fourths of them say they have such violent pains in their backs from windrowing cane that

18. *Freedom* 3:416–8 (quotation 417–8), 439–40n, 447–53 (quotation 452–3). See also *Freedom* 3:426–9, 438–9; Duganne, *Camps and Prisons*, 62–6; Nathaniel Prentice Banks, *Emancipated Labor in Louisiana* (New York, 1864), 7.

19. The discussion in this and the following paragraphs is based upon entries between October and December 1863, in Plant. Diary 36, WJMP. Quotation at Nov. 27.

they can not work longer at it." By mid-November, plantation operations had degenerated to the point where Minor threw up his hands in disgust. "The wish of the negro is now the white man's law," he fumed. "A man had as well be in purgatory, as attempt to work a sugar plantation under existing circumstances."[20]

In the old days things had been different. "Pains in their backs" had not kept slaves from work. The mill was not shut down because it ran out of cane juice, and the juice did not run out because slaves had worked poorly. Instead, slaves had toiled under the lash seven days a week, in addition to working night watches, and children and the elderly had not escaped their share of labor. Minor's ordeal further convinced him that trying to make sugar with free labor was an absurd proposition. At one point, he calculated that under the present system it would require four months to harvest the crop—a month longer than it had taken "before the negroes got to think themselves free." Minor concluded that his experience "settle[d] the question in the negative" whether free labor could make sugar in Louisiana. He could not admit to himself the possibility that his former slaves worked so poorly precisely because he refused to think of them as such.[21]

Army labor policy in 1863 had been at best an improvised response to the immediate problems of returning fugitive slaves to work and resuscitating the plantation economy. Born of expediency, it was not intended as a blueprint for the future. Although Nathaniel Banks had attempted to take laborers' rights into account when formulating his labor program, his desire to gain planters' support in reconstructing Louisiana compelled him to give greater weight to their concerns than to those of former slaves. Banks's reward was censure by planters, whose determination to preserve slavery and reestablish control over labor ignited their workers' defiance and precipitated further collapse of plantation regimen. As 1864 dawned, Banks was forced to rethink elements of his labor policy.

In doing so, Banks contended with a host of other critics. Affairs in Louisiana had drawn the heightened attention of northerners, many of whom did not like what they saw. Abolitionists and Radical Republicans in particular disparaged army labor policy as slavery in all but name. Nearby, members of the New Orleans free black community vehemently criticized army policy. Presuming to speak for the mass of illiterate, propertyless plantation laborers, whose interests they did not necessarily share, the black elite denounced the restrictive provisions of army policy. Two free black men in particular, Louis Charles Roudanez and Paul Trévigne, took the lead. They, along with the white Belgian émigré Jean-Charles Houzeau,

20. Ibid., Nov. 5, 14, 1863.
21. Ibid., Nov. 14, 1863.

published two newspapers—the French-language *L'Union* and its successor, the bilingual *New Orleans Tribune*—in which they castigated Banks and other federal officials for coddling planters while ignoring the plight of former slaves. With his policy seemingly under attack from all sides, Banks chose to implement a revised labor policy that still hedged on the former slaves' legal status but nonetheless considerably expanded their rights as workers.[22]

Banks presaged his course in January 1864 by suspending all slavery provisions of Louisiana's antebellum constitution and laws. In early February, he issued his new labor policy, General Order 23, which marked a pivotal point for free labor in the sugar region. Banks continued to perform intellectual somersaults in trying to reconcile planters' avowed need to control labor with certain tenets of free labor, but he also conceded that any workable labor system could not ignore workers' demands. These measures anticipated the work of the upcoming constitutional convention— due to meet that spring under auspices of Lincoln's Ten Percent Plan and to be shepherded by Banks himself—in which Louisiana Unionists were expected to abolish slavery. As his new labor policy made clear, Banks envisioned an apprenticeship system that would assist slaves in making the transition to freedom.[23]

22. On the *Tribune*, see Jean-Charles Houzeau, *My Passage at the New Orleans* Tribune: *A Memoir of the Civil War Era*, ed. David C. Rankin, trans. Gerard F. Denault (Baton Rouge, 1984), and William P. Connor, "Reconstruction Rebels: The *New Orleans Tribune* in Post–Civil War Louisiana," *LH* 21 (spring 1980): 159–81. There is a considerable literature on the New Orleans free black community during the Civil War era, including John W. Blassingame, *Black New Orleans, 1860–1880* (Chicago, 1973); Caryn Cossé Bell, *Revolution, Romanticism, and the Afro-Creole Protest Tradition in Louisiana, 1718–1868* (Baton Rouge, 1997); Donald E. Everett, "Demands of the New Orleans Free Colored Population for Political Equality, 1862–1865," *LHQ* 38 (April 1955): 43–64; David C. Rankin, "The Origins of Black Leadership in New Orleans during Reconstruction," *JSH* 40 (August 1974): 417–40; and Charles Vincent, *Black Legislators in Louisiana during Reconstruction* (Baton Rouge, 1976). Some scholars assume that the free people of color automatically became spokesmen for plantation laborers and that their critique of army labor policy articulated laborers' thinking. While such criticism, to a degree, resonated throughout the countryside and expressed the will of former slaves, free people of color and plantation laborers did not always share common interests, nor did the former necessarily speak for the latter. These two groups occupied different social universes before the war, and tensions between them would continue for years after it. Moreover, free-black criticism of the labor system was ambivalent, taking issue with white assumptions about black incapacity for independence but also reflecting conventional fears about vagrancy. Schmidt, *Free to Work*, 169–75; Ted Tunnell, "Free Negroes and the Freedmen: Black Politics in New Orleans during the Civil War," *Southern Studies* 19 (spring 1980): 5–28.

23. In overseeing the constitutional convention, Banks acted under Lincoln's Proclamation of Amnesty and Reconstruction, issued on December 8, 1863, which outlined the steps for Confederate states to rejoin the Union. Once a number of persons equivalent to 10 percent of votes cast in the 1860 presidential election had taken an oath of allegiance, which included a

From the former slaves' perspective, General Order 23 significantly improved upon preceding army policy. Laborers were no longer referred to as slaves, and monthly wages were raised from $2 to $8 for male workers. Planters and laborers again might agree to share-wage arrangements, but laborers were to receive a one-fourteenth share of the proceeds of the crop, up from the previous year's share of one-twentieth. Though laborers and their dependents would continue to receive basic necessities, Banks also recognized laborers' desire to engage in independent production by allotting families garden plots of up to one acre. Most importantly, laborers were free for the first time to choose their employers. Banks thus established the rudiments of a free-labor market in the sugar region.

At the same time, Banks was hardly blind to planters' concerns. Designating work a "public duty" and idleness a "crime," he dictated that laborers must sign and adhere to labor contracts. They could not leave the plantations except under guidelines established by the provost marshal of each parish. Any laborer who violated his or her contract would be put to work on the public roads without pay. Banks's order also directed that one-half of laborers' monthly wages be held in reserve until year's end. Designed to ensure that laborers remain to complete the crop, the policy of withholding pay showed the army's willingness to provide planters with means to control their workers. This provision would have profound implications for free labor's development over the next decade: unable to compel their workers physically to stay through the crop season, planters after the war would withhold wages as the only way to do so. Regarding the former slaves' legal status, General Order 23 said nothing. Despite its shortcomings from both planters' and laborers' viewpoints, however, it signaled a major step forward for free labor by laying the groundwork for a future labor market. The order did not end daily labor conflict, but Banks believed he had assuaged planters' fears about making sugar without coerced labor while guaranteeing the former slaves' rights as laborers.[24]

---

provision to abide by all federal measures concerning slavery, such Unionists could create a loyal state government that presumably would abolish slavery. By early 1864, the requisite number of persons had taken the oath in Louisiana, and Lincoln had directed Banks to organize a government and hold a constitutional convention. For the proclamation, see Richardson, *Messages and Papers*, 8:3414–6.

24. The text of General Order 23 appears in U.S. War Department, *War of the Rebellion*, 34, pt. 2, 227–31. In addition to the criticism they sparked at the time, Banks's 1863 and 1864 labor policies have also been debated by historians. For various interpretations, see Cox, *Lincoln and Black Freedom;* Dawson, *Army Generals;* Gerteis, *Contraband to Freedman;* McCrary, *Lincoln and Reconstruction;* Messner, *Freedmen and Ideology of Free Labor;* Ripley, *Slaves and Freedmen;* Tunnell, *Crucible of Reconstruction.* Banks was deeply conservative, and his policies were driven by his 1864 presidential hopes. Nonetheless, some recent criticism of his labor policies is predi-

Banks's new labor policy left almost nothing for planters and laborers to negotiate, but former slaves jumped at the chance to deal with former owners as
equals. Laborers whose employers had not yet settled with them for the previous
year refused to contract until they were paid, further delaying planting season.
One local provost marshal's office, a planter observed, was "thronged with negroes
claiming their payment with masters." Laborers who contracted, moreover, did so
only after they had had a chance to discuss the terms of their employment. Those
on one plantation elected a leader, the same planter noted, "to represent them before the Prost. Marshall tomorrow to make the contract." [25]

Laborers would have been disappointed to learn that their contracts had not
always been equitably negotiated. Instead, planters in certain localities colluded to
prevent internecine competition and impede development of a labor market.
Lafourche district planters met in late February, as one of them noted, "to adopt
some system which will secure uniformity of action in the employment of laborers." Rejecting monthly wages, they pledged to contract under share-wage
arrangements and agreed not to hire one another's former slaves, thereby negating
the laborers' right to chose where to work and violating the spirit if not the letter
of army policy. At the same time, planters in St. Mary Parish endorsed similar
measures. Such initiatives foretold what after the war would become a relentless
campaign by planters to mount a united front against labor. Only by acting in
unison, they believed, could they ever hope to keep their workers from gaining the
upper hand. "If planters don't stand by each other," one of them later predicted,
laborers "will become more and more exacting every year until in a short time we
will be the slaves and they the masters."[26]

Planters' sanctioning of share-wages connoted grudging accommodation to
reality rather than approval of the concept of compensated labor. Despite Banks's
efforts to secure them a work force, planters were more convinced than ever of the
incompatibility of free labor and sugar production. Insisting that "the thorough
control of ample and continuous labor" was essential to making sugar, W. W. Pugh

---

cated upon an ahistorical wish for immediate abolition rather than upon a recognition of the
wartime limitations under which Banks operated. One study that sees Banks's labor policies as
carefully crafted attempts to reconcile contradictory elements of antebellum northern free-labor
thought is Schmidt, *Free to Work*, chap 3.

25. Feb. 17, 20, 1864, A. F. Pugh Diary, Pugh Papers, *RASP*, ser. G. See also Feb. 14, 16–20, 24,
1864, Plant. Diary, Contract between Pugh and Augustin laborers, Feb. 18, 1864, and Contract
between Pugh and New Hope laborers, Feb. 29, 1864, Pugh Papers, *RASP*, ser. G; Feb. 9, 1864,
Plant. Diary (typescript), AFPP, *RASP*, ser. I.

26. Resolutions [Feb. or early Mar. 1864], and Mar. 13, 1864, Plant. Diary, Pugh Papers,
RASP, ser. G; Report, Feb. 20, 1864, Palfrey Papers, *RASP*, ser. I; Walter Pugh to AFP, Apr. 24,
1865, Pugh Papers, *RASP*, ser. G.

complained that only with corporal punishment could planters control their workers. Without it, he predicted, "[w]e shall have a repetition of the experience of the last year's rolling," when ex-slaves had worked poorly with planters unable to do anything about it. Pugh's solution was simple. "The saving of the growing crop is entirely dependent on the exercise of authority over the blacks," he asserted, "otherwise a large portion of the cane will be left to perish in the field." Without strict labor control, Pugh prophesied, planters had no future.[27]

Laborers defied planters' attempts to reestablish mastery. They continued to work at their own pace, for instance, kindling their former owners' anger. "Went over Augustin & New Hope today," observed A. F. Pugh. "On the former they are doing only soso on H. P. better as well as I could expect." Those on another plantation, he griped, "are doing so many things at a time, that but few are at work at any one thing." Pugh's affairs barely improved as the year progressed. His workers were still planting cane in April, and he estimated they would not begin hoeing it before mid-May—two months behind schedule. By September, when preparations for rolling should have been underway, the cane had not yet been laid by. Pugh had "the poorest crop" he ever saw.[28]

As workers became more experienced with noncoercive labor, and as they gained confidence—as well as greater rights—under the army's new policy, the terrain of freedom broadened to include a host of other issues besides that of the pace of work. Laborers, for example, demanded Saturday—either afternoons or the whole day—as their own. Having enjoyed Saturday afternoons to themselves under slavery, they refused to surrender this privilege. Banks's program did not explicitly set aside Saturday afternoons for laborers, but planters found themselves forced to relent to this demand. One overseer reported that the ex-slaves "are working tolerable well now I am obliged to give them saterday afternoon as it is the custom in the neighborhood." Some planters allowed them the whole day, as one noted in July 1864, "to work for them selves."[29]

By working for themselves on their own time, former slaves laid claim to the plantation's economic resources. William J. Minor's laborers, for instance, gathered wood and Spanish moss for their own use or sale, availed themselves of his mules, teams, and farm implements to work their garden plots, slaughtered his hogs, and sold his sheep. "[M]ost of them think, or pretend to think," Minor

27. [W. W.] Pugh to Capt. Rudyard (draft) [early 1864], Pugh Papers, *RASP,* ser. G. See also *Freedom* 3:517–21.

28. Feb. 25, Apr. 6, 28, 29, June 2, Sept. 1, Oct. 6, 1864, Plant. Diary, Pugh Papers, *RASP,* ser. G.

29. B. A. Johnson to AFP, May 7, 1865, Pugh Papers, *RASP,* ser. G; July 17, 1864, Erwin Diary, LSU. See also Aug. 22, Sept. 5, 1863, Plant. Diary 35, Oct. 2, 1863, Plant. Diary 36, WJMP; Mar. 19, Apr. 16, 1864, Erwin Diary, LSU.

complained, "that the plantation & every thing on it belongs to them." Ex-slaves saw these practices as traditional privileges to be preserved under the new system, whereas planters, discarding their customary paternalistic obligations, interpreted them as nothing less than expropriation of property. Nonetheless, if they wanted their workers' cooperation, they could do little but complain. Alternative economic activities allowed ex-slaves to supplement their monthly wages or assured them some income when working under share-wage arrangements. Former slaves consequently regarded such activities as essential to free labor.[30]

Also viewed as essential to free labor was the reduction of the time freedwomen spent working in the fields. Whether they were emulating the gender conventions of southern white society or repudiating an objectionable aspect of slavery is less important than the fact that they were forging their own notion of freedom. "Now, for the first time, the freedman seeks to realize the full advantages of home," Banks observed. "He asks of his employer that his wife shall not be sent to field labor; he wants her to stay at home and take care of his children, and is willing to work over hours to support them." Planters saw things differently. One minced no words in lambasting his female laborers' work habits. "They are idle, impudent, lose a great deal of time by feigning sickness," he complained, "and some refuse field work entirely." Although Banks made no provision for freeing black women of productive age from field labor, ex-slaves decided the issue for themselves.[31]

Some ex-slaves found that they had the power to evict their overseers, who had been their nemeses during slavery. Although most former slaves did not object to the overseer system in principle under the new order, in actual practice overseers were of special concern to them, since they continued to work in gangs. Ex-slaves could make life difficult for overseers whom they found objectionable for any reason. After receiving a complaint in late April 1864 that laborers on one plantation refused to work, the local provost marshal investigated and found them in "a riotous & insubordonete state." They had no cause of complaint, he believed, "except that they did not want to work on the plantation, with Mr Desbin as Overseer." Desbin stayed on, but others were less fortunate. When a new overseer tried to establish himself on the Bisland plantation in 1864, every former slave there assembled around the overseer's house and informed him, according to

30. Jan. 3, 1863, Plant. Diary 35, WJMP. See also Jan. 6, 7, Aug. 17, 20, 1863, Plant. Diary 35; Apr. 23, 1863, Plant. Diary 34; Oct. 14, 1863, Plant. Dairy 36; Oct. 8, 1864, Plant. Diary 33, all in WJMP; Col. S. R. Halobird to Maj. Carpenter, Feb. 17, 1863, McCollam Papers, SHC.

31. Banks, *Emancipated Labor,* 22; [W. W.] Pugh to Capt. Rudyard (draft) [early 1864], Pugh Papers, *RASP,* ser. G. See also June 28, 1864, Mar. 14, Apr. 12, 1865, Plant. Diary 33, WJMP; *Freedom* 3:535–6 (quotation 535), 489–91 (quotation 490).

Fannie Bisland that "he should not set foot in that house, that the quarter belonged to them and no d—— white man should live there." Warned that if he tried to remain the residents would "burn powder and lead round it all night," the overseer quickly left.[32]

Prohibited from coercing workers either directly or through overseers, planters increasingly resorted to marketplace incentives to gain cooperation. In doing so, they condoned the new relation to labor that they denounced so vehemently, and they belied their own claim that black people responded only to the threat of violence. "[T]he hands are clamoring for wages," Stephen Minor informed his father in March 1864. "I would advise sending up the money, *at once*, as they will stop work after tomorrow." The emergence of a cash nexus further corroded a paternalistic system that was steadily rotting away. Having entered into a share-wage arrangement with his workers, A. F. Pugh was soon compelled to make periodic cash advances to induce them to work. When he refused on one occasion to dispense any money, owing to what he deemed misconduct, hard feelings ensued. The workers "grumbled considerably," Pugh noted, "and seemed to think great injustice had been done them." With his workers angered, Pugh decided to avoid them for a few days "to let them cool down."[33]

Despite their grudging accommodation to free labor, planters were no more satisfied with the 1864 rolling season than they had been with those of the past two years. A. F. Pugh's workers moved "very slowly towards getting ready for rolling," he complained in mid-October. When they finally began cutting cane, they worked so sluggishly that Pugh was sure the cold weather would harm the cane crop before they finished. He therefore offered cash incentives, even though he believed his workers had already received more money than they deserved. "If they thought they were to get no more, I fear [the crop] would be lost." These inducements failed to have the desired effect, and by early November, when Pugh should have been cutting cane for the sugar mill, he had barely finished putting up seed cane. Only three weeks later did he induce his workers to begin cutting cane for the mill, after he had given them new shoes. Not long before, Pugh would have whipped slaves who jeopardized his solvency by working poorly. Now he had to bargain for their services.[34]

32. *Freedom* 3:489–90, 535. For other wartime episodes involving overseers, see *Freedom* 3:548–9; Nov. 5, 6, 8, 1862, Plant. Diary (typescript), AFPP, *RASP,* ser. I; Richard Pugh to Mary Pugh, Dec. 16, 1862, Richard L. Pugh Papers, LSU; George Hughes Hepworth, *The Whip, Hoe, and Sword; or, The Gulf-Department in '63* (Boston, 1864), 29–30; Parton, *Butler in New Orleans,* 540–2.

33. S. Minor to W. J. Minor, Mar. 21, 1864, WJMP; May 23, July 28, 30, 1864, Plant. Diary, Pugh Papers, *RASP,* ser. G.

34. Oct. 12, 14, 21, 29, Nov. 1, 25, 27, 29, Dec. 12, 1864, Plant. Diary, Pugh Papers, *RASP,* ser. G.

Even when the rolling season commenced, workers had little to do. "There will hardly be a grinding season," one journalist had accurately predicted, as the sugar industry hit bottom in late 1864. The yield of a scant 10,387 hogsheads seemed to offer further confirmation of planters' insistence that free labor was incompatible with sugar production. While this state of affairs undoubtedly resulted from the ex-slaves' refusal to work as they once had, the labor problem was only one among a triad of difficulties that planters encountered. In addition to having the new labor system imposed upon them, planters faced the destruction of war and the cumulative effects of successively poor harvests and planting seasons. Any of these factors alone could have thrown the industry into a tailspin; the three together were devastating. After more than two years of chaos, planters rightly saw themselves on the verge of annihilation.[35]

As though the planters did not face enough challenges, Louisiana Unionists approved a state constitution in September 1864 that formally abolished slavery. Because only a few thousand loyalists, mostly in New Orleans and its environs, participated in the constitution plebiscite, there was no pretending that it represented the will of all Louisianians. Moreover, the constitution immediately affected only the sugar region and the area along the Mississippi River, since the rest of the state remained under Confederate control. Nonetheless, even though in reality slavery was a thing of the past in the sugar region by fall 1864, former slaves now rejoiced in its legal demise.

Whereas planters celebrated neither slavery's abolition nor completion of the rolling season, ex-slaves—now truly freedmen—availed themselves of the shortened harvest to enjoy an extended Christmas holiday. "This is holyday week, and the negroes will not do anything before the first of Jan. if then," one planter lamented. Some, in fact, would not begin work until well into January. It was yet another change to which planters had to reconcile themselves. Freedmen would eventually expand the year-end holiday to include most of January, thus building upon a privilege they had traditionally enjoyed as slaves.[36]

Hoping to improve further upon earlier army labor policy, Nathaniel Banks had implemented a program in 1864 that broadened the rights of ex-slaves while it tried to ensure planters dependable labor. This attempt to harmonize the opposing interests of laborers and planters satisfied neither party. Planters continually announced their disapproval of free labor, insisting that it compromised their control of the work force and jeopardized their future. Freedmen resisted planters'

35. *DP,* Aug. 8, 1864.
36. Dec. 26, 1864, Plant. Diary, Pugh Papers, *RASP,* ser. G. See also Jan. 11–12, 1865, Plant. Diary (typescript), AFPP, *RASP,* ser. I; Dec. 24, 1863, Erwin Diary, LSU.

attempts to reenslave them, and they envisioned a labor system that preserved their customary privileges even as it guaranteed them the rights of free people. The events of 1864 inspired little confidence among planters in free labor's prospects. Nonetheless, although the sugar industry's future seemed doubtful as the year came to an end, a new labor system was slowly taking root in the region.

By early 1865, the nation's long travail seemed near its end. Abraham Lincoln had won reelection in November, and General Ulysses S. Grant's spring campaign against the Army of Northern Virginia augured the Confederacy's demise. Affairs in Louisiana, however, were uncertain. Despite the state's abolition of slavery, congressional opposition to Lincoln's Louisiana government kept the state's readmission to the Union in limbo. Plantation matters were also shrouded in ambiguity. In July 1864, Congress had transferred plantation supervision from the War Department to the Treasury Department. The difficulties attending such a change in the middle of the crop season were exacerbated by a misunderstanding between Benjamin F. Flanders, the Treasury Department's representative in Louisiana, and General Stephen A. Hurlbut, who had replaced Banks as military commander in September. Because of miscommunication and no small amount of bureaucratic wrangling, Flanders and Hurlbut each believed that the other would be responsible for supervising labor in 1865. Not until March did Lincoln direct military authorities in southern Louisiana to resume this responsibility, and only then were labor regulations for 1865 announced.[37]

Planters, hoping to influence army labor policy, seized upon the uncertainty surrounding plantation affairs. They vented their continuing frustration with free labor in public and in the press. A delegation of Lafourche district planters conferred with Flanders, according to one of them, "in regard to wages & management of negroes for the coming year." Terrebonne planters also met to discuss labor arrangements for the new year. "They all agree the present system has proved a complete failure," noted William J. Minor. Planters especially castigated the notion that black people might develop the internal drive necessary to any noncoercive labor system. "If increased pay would produce obedience, honesty and faithful labor, I for one would willingly submit to it," one planter contended, "but twenty year's experience convinces me that the negro has little, or no ambition to provide for the future." After meeting with planters in November 1864, Thomas W. Conway, superintendent of the Gulf Department's Bureau of Free Labor, believed most of them were of "a disposition to *grind* the negroes." Slavery was dead

37. This episode is summarized in *Freedom* 3:371–5. For more detailed elaboration, see Messner, *Freedmen and Ideology of Free Labor,* 61–112.

in Louisiana, but planters' insistence on reviving the old plantation regimen, Conway later noted, had created "a root of bitterness" that would be difficult to overcome.[38]

Planters who considered the present system a failure would have been even more disappointed by General Hurlbut's 1865 labor regulations, promulgated in early March. Although leaving intact most of Banks's labor policy, the new guidelines made several key changes. Male laborers would receive increased monthly wages of $10, $8, and $6, according to "class," and female laborers, $8, $6, and $5. Wages would be paid quarterly rather than monthly, one-half being held in reserve each quarter until completion of the crop. Thus, while Hurlbut freed planters from having to pay wages every month and kept intact their means for securing labor, he also endorsed regular wages. The regulations permitted share-wage arrangements that had already been agreed to, since the crop season was well underway, but the laborers' share was left for planters and workers to negotiate. Freedmen gained Saturday afternoons to themselves, but during the rolling season they were required to perform night watches and to work Saturday afternoons and Sundays for extra pay. Freedmen also enjoyed greater choice over the crops they grew in their gardens but were forbidden to keep animals other than domestic poultry. In trying to reconcile the interests of planters and freedmen, the new guidelines further consolidated monthly wage labor in the sugar region.[39]

Hurlbut's labor policy undoubtedly reflected the freedmen's growing preference for monthly wages, which manifested itself during the settling of 1864 accounts and contracting for 1865. A. F. Pugh, for instance, dreaded settling with his laborers, a task that he predicted would amount to a "Tug of War." He was right. Having toiled for a one-fourteenth share of the dismal 1864 crop, Pugh's workers had little to show for their efforts, and when they received their pay in mid-February, the scene was not pleasant. "I settled with the negroes today," he noted, "as was expected they are very much dissatisfied with what they got." Freedmen also voiced their unhappiness by refusing to begin the new crop season and demanding monthly wages, which promised them greater compensation and more frequent disbursement than did share-wage arrangements. By late February, Pugh, who preferred share-wages, was so anxious to begin planting that he improved his offer to a one-eighth share of the crop and garden plots of two acres.

38. W. W. Pugh to Judge Howell, Nov. 16, 1864, and Nov. 16, 21, 22, 1864, Plant. Diary, Pugh Papers, *RASP,* ser. G; Nov. 17, 1864, Plant. Diary 36, WJMP; *Freedom* 3:554–7 (quotation 555), 559–61 (quotation 560); U.S. Army, Dept. of the Gulf, Bureau of Free Labor, *The Freedmen of Louisiana: Final Report of the Bureau of Free Labor, Dept. of the Gulf, to Maj. Gen. E. R. S. Canby, commanding, by Thomas W. Conway* (New Orleans, 1865), 6–11.

39. *Freedom* 3:591–4.

Freedmen were unimpressed, however, and by early March, when Hurlbut announced the new labor regulations, they had yet to contract.[40]

Still hoping to convince his workers to accept share-wages, Pugh continued to haggle with them throughout March and early April. But the freedmen, exploiting leverage they had gained from the new guidelines, stood fast for monthly wages. "I had an interview with them today and laid before them my proposition of an eighth of the crop," he noted. "It was very distastefull to them, only a few of them were inclined to accept it." By mid-April, with the planting season all but gone, Pugh found himself with no choice but to accede to his workers' demands. "I have agreed with the negroes today to pay them monthly wages. It was very distasteful to me, but I could do no better," he complained. "Every body else in the neighborhood has agreed to pay the same and mine would listen to nothing else."[41]

In addition to monthly wage labor's gaining ascendancy in the sugar region by spring 1865, a pattern surfaced in negotiations between planters and freedmen that would become as familiar as the Bayou Teche two-step. Just as crop seasons overlapped, so did settling accounts for one year and contracting for the next. Aware of the effort the rolling season demanded, freedmen could express their dissatisfaction with a planter's offer for the new year by working slowly or not at all. Likewise, if displeased with the settlement after completing the crop, they might seek employment elsewhere as planting was to begin. The perils of sugar production had caused planters enough anxiety before emancipation; now they had to bargain with laborers who were free to leave. Despite the restrictions of army policy, freedmen were learning how to take advantage of the sugar region's emerging labor market.

As planters negotiated with workers, their course was piloted by two distinct but interrelated concerns. The first and most obvious involved the economic repercussions of compensating labor. Now that planters were forced to pay their workers, the form of remuneration assumed considerable importance, since monthly wages imposed a larger financial burden on planters than did share-wages. The proprietor of Uncle Sam plantation, for example, paid sixty freedmen who worked for one-fourteenth of the 1864 crop an average of $7.50—less than a

---

40. Feb. 19–20, 1865, Plant. Diary (typescript), AFPP, *RASP*, ser. I. See also Jan. 17–18, Feb. 2, 10–12, 15, 18, 22–23, 1865, Plant. Diary (typescript), AFPP, *RASP*, ser. I; Contract with freedmen (unsigned), [Mar.] 1865, [AFP] to Dear Sir, [late Feb. 1865], and A. B. Sharpe to AFP, Mar. 5, 1865, Pugh Papers, *RASP*, ser. G.

41. Apr. 13–14, 1865, Plant. Diary (typescript), AFPP, *RASP*, ser. I. See also Mar. 16, 21, 27–28, 30, Apr. 1–2, 5, 1865, Plant. Diary (typescript), Apr. 8, 11, 1865, Plant. Diary, AFPP, *RASP*, ser. I; B. A. Johnson to AFP, Apr. 9, 1865, Pugh Papers, *RASP*, ser. G.

single month's income in 1865, when Uncle Sam freedmen received monthly wages. Though opposed in principle to all forms of compensated labor, planters found monthly wages especially disagreeable, but faced with the freedmen's preference for monthly pay and the army's sanctioning it, there was little they could do. In order to have any hope of surviving under the new order, they had to undertake the most stringent fiscal measures in all other aspects of running their estates.[42]

While increased labor costs would now be a major consideration to planters, a second concern was less tangible, though equally compelling. They were determined to control the freedmen's personal conduct as well as their working lives. This impulse derived from planters' need to command labor, but it also originated in their obsession to dominate black people as they once had. Racism therefore commingled with concrete economic pressures in shaping planters' thinking. The paternalistic ethos was crumbling daily, but its dissolution did not preclude former slaveholders' continuing to aspire to mastery. In 1865, for instance, William J. Minor paid his best workers $12 per month plus their necessities. In return, freedmen vowed not only to labor faithfully but also to abide by strict rules that covered matters of personal behavior. They pledged "to *bind [them]selves*, to be *respectful* in [their] *deportment*, to *obey orders & comply with the rules & regulations* of the plantation." They also consented not to leave the plantation without a pass, nor to drink, gamble, or "use bad language." Planters may have been forced to pay their workers, but they wrested concessions that reinforced their personal authority in other ways.[43]

Despite the bitterness between them, planters and freedmen were symbiotically constructing a new order. Planters wanted work routines as close to those of slavery as possible, and they coveted the deference that their former slaves had once accorded them. But by achieving at best only partial success in these goals, planters slowly acclimated themselves to the new social environment. Freedmen, conversely, realized that any similarities between plantation life under slavery and free labor were both superficial and greatly outweighed by the differences. They acquiesced to strict rules governing work and deportment because they understood the discipline that sugar production required and because the regular wages they received endowed them with a sense of independence previously unimagined. In creating a new labor system, planters and freedmen were shackled to-

42. Register of Colored Persons, 1864; Payroll, Feb. 1, 1865; Agreement with Freedmen, 1865, Uncle Sam Plant. Papers, LSU.

43. Contract between William J. Minor and laborers [early 1865], and Mar. 2, 3, 1865, Plant. Diary 36, WJMP.

gether, incapable of acting independently from one another. Distasteful as it was, they moved in tandem, grudgingly and reluctantly, but inexorably forward.

Although wage labor's predominance in the sugar region was due in no small measure to the freedmen's acquiescence, a number of them instead hoped to escape the limitations of wage labor and the control that traditional sugar production entailed. In doing so, they anticipated the former slaves' desire for land—universal in the postwar South—and portended what would become a countervailing tendency in the sugar region. Freedmen in Terrebonne and Lafourche Parishes, for example, organized themselves into "labor companies" that tilled abandoned estates. In January 1865, a group of Terrebonne freedmen successfully petitioned a Treasury Department official to work one plantation; by April, an inspector reported them doing well. Freedmen on several Lafourche plantations, noted another treasury official, expressed "a great desire to cultivate the land on their own account." He observed that "without exception they promise diligence, good order, obedience to regulations, and the faithful care and return of the property entrusted to them." These and other attempts at independent, landed proprietorship turned out to be short-lived, since most of the abandoned plantations would be returned to their owners soon after the war. Nonetheless, they connoted a longing among certain freedmen for greater independence than sugar production allowed. Whereas most freedmen could abide the semblance between old and new work routines, others found it too strong to stomach.[44]

Freedmen worked relatively few abandoned plantations on their own. Instead, the federal government leased most of these estates to the many northerners who had come south in search of opportunity. At first, relations between freedmen and northern apostles of free labor went smoothly enough. But as northerners' opportunistic thirst for profit overrode any altruistic impulse to cultivate free labor in southern soil, the freedmen's mistrust of their "new masters" increased accordingly. Some former slaves even came to believe, remarked one federal official, that they "were better off with their old Masters and would be glad of his return." Thomas W. Conway likewise contended that "many of these new men are unprincipled & came down here with a little money, not intending to settle in the country, but merely to enhance their fortunes by a year's operation & to do so regardless of the laborers, their own dignity & behavior." Many freedmen discovered to their disappointment that northerners displayed no greater concern for

44. *Freedom* 3:572–3, 573n (quotation), 573–4, 617. On freedmen's efforts to form labor companies and work abandoned estates on their own in 1865 and early 1866, see Paul K. Eiss, "A Share in the Land: Freedpeople and the Government of Labour in Southern Louisiana, 1862–65," *Slavery and Abolition* 19 (April 1998): 46–89.

their dignity than had their former owners. The resulting conflicts belied the supposed consensus of interests between capital and labor central to free-labor ideology and strengthened planters' claims that sugar production could not be reconciled with free labor.[45]

Southern planters never tired of sounding that theme. Neither the Emancipation Proclamation nor slavery's abolition in Louisiana could induce them to retreat from their contention that they must be able to compel labor. "The difficulty has been to control the labor," William J. Minor testified before a federal commission investigating corruption in the Gulf Department in spring 1865. Describing sugar planting as "an artificial culture" in Louisiana, he explained that planters were "obliged to do certain things at certain times." Because they had to harvest the crop between October and January, "[t]he inability has been to get labour to take off the crop—that is to make the sugar within the time prescribed." Under free labor, freedmen refused to work as diligently as they had as slaves. Consequently, Minor insisted, in language that other planters echoed, that the state be allowed to enact laws governing labor without the federal government's interference.[46]

While publicly deploring their future prospects in a world without slavery, planters also despaired privately. Having been relegated to the sidelines since April 1862, they had had plenty of time to mourn the loss of their world. "If this war continues twelve months longer," one planter observed in fall 1863, "[t]he owners of the soil will make nothing, the lands will be sold for taxes, & bot in by Northern men, & the original owners will be made the beggars." A year later, A. F. Pugh also slipped into hopelessness. "I never have been so much depressed in mind since the commencement of this war," he lamented. "I can find no object, with which to turn my thoughts from the deepest gloom which depresses me. All is darkness with hardly a ray of hope in the future." Another year like 1864, Thomas W. Conway predicted, and "the old planting aristocracy would be gone." Planters remarked "that they cannot survive the shock which has come upon them from the war, the abolition of slavery, and the disheartening aspect presented in the loss of their fortunes, their sons, and their hopes, which are all swallowed up in the terrible grave dug for them by this huge rebellion." Anticipating their demise, Conway concluded that planters were "now preparing to give way to new capital and new proprietorship."[47]

45. *Freedom* 3:551–4 (quotation 553); see also 575–81. On northern planters in general, see Lawrence N. Powell, *New Masters: Northern Planters during the Civil War and Reconstruction* (New Haven, Conn., 1980).

46. *Freedom* 3:599–607. For similar statements by other sugar planters, see *Freedom* 3:607–13 (quotation 600).

47. Sept. 29, 1863, Plant. Diary 36, WJMP; Oct. 10, 1864, Plant. Diary, Pugh Family Papers, *RASP*, ser. G; Thomas W. Conway, *Annual Report of Thos. W. Conway, Superintendent, Bureau of*

Despair and predictions of their ruin notwithstanding, planters had not given up the hope of reviving their enterprise. In May 1865, Lafourche district planter William Littlejohn, who had taken refuge in Texas during the war, explored the possibility of returning to Louisiana. "I will thank you to inform me," he inquired of an acquaintance, "whether the negroes I left are all on the plantation & how they are disposed to behave, also whether there is any cane on the place & how much & again whether the machinery at my sugar house has been disturbed or taken away." No record of a response has survived, but encouraging answers could have been provided in reference to few estates. Those freedmen who had remained on the plantations were not disposed to behave in a manner that Littlejohn would have recognized, and if it were seed cane and a functioning sugar mill Littlejohn wanted, he would have been better advised to stay in Texas.[48]

Littlejohn and others could hardly have foreseen that decades would pass before the sugar industry recovered from war and emancipation. Whereas more than 1,000 sugar-making establishments had produced 460,000 hogsheads with a value of more than $25 million in 1861, in 1864, 231 estates produced about 10,000 hogsheads, valued at $1.9 million. Such losses were not caused simply by interruptions in production, since war, vandalism, and decay almost completely destroyed the industry's capital investment. Losses in slaves, animals, machinery, tools, farm implements, and buildings for the industry as a whole approached $190 million out of an estimated antebellum value of $200 million. Because the sugar region had boasted the antebellum South's most advanced technological development, the problem of rebuilding the industry's infrastructure became entwined with that of labor adjustment. Former slaveholders throughout the rest of the South also confronted a new labor system, but few did so amidst such desolation.[49]

The Civil War ended the way of life in southern Louisiana predicated upon sugar and slavery, but the Union's victory raised questions concerning the freedmen's status and the sugar industry's future. Although the war established important precedents, it had been but a dress rehearsal. Planters, freedmen, and northern reformers now prepared to debut in the drama of Reconstruction guided by a poorly drafted script.

Free Labor, Department of the Gulf, to Major General Hurlbut, Commanding, for the Year 1864 (New Orleans, 1865), 8–9. For similar sentiments, see Dec. 19, 1862, Plant. Diary (typescript), AFPP, *RASP*, ser. I; May 9, 1863, Lawrence Plant. Diary, Brashear Papers, SHC; Aug. 23, 1863, Erwin Diary, LSU; Mar. 16, 1864, Plant. Diary, Palfrey Papers, *RASP*, ser. I.

48. W. Littlejohn to E. E. Mathios, May 20, 1865, Martin-Pugh Collection, NSU.

49. Figures are from *De Bow's Review: After the War Series* 4 (September 1867): 239–40, and Prichard, "Effects of the Civil War," 321–2.

3

LAND AND LABOR AFTER THE WAR

[T]he Hand's Want to hire land from the Madame Nicholas
owner of the place. . . . But the Madam Says She would rather
See her plantation grow up in Weed's than let a Nigger Cultivate for his own use.
　　—Patrick O'Hare to Thomas W. Conway, October 11, 1865

The Civil War gave rise to monthly wage labor in southern Louisiana, but
the new system's persistence was not preordained. Many freedmen aspired
to landholding immediately after the war, and some planters were willing
to experiment with alternative labor arrangements. Nonetheless, while the search
for new ways to organize plantations in the southern Louisiana sugar country resembled developments in the cotton South, the range of alternatives available was
circumscribed by wartime precedents and by the demands of sugar production.
Moreover, because President Andrew Johnson's Reconstruction policy returned
former Confederates to power and forestalled land confiscation, planters and
freedmen battled over specific labor issues during late 1865 and 1866. In this contest, planters wielded the state's coercive power, which they used to try to control
their workers, but freedmen rose to the challenge. They petitioned the Freedmen's
Bureau for aid, exploited the developing labor market, and insisted upon their
rights as free Americans. The freedmen's success in these matters, considered
along with the demands of sugar production and the failure of land reform, account for wage labor's eventual dominance in the postbellum sugar region.

*　*　*

As the war ended, sugar planters attempted to rebuild their lives and industry. In doing so, they suffered particular hardship, since most of their expensive equipment, into which they had invested much of their antebellum wealth, had been destroyed or had fallen into disrepair. Cotton, rice, and tobacco planters also faced the difficulties of postwar readjustment, but loss of a cotton gin, though not negligible, did not compare with that of a sugar mill, and the cost of cottonseed paled against that of plant cane. Plantations without working sugar mills and seed cane were of little value.[1]

The South's credit shortage hampered rebuilding efforts. Collapse of the region's credit, which had been based on slave property, along with the failure of New Orleans's banks, factorages, and commercial houses, wreaked havoc with planters, who could no longer draw upon the city's commercial power. "My affairs are in a very bad condition," lamented A. F. Pugh in May 1865, "and I fear even if I am able to stagger through this year I shall have to give it up next year." Pugh's situation was hardly unique. "Father is undecided as to his future," noted Robert C. Martin Jr. in late 1865. Martin's main creditor was willing to grant a forbearance, but others, his son observed, "may not be so liberally inclined."[2]

With so many planters seeking credit, even liberally inclined financiers felt overwhelmed. Antebellum planters had relied on credit, and they found old habits hard to break. Too many, complained one observer in late 1866, "still look to New Orleans and the generosity of its merchants as their only hope." J. D. B. De Bow estimated in 1867 that planters collectively needed $25 million just to cover yearly operating expenses. Because such sums were unavailable in the South, only northern or European capital could save the sugar industry. Outside assistance, however, cut both ways: planters who secured northern financing risked foreclosure when crops failed. John Moore of St. Mary Parish entered into a partnership to work one of his plantations in 1866. After raising a poor crop, Moore sold the estate to a northern investor for a mere $60,000. "By the effects of the War," Moore lamented, "I am almost totally ruined."[3]

1. R. C. Martin Jr. to R. C. Martin, Aug. 3, 1866, Martin-Pugh Collection, NSU; Sept. 30, 1865, Erwin Diary, LSU; *De Bow's Review* 3 (March 1867): 308; Henry Latham, *Black and White: A Journal of a Three Months' Tour in the United States* (London, 1867), 177.

2. May 14, 1865, Plant. Diary (typescript), AFPP, *RASP,* ser. I; R. C. Martin Jr. to M. Martin, Oct. 29–30, 1865, Martin-Pugh Collection, NSU; Richard Holcombe Kilbourne Jr., *Debt, Investment, Slaves: Credit Relations in East Feliciana Parish, Louisiana, 1825–1885* (Tuscaloosa, Ala., 1995).

3. J. C. Patrick to W. Edwards & Co., Nov. 7, 1866, EJGP; *De Bow's Review* 3 (March 1867): 308, and 4 (September 1867): 238; J. Moore to Mrs. J. R. Snyder, Oct. 11, 1866, Kean-Prescott Family Papers, SHC; Legal Agreement between Moore and Johnson, and Lyon, Feb. 27, 1867, Weeks Papers, LSU.

To obtain funds necessary to recommence sugar production, many planters cultivated cotton instead. Most planters and freedmen had had some experience with it, and its high price after the war, along with its lower start-up costs, proved irresistible. In 1865 nearly every operating plantation in southern Louisiana grew cotton. "As the Planters have not the cane to plant they try cotton hoping to get a fair yield," reported a Freedmen's Bureau agent in early 1866. "If they do it will give them the means of procuring seed cane the coming year." Cotton was less predictable than sugarcane, because of the army worm, excessive rain, and ill-suited soil, but it provided many planters means to survive the precarious early postwar years and keep their estates. Vexing as its production was in southern Louisiana, cotton provided a meager return to planters desperate enough to try anything. For some, the little it provided turned out to be just enough.[4]

With much of their capital investment wiped out and almost forced to beg for loans, planters faced a bleak future. "[P]rospects very gloomy," A. F. Pugh complained in November 1865. "It all looks as dark as midnight to me with hardly a gleam of light appearing." To be sure, Pugh and others would confront some difficult days. Nonetheless, whether or not they realized it, planters by late 1865 had already overcome a major hurdle in preserving their former status within the new order. By that time, President Andrew Johnson had shown that he would not countenance land confiscation in the former Confederacy. Debate over land reform was beginning in fall 1865, but it was clear that any attempt to alter fundamentally the southern social order would have to surmount presidential opposition.[5]

It is axiomatic that most former slaves saw land as the linchpin to freedom. They envisioned land confiscation in particular as compensation for generations of unrequited toil under slavery. Since their sweat, blood, and suffering had cleared the land and had made it productive, justice demanded that they now enjoy the fruits of their past labors. Yet more important than overdue compensation was the belief that land ownership would secure a meaningful freedom. Embracing elements of northern free-labor ideology that emphasized productive property as the cornerstone of economic independence, most freedmen hoped eventually to become landed proprietors. They considered access to land less a matter of settling old scores than of looking to the future.

Many freedmen of the sugar region likewise yearned for a freedom rooted in

4. C. E. Merrill to A. F. Hayden, Mar. 20, 1866, Narrative Trimonthly Reps. of Business Transacted, ser. 1603, Agt & ASAC, Franklin, BRFAL. Comments about cotton production by planters, Freedmen's Bureau agents, and others are so numerous as to be impossible to cite. For examples, see Erwin Diary and WJMP, and Inspection Reps., Plant. Dept., vol. 90, ser. 1409, AC, BRFAL.

5. Nov. 22, 1865, Plant. Diary (typescript), AFPP, *RASP,* ser. I.

land. When wage labor had been established during the war, not all freedmen had acquiesced to it. Nor had they abandoned their dream that the federal government would dispense land. During the war, some groups of former slaves had worked abandoned plantations in cooperative ventures, showing their desire to gain access to productive property and avoid wage labor. Although wage labor made greater progress than did land reform in the sugar region by spring 1865, the war's end reopened the land question.

The freedmen's desire for land received a boost in March 1865, when Congress created the Bureau of Refugees, Freedmen, and Abandoned Lands. A division within the War Department, the Freedmen's Bureau, as it came to be known, was charged with overseeing the transition from slavery to freedom in the South. Among the bureau's many responsibilities was that of dividing abandoned and confiscated plantations under federal control into forty-acre plots for distribution among freedmen. By spring 1865, the federal government held some 96,000 acres of land in Louisiana, mostly in the sugar region. Redistribution of this property would have furnished land to about 2,400 families—a modest beginning in remaking the sugar region, but a start.[6]

Prospects for distributing abandoned land, however, suffered a major setback only weeks after the war. Despite his harsh rhetoric against traitors, Johnson did not intend to bring social revolution to the South. In his May 1865 amnesty proclamation, he offered pardon and restoration of property rights, excepting slaves, to former Confederates who swore allegiance to the Union and recognized slavery's abolition. Johnson exempted certain classes of persons from his amnesty, including most of the planter elite, but such persons could apply to him for special pardons. Despite Johnson's proclamation, General O. O. Howard, the Freedmen's Bureau commissioner, instructed bureau officials in summer 1865 to begin parceling out abandoned property. Following Howard's lead, Thomas W. Conway, who had overseen wartime free labor and who now headed the bureau in Louisiana, invited freed families and "associations" of freedmen to apply for land. Within weeks, hundreds of applications—representing thousands of Louisiana freedmen—flooded bureau headquarters, as word spread that the federal government intended to make good on its pledge to distribute land.[7]

---

6. On the amount of government-held land in Louisiana, see 39th Cong., 2nd Sess., House Executive Document 1, p. 708. On the Freedmen's Bureau, see George R. Bentley, *History of the Freedmen's Bureau* (Philadelphia, 1955) and William S. McFeely, *Yankee Stepfather: General O. O. Howard and the Freedmen* (New Haven, Conn., 1968). On the Louisiana Freedmen's Bureau, see Howard A. White, *The Freedmen's Bureau in Louisiana* (Baton Rouge, 1970), and John Cornelius Engelsman, "The Freedmen's Bureau in Louisiana," *LHQ* 32 (January 1949): 145–224.

7. Richardson, ed., *Messages and Papers* 8:3508–10; Circular No. 10, Aug. 28, 1865, in 39th Cong., 1st Sess., House Executive Document 70, p. 19; List of Applications of Freedmen and

The freedmen's hope of attaining the promised lands soon suffered a second, crippling blow. In September 1865, Johnson ordered bureau-controlled property returned to its former owners once they had received presidential pardons, which by this time he was dispensing quite freely. Within a year, the bureau in Louisiana returned to its original owners virtually all the land it held. In doing so, it effectively suppressed the various cooperative ventures that freedmen had undertaken on abandoned estates throughout the region. By restoring property to the old elite, Johnson not only subverted the will of Congress but also undermined prospects for fundamental change in the South. Further, Johnson also had Howard remove officials, including Conway, who did not share his vision of the bureau as a vehicle for property restoration. Following Conway's dismissal in October 1865, more conservative men headed the bureau in Louisiana.[8]

Although Johnson's actions appeared to kill the chances of confiscation, freedmen continued to express their desire for land. In December 1865, one Union officer found a "spirit of discontent" among freedmen in Terrebonne Parish, many of whom had "form[ed] ideas & hopes from the general government, which had not been realized. . . . Every man became impressed with the idea that he was soon to become a landed proprietor." Freedmen throughout the region squatted on unimproved swampland or on unclaimed estates. Some even refused to vacate plantations when ordered to do so by pardoned former owners. So convinced were freedmen of an impending land redistribution that the Freedmen's Bureau for Louisiana issued a circular in December 1865 attempting to dispel this idea.[9]

Agitation over land also prompted the initial stirrings of black political mobilization in the countryside. To their employers' annoyance, freedmen left work and gathered in towns to hear speakers and to debate the questions of Reconstruction—including that of land confiscation. Their political mobilization was further driven by unofficial "elections" that Louisiana's small group of Radical Republicans sponsored in early November 1865 to discredit presidential Reconstruction. Coinciding with regular elections for state officials and members of Congress, these Radical elections included black men, whom Johnson had ex-

---

Refugees for Government Lands, in accordance with Circular No. 10, FSSP: A-8808. On Conway, see McFeely, *Yankee Stepfather,* chap. 9.

8. On the return of abandoned and confiscated property in Louisiana, see 39th Cong., 2nd Sess., Senate Executive Document 6, p. 69; 39th Cong., 2nd Sess., House Executive Document 1, p. 708. On Conway's removal, see McFeely, *Yankee Stepfather,* 174–5.

9. T. Kanady to Z. K. Wood, Dec. 28, 1865, FSSP: C-655; Circular No. 34, Dec. 27, 1865, in 39th Cong., 1st Sess., House Executive Document 70, pp. 35–7. See also W. E. Dougherty to D. G. Fenno, Nov. 7, 1865, and M. A. Reno to A. A. Milliken, Dec. 22, 1865, enclosed in M. A. Reno to A. R. Houston, Jan. 2, 1866, FSSP: A-8562, A-8509.

cluded from Reconstruction. Although they lacked any legal basis, the Radical elections enabled freedmen to voice their hope for gaining land.[10]

Inevitably, freedmen formed from this political activity somewhat inflated ideas concerning land confiscation, especially since white Radicals agitated on the question. Freedmen were easily misled because of their land aspirations. "The whole Parish was in an uproar," reported the provost marshal for Assumption Parish after the November elections. Certain white Unionists had convinced former slaves that they were entitled to vote and that they had to choose between two candidates for Congress, "secessionist" and Republican. They believed that "[i]f the Secessionist was elected, they would again be slaves," whereas "[i]f the Republican candidate was elected, all the secessionists plantations would be divided among the Freedmen." In truth, freedmen had as much chance of gaining control over the plantations, secessionist or otherwise, as they had of being literally reenslaved, but in November 1865 they believed both outcomes possible.[11]

As the freedmen's fears of actual reenslavement were overblown, so their continuing hopes of gaining land were also misplaced. To be sure, Congress had not been in session since the war's end and thus had not yet addressed the question of land confiscation, but the damage from Johnson's restoration policy had been done, since it sabotaged what would prove to have been the freedmen's best opportunity to gain land. It also altered the dynamics of Reconstruction by putting land reform's advocates on the defensive. If the federal government merely restored land to which it could claim firm legal title, what hope was there for outright confiscation of rebel property? Johnson's course likewise emboldened former Confederates to resist any measures beyond the minimal requirements he had set for the southern states' readmission to the Union—ratifying the Thirteenth Amendment to the U.S. Constitution abolishing slavery, rescinding ordinances of secession, and repudiating Confederate debts. By the time the 39th Congress convened in December 1865, advocates of land reform faced an uphill fight.

10. On freedmen's political mobilization in late 1865, see W. E. Dougherty to L. Crooker, Oct. 18, 1865, J. Rhodes to B. B. Campbell, Oct. 21, 1865, and W. E. Dougherty to L. Crooker, Nov. 6, 1865, FSSP: A-8577, C-653, C-805. On the unofficial elections, see Taylor, *Louisiana Reconstructed,* 76–9. On May 29, 1865, the same day he issued his amnesty proclamation, Johnson issued a second proclamation appointing a provisional governor for North Carolina and spelling out the process for creating loyal state governments. This proclamation became the model for naming provisional governors in several other ex-Confederate states. Louisiana had a Unionist government at the time, with J. Madison Wells as governor, so no provisional governor was appointed. But because much of Louisiana had been under Confederate authority when the war ended, state and congressional elections were held in fall 1865. Wells was reelected governor. For Johnson's proclamation, see Richardson, *Messages and Papers* 8:3510–2.

11. J. W. Greene to C. W. Lowell, Nov. 23, 1865, FSSP: C-808.

Predictably, freedmen felt most keenly the consequences of Johnson's policy. The failure of land reform forced them to think more realistically about how best to secure a meaningful freedom given their circumstances. Expectations of change through land acquisition would have to give way to more pragmatic considerations of daily working and living conditions. Freedmen of the sugar region, along with their counterparts elsewhere in the South, had dared to imagine themselves as landowners, but the events of fall 1865 awoke them from that dream.

Planters survived land confiscation, but they still confronted the challenge of labor control in a world without slavery. In doing so, they exhibited both accommodation and resistance to the new order. Whereas during the war planters had strived to reestablish mastery and insisted that only by compelling labor could they make sugar, after the war most planters conceded slavery's legal demise but called for state regulation of labor. Likewise, with slavery dead most planters jettisoned their paternalistic obligations, which had largely withered away during the war, and began assuming the role of employer. Nonetheless, many not only continued to aspire to mastery but also allowed vestiges of paternalism to influence their thinking and behavior. Planters were thus both individually and collectively beset by an internal conflict as profound as the one between paternalism and profitability that had plagued them before the war. And most of them hoped to preserve what they could of the old order while adjusting to the new.[12]

For some, preserving the old mattered most. They insisted that free labor was a hopeless proposition and adamantly opposed it. This attitude derived in part from their refusal to surrender dominance over black people, but it also resulted from an inability to engage their workers as equals who must receive compensation for their labor. "The whites were as ignorant of the true nature of the [free-labor] system as the blacks," journalist John T. Trowbridge observed in late 1865. "Capitalists did not understand how they could secure labor without owning it, or how men could be induced to work without the whip." A Freedmen's Bureau agent near New Orleans reported that "the planters are bitter opponents of the free-labor system in any phase it may assume." They were "to a man haters of our government," he added, and "unhesitatingly condemn any and all of its measures that have been adopted in opposition to slavery."[13]

12. On planters' views after the war generally, see Dan T. Carter, *When the War Was Over: The Failure of Self-Reconstruction in the South, 1865–1867* (Baton Rouge, 1985), 147–75, and Roark, *Masters without Slaves*, chaps. 4 and 5.

13. J. T. Trowbridge, *A Picture of the Desolated States: And the Work of Restoration, 1865–1868* (Hartford, 1868), 408, 411; W. Dougherty to D. G. Fenno, Nov. 7, 1865, Letters & Telegrams Received, ser. 1303, AC, BRFAL. See also July 24, 1865, Erwin Diary, LSU; P. O'Hare to T. W.

Other planters adjusted to free labor with surprising equanimity. Rather than continue an exercise in futility, they reconciled themselves to the new order and determined to make the most of it. "[T]he majority of Planters are endeavoring to accommodate themselves to the new labor system," noted an officer near New Orleans in July 1865. "Many of the plantations are in a high state of cultivation and the laborers work cheerfully in all cases where they are properly cared for." In spring 1866, the bureau agent for St. Mary Parish also noted a marked difference in planters' attitudes toward their workers. "[The freedmen] tell me . . . that there has been a great change in their Master Man as they call their Employers," he reported. "[H]e treats them like a gentleman and tells them the truth which he did not do before the surrender." Finally understanding that freedmen worked better when treated as free people and not as slaves, some planters acceded to what was in effect already a fait accompli.[14]

For planters, concomitant with accepting slavery's abolition was the abandonment of their responsibilities as paternalistic slaveholders. Forced now to deal with labor power as a commodity, they could ill afford to let personal attachments sway them if they hoped to survive the cold, hard logic of the capitalist market. "Within the last three or four days, some eight or ten negroes have returned . . . some bringing their wives, who never belonged to the place," one planter complained in September 1865. "[I]t is impossible to let this thing go on, there is nothing in the plantation to feed them with, and not work enough to keep them busy." Sounding more like an employer than a paternalistic slaveholder, he resolved "to turn them off." The same month, a Union officer told of a planter evicting from his estate relatives of black soldiers, leaving them "in a starving condition." This act, he believed, was "part of a general plan to turn upon the hands of the Government all the Old people and the wives and children of Soldiers." Forced now to deal with labor through the objective

---

Conway, Oct. 11, 1865, FSSP: A-8582; R. C. Martin Jr. to M. Martin, Sept. 10, 1865, R. C. Martin Jr. to R. C. Martin, Aug. 3, 1866, and R. C. Martin to R. C. Martin Jr., Aug. 20, 1866, all in Martin-Pugh Collection, NSU; Kenneth E. Shewmaker and Andrew K. Prinz, eds., "A Yankee in Louisiana: Selections from the Diary and Correspondence of Henry R. Gardner, 1862–1866," *LH* 5 (summer 1964): 292–3.

14. [W. E. Dougherty] to L. Crooker, July 5, 1865, FSSP: C-806; [?] to A. F. Hayden, Mar. 10, 1866, Narrative Trimonthly Reps. of Business Transacted, ser. 1603, Agt & ASAC, Franklin, BRFAL. See also W. E. Dougherty to D. G. Fenno, Nov. 7, 1865, FSSP: A-8562; Rep. of J. F. Harrison, Sept. 15, 1865, vol. 90, p. 93, Inspection Reps., ser. 1409, Plant. Dept., AC, BRFAL, and W. H. Webster to L. H. Warren, Feb. 29, 1868, vol. 284, pp. 69–83, Monthly Reps., ser. 1594, SAC of the 3rd Subdist., Franklin, BRFAL; Trowbridge, *Picture of the Desolated States,* 413–4; Giulio Adamoli, "New Orleans in 1867," *LHQ* 6 (April 1923): 274; *Franklin Planters' Banner,* Sept. 2, 1865, reprinted in *DP,* Sept. 13, 1865.

medium of the market, many planters refused to allow paternalism to affect their judgement. Thus market relations stripped freedmen of what little personal protection they had once enjoyed.[15]

Nonetheless, many former slaveholders, as well as a fair number of freedmen, found paternalism's legacy too much to overcome so soon after emancipation. The personal bond between master and slave, which had both fostered and been nurtured by paternalism, often proved difficult to break. Paternalism continued to color relations between planters and freedmen, who engaged each other through the prism of their previous experiences as masters and slaves. In early 1866, for instance, William J. Minor's contract negotiations with his workers became so acrimonious that many of them left in disgust. "The negro is certainly the greatest hypocrite & the best actor in the world," Minor angrily concluded. Some time later, though, the hard feelings on both sides had abated. "A number of our old hands came to see us to day," Minor noted. "They all say they are sorry they left & would come back if they could. Will certainly come back next year." However great a change they had undergone, neither planters nor freedmen could escape entirely paternalism's hold. Only in theory did the market's impersonal relations replace slavery's personal attachments.[16]

Whatever their opinions on free labor or paternalism, planters all but unanimously agreed that solving what came to be known as "the problem of labor" required state action. "Slavery as an institution has probably left us, but the management of 'free labor' will probably be controlled by State legislation," observed W. W. Pugh soon after the war. State power might afford "a good substitute for the late institution," he added, "provided we can control the labor so as to get a quid pro quo for our investment." A journalist spoke for planters when he wrote: "[G]ive the State control of the labor question, and, in a very short time the plantations of Lower Louisiana . . . will again smile with rich harvests." Having already sounded the theme of state regulation during the war, planters continued to do so for many years after it.[17]

15. R. L. Eastin to J. Moore, Sept. 16, 1865, Weeks Papers, LSU; H. N. Frisbie to T. W. Conway, Sept. 18, 1865, FSSP: C-913. See also Whitelaw Reid, *After the War: A Tour of the Southern States, 1865–1866* (1866; reprint, New York, 1965), 463–4.

16. Jan. 6–14, 1866, Mar. 25, 1866, Plant. Diary 36, WJMP. See also W. T. Palfrey to J. G. Palfrey, June 29, 1865, Palfrey Papers, *RASP*, ser. I; D. Avery to D. D. Avery, Nov. 21, 1865, Avery Family Papers, SHC.

17. W. W. Pugh to R. C. Martin, June 23, 1865, Martin-Pugh Collection, NSU; *Plaquemine Iberville South,* June 9, 1866. See also C. L. Norton to C. T. Christensen, June 27, 1865, and W. E. Dougherty to D. G. Fenno, Nov. 7, 1865, FSSP: C-948, A-8562; *DP,* Nov. 17, 26, 1865, Feb. 2, 1866; *Franklin Planters' Banner,* Sept. 2, 1865, reprinted in *DP,* Sept. 13, 1865; J. Moore to W. F. Weeks, Dec. 8, 1865, Weeks Papers, LSU.

Planters assumed they would handle the reins of power as they had before the war, and Andrew Johnson did not disappoint them. They soon wielded authority bestowed by Johnson to subdue their workers. In late summer 1865, planters reactivated the state militia and revived the old patrol system to arrest freedmen who moved about without their employers' permission. Armed, mounted, and often donning their Confederate uniforms, patrol members preyed upon freedmen mercilessly. Observing no difference between antebellum patrols and the new ones, freedmen petitioned federal authorities for protection and vowed to take matters into their own hands. After investigating affairs in Terrebonne Parish in December 1865, a federal officer reported freedmen convinced that the patrols were designed "to crush out what freedom they now enjoy and reduce them once more to comparative slavery." Unless restrictions were placed on patrols, he predicted, "the most fearful results will ensue, as the blacks unhesitatingly avowed their determination . . . to resist and if necessary, meet force with force." Although federal officials intervened to prevent egregious violations of the freedmen's civil rights by patrols, such patrols continued to harass freedmen during presidential Reconstruction.[18]

In addition to relying upon law enforcement to gain control of former slaves, planters used the law itself in an effort to shape the labor market to their advantage. Their thinking on how best to regulate the new labor system reached its apotheosis with the state legislature's enactment of the infamous Black Codes in late 1865 and early 1866. While the Black Codes defined the freedmen's legal rights, they were primarily designed to keep freedmen working on plantations and to reestablish planters' authority over them. They contained no provisions that addressed the specific problem of applying free labor to sugar production, and in that sense they represented values and assumptions that sugar planters shared with the South's other former slaveholders. Nonetheless, because sugar planters assisted in framing them, the codes reflected both their hostility toward free labor as well as their hope that state power could serve as a viable substitute for slavery. The codes had limited practical impact during their brief life-span, however, and the 1866 Civil Rights Act, enacted in April over Johnson's veto, effectively negated them. Despite their failure to hinder the labor market's development, the Black Codes were replete with symbolic importance. They ultimately proved to be the sugar planters' boldest and most systematic attempt during Reconstruction to rectify "the problem of labor."[19]

18. T. Kanady to Z. K. Wood, Dec. 23, 1865, FSSP: C-655. See also Kanady to Wood, Dec. 28, 1865, and H. Scofield to Wood, Dec. 30, 1865, FSSP: C-655, C-656.

19. Louisiana's Black Codes are in 39th Cong., 2nd Sess., Senate Executive Document 6, pp. 181–7. On the southern black codes in general, see Theodore Brantner Wilson, *The Black Codes of the South* (University, Ala., 1965) and Carter, *When the War Was Over*, 187–91, 216–31.

* * *

Both the freedmen's desire for land and the planters' hopes of using the state to regulate labor were thwarted during late 1865 and 1866. Consequently, for the remainder of presidential Reconstruction, conflict between planters and freedmen focused on more immediate concerns, such as labor's geographic mobility, settling accounts and contracting, and white supervision of labor. Yet these quotidian issues also assumed larger significance. Not only did they illustrate the struggle between freedmen's desire for autonomy within sugar production and planters' paramount goal of controlling labor, they were also the main nodes of conflict until Radical Reconstruction reconfigured the political landscape in early 1867.

Although wartime free labor laid the groundwork for a future labor market, it had barely recognized laborers' right to seek the best terms of compensation. Laborers enjoyed little leverage in negotiating contracts, being more or less compelled to work for their former owners. Furthermore, the withholding of half their wages until year's end, along with federal officers' determination to keep them at work, effectively hindered laborers' midseason mobility. In the weeks after the war, military officials kept intact the restrictive features of army labor policy by ordering freedmen to remain on their home plantations. Responding to freedmen's protests throughout the South, the War Department in July 1865 forbade military commanders to impose discriminatory restraints upon the freedmen's movement. Freedmen under contract were required to fulfill their agreements, but otherwise military officials could no longer interfere with their mobility.[20]

Because of their wartime experiences, freedmen of the sugar region did not join the mass movement throughout the South in summer 1865 of ex-slaves who had been freed suddenly at war's end. Instead, those who left their plantations in southern Louisiana did so for the specific purpose of obtaining better wages, thereby demonstrating, much to planters' consternation, that they had begun to master the labor market. "[P]arties of the wood trade are frequently in the habit of inducing negroes to leave the plantations and go into their employ at a rate of wages much higher than that paid by the planters," reported a federal officer in June 1865, "thus, the negroes are constantly breaking their agreements with the planters, and in many instances have conducted themselves with insubordination." Planters quickly complained to military officers and Freedmen's Bureau agents

---

20. For an example of an order designed to prevent freedmen from leaving plantations in the early postwar period, see Gen. Orders No. 2, Office Provost Marshal Par. Jeffr. and Orleans R[ight] B[ank], enclosed in W. E. Dougherty to L. Crooker, June 27, 1865, FSSP: C-806. For the War Department order prohibiting discriminatory restrictions on movement, see Steven Hahn, Steven F. Miller, Susan E. O'Donovan, John C. Rodrigue, and Leslie S. Rowland, eds., *Freedom: A Documentary History of Emancipation, 1861–1867,* ser. 3, vol. 1, *Land and Labor: 1865* (Cambridge, U.K., forthcoming), chap. 2.

about a labor policy that, as one of them put it, gave "the laborer permission to go & come as he pleased & when he pleased." In truth, freedmen did not move about quite as freely as planters alleged, since part of their wages was withheld and military officials did not balk at enforcing labor contracts. In those cases when freedmen left for a better offer, however, planters had to weigh the time and effort it would take to get them back against the deterioration in plantation discipline that would inevitably result if they did nothing about it.[21]

The fledgling labor market owed its existence in no small measure to the Freedmen's Bureau. Whereas the bureau failed to provide freedmen with land, it achieved greater success in fostering development of a labor market essential to free labor. Nurturing free labor in the South proved to be a daunting challenge. Military necessity had impeded its progress during the war, and planters' and freedmen's wartime experiences hardly inspired confidence in its future prospects. Nonetheless, the war's end removed the fetters of military necessity and left planters and freedmen at liberty to engage one another as putative equals within a free and open marketplace. Freedmen's Bureau officials assumed responsibility for instructing both parties in the ways of a labor system predicated upon voluntary contracts and the capitalist market.[22]

Freedmen's Bureau officials believed that ex-slaves and planters would eventually recognize free labor's benefits. In order to facilitate this process, the Freedmen's Bureau promulgated labor regulations in December 1865. Retaining some features of wartime free labor, the bureau's regulations parted from it by not prescribing wage rates. Instead, they declared it the freedmen's "duty" to "obtain the best terms they can for their service" and left them free to choose their employers. By retaining the practice of reserving half wages until year's end, the bureau conceded planters' need to have some means to control labor. The regulations also echoed wartime free labor by defining a month's labor as twenty-six days of ten hours each (except during the rolling season) and by directing that freedmen receive their necessities as well as half-acre plots per family. These regulations remained in effect throughout the bureau's existence, and although bureau agents enforced them to varying degrees, freedmen came to see the bureau as guarantor of their freedom. They did not hesitate to petition its agents for assistance.[23]

21. W. E. Dougherty to L. Crooker, June 5, 1865, and W. J. Minor to E. R. S. Canby, June 29, 1865, FSSP: C-806, C-578. See also A. Morse to Cole, Sept. 4, 1865, FSSP: A-8502, and J. Moore to Mrs. J. R. Snyder, Oct. 11, 1866, Kean-Prescott Papers, SHC.

22. For elaboration on this point, see John C. Rodrigue, "The Freedmen's Bureau and Wage Labor in the Louisiana Sugar Region," in *The Freedmen's Bureau and Reconstruction: Reconsiderations*, ed. Paul A. Cimbala and Randall M. Miller (New York, 1999), 193–218.

23. Circular No. 29, Dec. 4, 1865, in 39th Cong., 1st Sess., House Executive Document 70, pp. 30–3; A. Baird to O. O. Howard, Dec. 20, 1865, FSSP: A-8746.

The bureau's labor regulations defined the boundaries within which contracting for 1866 took place. The interrelated routines of settling accounts for one year and negotiating contracts for the next had become familiar to planters and freedmen during the war, but late 1865 and early 1866 was the first time that the parties were free to make arrangements without direct military oversight. Consequently, the transitional period between crop seasons witnessed a flurry of activity as planters settled with freedmen and offered terms, while freedmen demanded higher wages, refused to contract, and sought better offers. Negotiating contracts for 1866 demonstrated that neither militia patrols nor Black Codes could forestall the labor market's development.

Planters throughout the sugar region reported freedmen's dissatisfaction with the 1865 settlements and their refusal to contract for 1866. A. F. Pugh's travails in contracting with his workers epitomized planters' and freedmen's experiences. After limping through his rolling season in a mere two weeks, Pugh undertook in early January "the very disagreable duty of paying off negroes & hiring them for another year." He made little progress in contracting. "Had a talk with the negroes . . . about hiring them and found them very unreasonable," he later noted. Pugh proposed paying his best workers $12 per month, and only after much effort did he persuade them in mid-January to accept those terms. Thus the freedmen failed to wrest higher wages from Pugh, but they had forced him to deal with them as equals. For both sides, it was an invaluable lesson in hard bargaining.[24]

Freedmen's unwillingness to contract in early 1866 also stemmed from their aversion to arrangements that they feared would bind them to particular plantations for the year. Even when they agreed to wage rates their employers offered, they hesitated to sign annual contracts, preferring to work on a monthly or weekly basis. "I am now paying from $10 to $15 for men & from $6 to $10 for women," noted a Lafourche Parish planter. "I do not apprehend any difficulty in keeping the hands, although they are unwilling to sign the contract." The matter of annual labor contracts would remain a point of contention for several years. Having once been bound to plantations by other means, freedmen were suspicious of anything that appeared to violate their freedom; they even distrusted bureau agents' admonitions that written contracts imposed obligations on planters and thus offered them protection.[25]

24. Jan. 6, 12, 14, 16, 1866, AFP Diary, and Agreement with freedmen, Jan. 15, 1866, Pugh Papers, UT. See also Oct.–Dec. 1865, AFP Diary (typescript), AFPP, *RASP,* ser. I; J. E. Pugh to AFP, Nov. 4, 14, 1865, Pugh Papers, *RASP,* ser. G; Jan.–Feb. 1866, AFP Diary, Pugh Papers, UT; Nov. 8–11, 16, 1865, Erwin Diary, LSU; Nov. 14, 17, 1865, Plant. Diary, Palfrey Papers, *RASP,* ser. I.

25. J. Selby to C. Mathews, Mar. 10, 1866, Charles L. Mathews and Family Papers, LSU. See also C. C. Weeks to Bud, Dec. 7, 1865, Weeks Papers, LSU; T. Kanady to Z. K. Wood, Dec. 23,

In noting that freedmen wanted "to draw the whole of their monthly pay when due," a Freedmen's Bureau agent near New Orleans touched upon another issue that became a flash point in late 1865 and early 1866 and continued to smolder during the 1870s: the withholding of half wages until year's end. Inaugurated under wartime free labor and sanctioned by the bureau, the practice provoked contrasting responses from planters and freedmen. The former maintained that it was the only way to compel workers to fulfill their contracts; the latter countered that it forced them to remain with undesirable employers and thus effectively reenslaved them. "All freedmen object to being only paid half of their wages at the end of the month or quarter, and in many cases refuse to receive it unless paid the full amount," noted a bureau agent in late 1865. "They become dissatisfied and leave the plantation and go to the city [New Orleans] to work on the levee, or steamboats, or at anything else where they can obtain higher wages and receive pay more frequently." Planters who paid in full every month courted trouble, he added, since doing so enabled freedmen to leave the plantations and remain away until they had spent their money, "when they may or may not return, according to circumstances." Freedmen deemed withholding part of their pay as compromising their freedom, but for employers it approached the absurd to operate a sugar plantation without being assured labor through the crop season. The issue thus bespoke planters' and freedmen's conflicting visions of free labor.[26]

One last feature of the new labor system to emerge from contracting for 1866 involved the extension of the portion of the Christmas holiday that stretched into the new year. Freedmen had begun during the war to expand the traditional year-end break from the first week in January to as much as two weeks. After the war they extended it further to include most of the month. Planters complained about this practice at first, but they eventually resigned themselves to it, since it met both their own and the freedmen's needs. By year's end, everyone on the plantation needed a rest following the physical and emotional strain of the harvest. Moreover, until the new crop year began in earnest, there remained relatively light tasks to perform. Planters shipped the sugar crop, made financial arrangements with their factors, and settled laborers' accounts; some freedmen cleaned, repaired,

---

1865, FSSP: C-655; Jan. 1, 15, 20, 1866, Plant. Diary, Palfrey Papers, *RASP*, ser. I; draft of labor contract, 1866, Weeks Papers, LSU; Feb. 1, 9, 1866, Bayside Plant. Records 2 (typescript), SHC; J. M. Davidson to AFP, Feb. 12, 1866, Pugh Papers, UT; John Richard Dennett, *The South As It Is: 1865–1866,* ed. Henry M. Christman (New York, 1965; reprint, Baton Rouge, 1995), 317, 325–6.

26. Trimonthly Rep. of W. E. Dougherty, Jan. 10–20, 1866, FSSP: A-8690; W. Dougherty to D. G. Fenno, Nov. 7, 1865, Letters & Telegrams Received, ser. 1303, AC, BRFAL. See also J. A. Bird to E. Cousinard, Jan. 30, 1866, Edward Cousinard Papers, LSU.

and closed down the sugar mill, prepared for planting, and performed general maintenance, while others rested and lived off their back wages. Planters and freedmen also bargained over new contracts. Freedmen who were unhappy with a planter's offer left in search of a better one, while planters assembled a work force. Since Louisiana's environment dictated that spring planting begin by late January, planters and freedmen came to think of that month as a time of physical and psychological renewal. Only if work on the new crop had not started by early February did planters become alarmed.[27]

Although common interests might explain particular attributes of free labor, affairs between planters and freedmen far more often reflected what a Union officer called "mutual suspicions and fears." One issue that repeatedly provoked this animosity after the war was supervision of freedmen's labor by white overseers. As had been the case during the war, freedmen objected neither to overseers nor to working in gangs under their direction. Rather, they challenged the authority of overseers who insisted on treating them as though they were still slaves. After the war, the freedmen's sensitivity to mistreatment increased, to include not only physical abuse but also harsh language, especially when directed toward freedwomen, as well as orders given in a scornful manner. Most observers remarked how diligently freedmen worked when treated fairly and decently. It was equally certain that trouble ensued when freedmen felt themselves abused. Despite bureau agents' admonitions and freedmen's protests, as well as their own experiences, overseers learned only with difficulty that abuse spawned not good and faithful labor but disruption of plantation operations.[28]

Mistreatment and abuse, to be sure, were open to any number of definitions after the war. Nonetheless, freedmen refused to tolerate what they considered ill treatment, and they petitioned the Freedmen's Bureau when subjected to it. The freedman, a Union officer reported in late 1865, "will not tamely submit to a tithe of the wrongs which he bore patiently while a slave." The bureau agent for St. Mary Parish observed in April 1866 that freedmen were "in noways intimidated"

27. Time entries, Dec. 1865–Jan. 1866, Scrapbook 10, Col. W. W. Pugh and Family Papers, LSU; Jan. 15, 1866, Plant. Diary, Alexandre E. DeClouet Papers, LSU; Dec. 25, 1865, Jan. 1–3, 1866, Erwin Diary, LSU.

28. C. L. Norton to C. T. Christensen, June 27, 1865, FSSP: C-948. For comments that freedmen worked well when treated fairly, see reports of D. H. Reese, Aug. 25, 1865, vol. 90, pp. 3, 5; E. C. Baxter, Aug. 28, 29, 1865, vol. 90, pp. 33, 35; and S. R. Oren, Sept. 8, 1865, vol. 90, p. 71, all in Inspection Reps., ser. 1409, Plant. Dept., AC, BRFAL; T. Kanady to Z. K. Wood, Dec. 23, 28, 1865, FSSP: C-655; J. H. Brough to A. F. Hayden, May 1, 1866, vol. 262, p. 2, LS, ser. 1577, Agt & ASAC, Donaldsonville, BRFAL. For freedmen's objections to what they believed to be abuse, see Aug. 30, Sept. 2, 1865, Plant. Diary (typescript), AFPP, *RASP,* ser. I; R. C. Martin Jr. to M. Martin, Oct. 29–30, 1865, Martin-Pugh Collection, NSU.

by overseers' abuse and "would report anything of the kind if it were practiced." That May, an overseer in Jefferson Parish, one Mr. White, complained to a local bureau agent that freedmen had left the plantation for higher wages elsewhere. When summoned before the agent, however, the freedmen explained that they had left because White was "never satisfied with their work and always expects more than they can perform." The agent judged White to be at fault, since "he has been an overseer about thirty years and is not managing the freedmen under the new system."[29]

Sustained by the efforts of the Freedmen's Bureau to defend their rights and to remake the South on a free-labor basis, former slaves shaped wage labor by contesting the terrain of freedom within it. Freedmen did not achieve all they wanted in their struggles with planters over freedom of movement, contracting, and treatment by overseers, but they prevented planters from reestablishing mastery over them. Yet even as many freedmen vied to fashion a wage-labor system they could countenance, others explored alternate arrangements. The unsuccessful search for viable alternatives to wage labor helps explain its triumph in the sugar region.

Despite its significance, land reform's failure does not alone explain why wage labor prevailed over tenancy or sharecropping in the sugar region. Immediately after the war, wage labor and centralized plantation routine characterized the cotton South. Freedmen there, however, eventually repudiated wage labor and the old work routines, whereas freedmen in the sugar region did not. In examining the divergence between the cotton and sugar regions, the key question is why freedmen eschewed wage labor in the former as much as why they acquiesced to it in the latter.

The emergence of sharecropping and tenancy in the cotton South is a familiar if complicated story. Planters at first hoped to reorganize their estates on a basis as close to slavery as possible. Freedmen, however, objected to a plantation system that resembled too closely the one they had known as slaves. They rejected gang labor under white overseers and instead pushed for access to land. Cotton planters initially opposed renting land to freedmen, but the freedmen's unstinting resis-

29. H. Scofield to Z. K. Wood, Dec. 30, 1865, FSSP: C-656; C. E. Merrill to A. F. Hayden, Apr. 30, 1866, Narrative Trimonthly Reps. of Business Transacted, ser. 1603, Agt & ASAC, Franklin, BRFAL; Monthly Rep. of R. Folles, May 31, 1866, Reps. of Asst. Inspector of Freedmen, ser. 1458, Agt & SAC, Algiers, BRFAL. See also Rep. of J. F. Harrison, Sept. 15, 1865, vol. 90, pp. 95, 99, Inspection Reps., ser. 1409, Plant. Dept., AC, BRFAL; C. L. Norton to B. B. Campbell, June 21, 1865, A. M. Malsie to A. F. Hayden, Aug. 28, 1866, and [R. Folles] to A. F. Hayden, Sept. [?], 1866, FSSP: C-947, A-8513, A-8694; R. C. Martin Jr. to R. C. Martin, Aug. 3, 1866, Martin-Pugh Collection, NSU.

tance to gang labor, as well as planters' own financial difficulties following unan-ticipated crop failures in 1866 and 1867, eventually compelled them to relent. The transition to sharecropping and tenancy in the cotton South occurred not over-night but rather after an extended period during which planters and freedmen ex-perimented with a wide array of possibilities. In one of history's ironies, freedmen in the cotton South championed sharecropping as a temporary expedient toward the goals of landholding and economic independence. But planters, despite their weakened status after the war, managed to mobilize their still-considerable re-sources in order to manipulate sharecropping arrangements to their advantage, enabling them to control the New South's plantation system.[30]

Freedmen and planters in the sugar region also experimented with alternatives to wage labor after the war. Building upon wartime precedents, some worked in share-wage arrangements. Freedmen collectively received a share of the crop's proceeds, usually between one-third and one-half, which they divided among themselves. Deciding between monthly wages or share-wages involved many factors and re-sulted from intense negotiations between planters and freedmen, neither of whom necessarily preferred one arrangement over the other. Suffering under financial hardship and unable to meet a monthly payroll, some planters favored share-wages while their workers demanded monthly wages; in other cases, planters wanted to pay wages while freedmen, according to one planter, were "bent on working on shares." Moreover, planters and freedmen tested alternative ways of organizing labor. Some freedmen were hired by the task while others worked in squads that cultivated a set acreage. Such arrangements were destined to become exceptions in the sugar region, but they suggest a willingness among some planters and freedmen to envision alternatives to wage labor and centralized plantation regimen.[31]

30. No effort is made here to cite the voluminous literature on sharecropping's origins and de-velopment. See the works cited in the Introduction, notes 1–4, as well as the work of Harold D. Woodman, including "New Perspectives on Southern Economic Development: A Comment," *AH* 49 (April 1975): 374–80; "Sequel to Slavery: The New History Views the Postbellum South," *JSH* 43 (November 1977): 523–54; "Post–Civil War Southern Agriculture and the Law," *AH* 53 (January 1979): 319–37; "Postbellum Social Change and Its Effects on Marketing the South's Cotton Crop," *AH* 56 (January 1982): 215–30; and "How New Was the New South?" *AH* 58 (October 1984): 529–45. For views that differ somewhat from those presented here, see Stephen J. DeCanio, *Agriculture in the Postbellum South: The Economics of Production and Supply* (Cambridge, Mass., 1974); Robert Higgs, *Competition and Coercion: Blacks in the American Economy, 1865–1914* (Cambridge, U.K., 1977); Joseph D. Reid Jr., "Sharecropping As an Understandable Market Response: The Post-Bellum South," *Journal of Economic History* 33 (March 1973): 106–30; Ralph Shlomowitz, "The Origins of Southern Sharecropping," *AH* 53 (July 1979): 557–75.

31. J. White to L. H. Warren, Feb. 29, 1868, vol. 384, pp. 38–41, Trimonthly Reps., ser. 1789, ASAC, New Iberia, BRFAL; R. Daigre to EJG, Dec. 10, 1866, EJGP; R. W. Mullen to L. H.

Nonetheless, although sugar production did not preclude alternatives to wage labor, certain factors inherent in growing cane, converting its juice into sugar, and marketing the crop all militated against sharecropping and tenancy. Coordination between field and mill during the rolling season, as well as the collective processing of cane, created obstacles difficult to surmount. They were compounded by the question of dividing the crop, especially when its quality could vary dramatically, even within a single hogshead. Deciding how to apportion shipping and insurance fees, commissions, and other costs associated with marketing the crop also confounded planters and freedmen. Such problems were not insolvable, as other sugar-producing societies have demonstrated. For centuries, Brazilian farmers and tenants have grown sugarcane and sold it to centralized mills. Likewise, the Cuban sugar planters adopted a variant of sharecropping after the emancipation of their slaves. However, the fact remains that while the failure of sharecropping and tenancy to take root in the sugar region did not owe to crop determinism, certain features of sugar production worked against alternative arrangements.[32]

The practical complications of applying sharecropping or tenancy to sugar production both reinforced and were reinforced by planters' ingrained conservatism. Considering sugar production an indivisible process, they regarded grow-

---

Warren, Sept. 10, 1868, vol. 206, pp. 21–6, Trimonthly Reps., ser. 1604, Agt & ASAC, Franklin, BRFAL. John Richard Dennett noted in 1866 that the vast majority of sugar plantations he visited utilized monthly wages. Dennett, *The South,* 317. For examples of share-wage arrangements, see Reps. of M. Hawke, Aug. 22, 1865, vol. 90, pp. 13–4, R. K. Diossy, Aug. 28, 1865, vol. 90, pp. 45, 47, and D. H. Reese, Aug. 25, 1865, vol. 90, pp. 5, 7, all in Inspection Reps., ser. 1409, Plant. Dept., AC, BRFAL; R. W. Mullen to L. H. Warren, Mar. 10, 1868, vol. 276, pp. 47–9, LS, ser. 1598, Agt & ASAC, Franklin, BRFAL; R. Daigre to EJG, Dec. 10, 1866, EJGP; Contract, Jan. 1, 1866, Joseph Kleinpeter and Family Papers, LSU; Contract, June 4, 1867, Slack Papers, SHC; Feb. 10, 1868, Plant. Diary, Palfrey Papers, *RASP,* ser. I. On the squad system, see Ralph Shlomowitz, "'Bound' or 'Free'? Black Labor in Cotton and Sugarcane Farming, 1865–1880," *JSH* 50 (November 1984): 569–96.

32. For examples of the myriad difficulties involved in dividing and marketing the sugar crop and reconciling laborers' accounts under share-wage arrangements, see J. H. Brough to J. M. Lee, Dec. 4, 1867, vol. 263, pp. 149–50, LS, ser. 1577, Agt & ASAC, Donaldsonville, BRFAL, and R. W. Mullen to L. H. Warren, Feb. 29, Mar. 20, 31, Apr. 10, 1868, vol. 276, pp. 43–5, 51–4, 57–61, 65–71, LS, ser. 1598, Agt & ASAC, Franklin, BRFAL. On Brazilian sugarcane farmers, see Stuart B. Schwartz, *Sugar Plantations in the Formation of Brazilian Society: Bahia, 1550–1835* (Cambridge, U.K., 1985). On sharecropping on Cuban sugar plantations after emancipation, see Rebecca J. Scott, *Slave Emancipation in Cuba: The Transition to Free Labor, 1860–1899* (Princeton, N.J., 1985), 104–5. Scholars have noted the difficulty of applying sharecropping to sugar production in Louisiana; see Mark D. Schmitz, "The Transformation of the Southern Cane Sugar Sector, 1860–1930," *AH* 53 (January 1979): 270–85; Shlomowitz, "'Bound' or 'Free'?" 595; and Sitterson, *Sugar Country,* 241.

ing cane and converting its juice into sugar as inseparable. Their previous experiences also convinced them that sugar production could only be conducted with large concentrations of land, labor, and capital. In this respect, planters were correct, since economies of scale were essential to sugar production. Yet if custom shaped planters' attitudes, so too did racism and the refusal to allow black people to exercise independent initiative. Thus the traditions to which sugar and slavery gave rise fused with structural impediments to produce an inertia that proved almost impossible to overcome. Given what planters had already experienced, their aversion to new ways of organizing operations, far from being irrational, is understandable.

If planters' thinking explains in part the dominance of wage labor and centralized regimen, so too does the freedmen's. Freedmen understood the importance of coordinated work routines in sugar production, but they envisioned a free-labor system that ensured them autonomy within its bounds. They submitted to the discipline sugar making required so long as they received pay for their labor and were not driven as slaves. As freedmen tolerated wage labor during and after the war, they found it to be more remunerative than share-wages. "Where the agreement is for share of crop or nett proceeds," explained a Freedmen's Bureau agent in 1866, "there will be dissatisfaction as the crop will not more than pay expenses, and the freedmen will not get anything." Nonetheless, just as freedmen in the cotton South thought sharecropping a temporary step toward landholding, many freedmen in the sugar region expected wage labor to enable them eventually to acquire property. They initially viewed wage labor as an acceptable alternative to independent proprietorship, especially when compared to slavery. Once in place, however, wage labor gained a momentum that proved to be unstoppable. Like their compatriots in the cotton South who pushed for sharecropping without anticipating the consequences, freedmen in the sugar region acquiesced to wage labor unaware of how their decisions would affect the future.[33]

Wage labor's triumph in the sugar region also reflected the transformation of northern free-labor ideology after the Civil War. Free-labor proponents who had previously espoused ownership of productive property as critical to economic independence now celebrated a laborer's freedom to sell his or her services within the capitalist market. The head of the Freedmen's Bureau in Louisiana declared in November 1865 that "the matter of wages must depend on the law of supply and

33. A. M. Malsie to W. H. Sterling, Oct. 23, 1866, vol. 261, pp. 9–10, LS, ser. 1571, Agt, Donaldsonville, BRFAL. See also J. W. Keller to J. M. Lee, Nov. 20, 1867, vol. 275, pp. 101–3, LS, ser. 1598, Agt & ASAC, Franklin; J. H. Brough to A. H. Clements, Dec. 1, 1867, vol. 263, p. 147, LS, ser. 1577, Agt & ASAC, Donaldsonville; and R. W. Mullen to L. H. Warren, Sept. 20, 1868, vol. 286, pp. 26–30, Trimonthly Reps., ser. 1604, Agt & ASAC, Franklin, all in BRFAL.

demand." This transformation resulted in part from the monumental changes northern society underwent during the war, but it also ensued from the attempt to recast southern society on a free-labor basis without providing land or other productive property to freedmen. Born of the effort to reconcile free-labor principles with sugar production, wage labor did not contradict northern free-labor ideology but instead helped to transform it.[34]

By early 1867, the new order's course was about to take another unexpected turn. The break between Johnson and Congress over Reconstruction precipitated passage of the Reconstruction Acts. By imposing military rule upon the former Confederate states and making black suffrage a requirement for their readmission to the Union, Radical Reconstruction irrevocably changed the dynamics of the postwar social order. The question of black suffrage was not new in Louisiana; a small group of New Orleans Radicals and the city's free men of color had pushed unsuccessfully for it during the war. Now mandated by the federal government, black suffrage would come to the state, further shifting the balance of power on plantations.

34. Circular No. 26, Nov. 7, 1865, in 39th Cong., 1st Sess., House Executive Document 70, p. 29. On northern free-labor ideology before the Civil War, see Foner, *Free Soil;* Glickstein, *Concepts of Free Labor;* and Schmidt, *Free to Work*, chaps. 1 and 2. On the transformation of free-labor thought after the Civil War, see Eric Foner, *Reconstruction: America's Unfinished Revolution, 1863–1877* (New York, 1988) and Schmidt, *Free to Work*, chap. 6.

❦4❧

SUGAR AND SUFFRAGE

The freedmen have the stamina to maintain their views politically, and defend the principles they advocate, which as a matter of course the planter contends against, and tries to run them to the belief of his creed.

—John H. Brough to Lucius H. Warren, September 11, 1868

The advent of Radical Reconstruction reconfigured the sugar region's political landscape, as southern Louisiana experienced a groundswell of black grassroots mobilization in 1867 and 1868. Freedmen formed political organizations, held rallies and engaged in debate, registered to vote and voted en masse, and banded together to shield themselves from external foes and maintain unity within the black community. This mobilization infused politics into freedmen's working lives, as disputes over seemingly mundane matters raised the larger question of who ultimately wielded decision-making authority on plantations.

Although these two developments—grassroots political mobilization and its effect on labor relations—occurred throughout the entire postbellum South, they had consequences specific to the sugar region. Centralized plantation regimen provided a solid foundation for black grassroots political activity, since freedmen who lived and worked together could unite in moments of crisis. This mobilization in turn galvanized freedmen's efforts to gain a measure of control over their working lives even as they labored within the sugar plantation's closely coordinated routine. By definition a collective endeavor, politics both reinforced and was reinforced by the freedmen's concerted campaign to shape labor relations. The combination of politics and labor activism that prevailed in the South during Radical Reconstruction enabled freedmen of the sugar region to put forward a formidable front in reorganizing labor.

The implications of black political power provoked desperate responses from planters, who increasingly resorted to extralegal methods to obstruct black politics and reestablish control over their workers. Freedmen combated planters' efforts to curtail their freedom, but the violence pervading Louisiana during summer and fall 1868 revealed the tenuousness of that freedom. The first postwar presidential campaign unleashed a wave of intimidation and violence that exposed the limits of black political power even as it demonstrated the freedmen's resolve to exercise their rights as American citizens.

At the very moment the 1867 crop season commenced, the freedmen's impending ascent to political power was about to revolutionize relations between them and the planters. Over presidential opposition, the Republican-dominated Congress passed the Reconstruction Acts, mandating the process by which former Confederate states could return to the Union. Effectively superseding civilian governments created by Lincoln during the war or by Johnson in 1865, congressional Reconstruction imposed military rule on the South, dividing it into five military districts, with Louisiana and Texas making up the Fifth Military District. District commanders would organize elections—in which black men would participate but from which many antebellum political leaders were barred—to select delegates to a state constitutional convention. This convention would frame a new constitution that provided for black male suffrage and that registered voters (including black men) had to approve. Elections would then be called for a new state government, which would ratify the Fourteenth Amendment to the U.S. Constitution, whereupon the state could seek readmission to the Union. Though each side viewed the matter very differently, both freedmen and planters believed black suffrage would bring revolution to southern Louisiana.[1]

Black suffrage transformed the entire South, but its repercussions were of special significance in southern Louisiana, where in 1860 the black population had outnumbered the white by about 90,000 to 60,000. Black majorities in several sugar parishes became powerful voting blocs, which translated into potential black dominance of both state and parish offices. Some sugar parishes sent black representatives to the state legislature throughout Reconstruction, and former slaves came to exercise powers of local law enforcement, participate in the state

---

1. Original Reconstruction Act in U.S., *Stats. at Large of USA* 14:428–9. Several supplemental measures were later passed that addressed oversights in the original act. On the Reconstruction Acts in Louisiana, see Taylor, *Louisiana Reconstructed*, 129–34.

militia, and control or influence local and parish administration. By creating a black majority in the sugar region before the Civil War, planters had inadvertently laid the foundations for black political power after it.[2]

The implications of that power went beyond voting or even officeholding. Political mobilization and the contest over labor together ignited a firestorm more intense than either could have produced alone. Plantations hosted large concentrations of workers, enabling freedmen to band together for mutual support and protection; the latter organized political "clubs," such as Union Leagues, with greater success than was possible in areas where the black population was dispersed. Freedmen engaged in debate at political rallies in nearby towns and on their home plantations. These events were attended not only by black men but also by black women, who despite their disfranchisement participated in all political activities other than voting. Decisions made in club meetings or at larger gatherings involved both abstract political matters and immediate concerns about daily life, and because such decisions expressed the will of the entire black community, discipline and unity could be maintained. The collective organization of life and labor on sugar plantations thus provided a fertile breeding ground for black grassroots politics, which in turn fueled freedmen's efforts to gain control over their own labor. Freedmen may have felt frustration at times over living and working in a manner that resembled their former condition, but defining freedom in communal terms rather than as a matter of individual autonomy gave them leverage in contesting plantation regimen.[3]

Planters stood by in spring 1867 and watched many of their former slaves register to vote, the first step toward incorporating black suffrage into the state's organic law. Inchoate black political activity had emerged as early as fall 1865, but Radical Reconstruction intensified and focused it. "All the Negroes went down to Mr. Keepers to get registered as Voters," noted an Iberville Parish planter. "The

2. Louisiana's 1860 population was divided almost equally between white and black, but by 1870 there would be a slight black majority, making Louisiana, Mississippi, and South Carolina the only states with black majorities during Reconstruction.

3. For a similar view, see Rebecca J. Scott, "'Stubborn and Disposed to Stand Their Ground': Black Militia, Sugar Workers, and Dynamics of Collective Action in the Louisiana Sugar Bowl, 1863–87," in *From Slavery to Emancipation in the Atlantic World*, ed. Sylvia R. Frey and Betty Wood (London, 1999), 103–26. Julie Saville has also explored black political mobilization, focusing on its ritualistic qualities, in "Rites and Power: Reflections on Slavery, Freedom, and Political Ritual," ibid., 81–102, and in "Grassroots Reconstruction: Agricultural Labour and Collective Action in South Carolina, 1860–1868," *Slavery and Abolition* 12 (December 1991): 173–82. For further discussion of some of the issues raised in this chapter, see John C. Rodrigue, "Labor Militancy and Black Grassroots Political Mobilization in the Louisiana Sugar Region, 1865–1868," *JSH* 67 (February 2001): 115–42.

colored people call on me very often to get advice in regard to voting," the Freedmen's Bureau agent at Thibodaux reported. "I always advise them to hold frequent meetings and on election day have some one at the polls who can tell if they are giving the proper vote." William T. Palfrey likened this burgeoning political movement to a recent inundation in St. Mary Parish. "I look upon this flood of water as nothing compared to the political flood of fanaticism & anarchy, now sweeping over & desolating the land," he groused. "The former will subside, the latter will swell more & more."[4]

Freedmen's political mobilization immediately affected their attitudes and actions toward plantation labor, as black political power obliterated prevailing relations between planters and ex-slaves with a fury that nearly matched emancipation itself. Planters "complain bitterly of the discontent and uneasiness exhibited by the Freedmen on account of their new political relations," the bureau agent for Iberville Parish reported, which "affect their laboring ideas to some extent." Another agent noted that "many cases of difficulty arise from a petty prejudice of the whites against the blacks on account of the recent elevation (political) of the latter class." Planters interpreted words and acts by freedmen as "intended insolence which *formerly* they did not notice," while freedmen were "making themselves obnoxious by their remarks and actions."[5]

Planters' complaints served as an invaluable gauge of the connection between politics and freedmen's "laboring ideas." However self-serving, such murmuring also reflected planters' awareness that black politics threatened their attempt to control labor. The immediate effect of black political activity was disruption of agricultural operations, which would have devastating consequences for the crop. The long-term threat involved potential loss of the postemancipation labor settlement. Planters quickly pinpointed the link between agricultural struggle and freedmen's political power. Understanding that the fate of their plantations rested in the political arena as well as in the sugarcane fields, planters tried to intimidate their workers in hopes of impeding black politics. Some discharged individuals whom they singled out as "ringleaders," while others forced substantial numbers of workers to leave the plantations, although doing so jeopardized their crops. Such tactics meant the sacrifice of short-term profits in order to achieve the long-term goal of controlling labor. Yet planters' motivations arose from more than

4. June 11, 1867, Erwin Diary, LSU; J. D. Rich to H. C. Warmoth, Apr. 12, 1867, Warmoth Papers, SHC; May 1, 1867, Plant. Diary, Palfrey Papers, *RASP,* ser. I. See also Apr. 13, 1867, AFP Diary, Pugh Papers, UT; May 3, 1867, Plant. Diary 2, DeClouet Papers, LSU.

5. F. A. Osbourne to G. F. Schayer, June 20, 1867, vol. 425, [no page no.], LS, ser. 1842, Agt & ASAC, Plaquemine, BRFAL; W. H. Webster to W. Sterling, June 10, 1867, vol. 217, p. 117, LS, ser. 1490, ASAC, Baton Rouge, BRFAL.

economic concerns: their actions underscored an enduring racist dimension to their thinking. They were determined to reassert authority over labor and over black people.[6]

Freedmen responded to intimidation with a unity that reflected their growing political acumen. In June 1867, for example, planter John Andrews of Iberville Parish reported to the local Freedmen's Bureau agent that after he had discharged John Williams and Alex Menken, the rest of his laborers refused to work. Williams belonged to a political organization known as the "Moses Club" and had been ordered, along with Menken and others, to embark on an electioneering tour by the club's president, George Deslonde. The crop needed attention, so Andrews asked the freedmen to delay their tour, but they insisted on going since "George Deslonde had ordered it." Believing plantation discipline would be compromised by such behavior, Andrews discharged Williams and Menken.

The following morning, however, the other employees quit work and announced that unless Williams and Menken were reinstated they would leave. Faced with potential loss of his entire work force, Andrews summoned the bureau agent, who "found that the laborers were determined to leave unless the two men were retained." Deciding that an amicable course was best, the agent discussed the matter with both parties and succeeded in restoring jobs to Williams and Menken and in persuading the laborers to resume their duties. Emboldened by what they saw as victory, the freedmen redoubled their political activity, later holding a July 4th barbecue.[7]

Despite planters' efforts to obstruct black political power, the freedmen's activities intensified throughout summer 1867, as elections for delegates to the constitutional convention approached. General Philip H. Sheridan, military district commander, scheduled elections for September 27 and 28 to decide whether or not to hold a convention and to select delegates to serve in it. "There is nothing of interest going on here except that the Negroes (generally) are having meetings and electioneering for the different candidates for the convention," Andrew H. Gay informed his father. "I saw about 20 on Horse back yesterday with the Stars & Stripes floating over them on their way to Grosse Tete to have a large meeting and speeches were to be made by Kenyon & others." The bureau agent at Baton Rouge reported that "all the freedmen are taking great interest in political mat-

6. M. Smith to Hartstaff, June 11, 1867, Letters & Telegrams Received, ser. 1303, AC, BRFAL; J. White to [?], Apr. [30], 1868, vol. 384, pp. 56–60, Trimonthly Reps., ser. 1789, ASAC, New Iberia, BRFAL.

7. F. A. Osbourne to G. F. Schayer, June 20, 1867, vol. 425, [no page no.], and Osbourne to L. O. Parker, July 24, 1867, vol. 426, pp. 12–3, both in LS, ser. 1842, Agt & ASAC, Plaquemine, BRFAL.

ters"—indeed, "almost too much," he added, "for they often neglect their crops & other work to attend political meetings at times when their work is most required." [8]

The election results were a foregone conclusion. Not only did Louisiana have a slight black majority, but the vast majority of white men were either prohibited from registering to vote or boycotted the election entirely, since participation to their minds would have legitimized what they believed an abomination. Nonetheless, the drama of black men casting their first ballots precluded any sense of anticlimax. Statewide, 75,000 ballots were cast in favor of the constitutional convention and only 4,000 against it; half of the ninety-eight delegates elected to the convention were black, and all but two were Republicans. In the sugar region, where every parish except St. Charles elected at least one black delegate, a total of eighteen black delegates were elected. However predictable, the election results were revolutionary. [9]

Confronting the unthinkable, planters wondered what black political power portended. "The *present political* condition of the country, and what it will be the next year," a neighbor remarked to Edward J. Gay, "you I have no doubt can form a better opinion than myself, and what effect it will have on the Labor for the next year." The effects of the election could already be seen. Because of the preaching of "low, mean, unprincipled demagogues," one bureau agent observed after the election, "the labor today is not as it was a month ago: not near so easily governed, nor can it be commanded owing to the political state of affairs." This condition, he believed, would have deplorable consequences: "[S]hould these demagogues continue to harass the minds of and keep at fever heat the Freedmen, labor will become disorganized, demoralized and dissatisfaction will ensue." [10]

However unwittingly, the bureau agent identified a problem that would plague sugar planters for years to come: the "demoralization" of labor. Planters through-

8. A. H. Gay to EJG, Sept. 20, 1867, EJGP; W. H. Webster to L. O. Parker, Aug. 31, 1867, vol. 216, pp. 38–45, LS, ser. 1486, SAC of the 2nd Subdist., Baton Rouge, BRFAL. See also Sept. 1, 1867, Plant. Diary 2, DeClouet Papers, LSU; S. W. Purchase to W. H. Sterling, Sept. 30, 1867, vol. 284, pp. 27–39, Monthly Reps., ser. 1594, SAC of the 3rd Subdist., Franklin, BRFAL.

9. Sept. 27, 1867, Erwin Diary, LSU; Sept. 27, 28, 1867, Plant. Diary 36, WJMP; W. H. Webster to J. M. Lee, Sept. 30, 1867, vol. 218, pp. 52–61, LS, ser. 1490, ASAC, Baton Rouge, BRFAL. Making allowances for war casualties, emigration, and natural deaths, Joe Gray Taylor has estimated that of almost 95,000 white males twenty-one or older in Louisiana in 1860, 45,000 did not register to vote in 1867. Moreover, a large majority of those who registered did not vote. Taylor, *Louisiana Reconstructed*, 143–7. On the number of black delegates elected to the convention, see Vincent, *Black Legislators*, 226–7.

10. T. I. Garrett to EJG, Sept. 27, 1867, EJGP; J. H. Brough to W. W. Tyler, Oct. 1, 1867, vol. 263, pp. 102–6, LS, ser. 1577, Agt & ASAC, Donaldsonville, BRFAL.

out the South used this term to describe what they saw as the consequences of emancipation. Demoralized labor, they believed, not only suffered from low morale but also lacked discipline. No longer subject to corporal punishment, ex-slaves eschewed steady labor and refused to obey orders. Such complaints exposed a host of assumptions about race and labor, yet when sugar planters used the term they were describing a real phenomenon. Sugar production required a group of individuals to strive together toward a common goal, from which emerged a collective identity or an esprit de corps. Because a work force's morale reflected this collective spirit, what planters called demoralization might also be described as dispiritedness. As is true of all collective endeavors—from battlefield to political campaign to sporting arena—morale is fragile. Once demoralization set in among sugar workers, it could spread like wildfire. Evidenced not by laborers' complete refusal to work but by their unwillingness to do so with the élan that sugar making required, demoralization could have disastrous consequences, especially during rolling season. Slaveholders had combined coercion with incentives to combat demoralization, but planters now had to find new ways of maintaining morale. Black political activity, to their minds, was more likely to increase demoralization than decrease it.

Even as Radical Reconstruction transformed the political landscape, notions implicit in planters' complaints about demoralization clashed with the freedmen's own ideas about labor. The freedmen's political elevation reinforced their determination to gain autonomy within the sugar plantation's operating system, whereas planters were as intent as ever to reestablish labor control. During 1867 and 1868, conflict between planters and freedmen manifested itself on two broad planes: the labor market and its effect on wages, and the reconstitution of plantation routine. Although both parties had become familiar with these issues since emancipation, the freedmen's political mobilization shifted the terrain on which they were contested.

Planters' approaches to the labor market reflected lingering divisions among them regarding free labor. With no alternative, most continued their slow but steady adjustment to the new order. Others, however, found bargaining for the labor of people they once owned too much to bear. Slavery and paternalism were dead, but class antagonisms exacerbated both persisting resentments born of slavery and racial tensions arising from emancipation. "This is a horrible business," raged one planter. "I certainly have never done any thing more humiliating than mixing with those miserable drunken wreches and talking on terms of familiarity in order to obtain their services." The northern jurist Joseph P. Bradley, who toured southern Louisiana in spring 1867, considered many planters incapable of adapting to the new labor system. "That many plantations will go to ruin is very clear," he predicted, before labor returned to a "normal condition." [11]

Determining what constituted a "normal condition" was the very point planters and freedmen contested. As both parties learned how to negotiate terms of employment, a functioning and recognizable labor market gradually took shape. Planters were aware that they were creating a potentially self-destructive bidding war, since labor was free to seek the best terms possible. The unwritten code that one did not meddle with a neighbor's workers proved illusory, as the vicious circle of competition and enticement among those eager to hire labor played into freedmen's hands. Even planters who avoided competing for labor within their own parishes willingly sought workers in other sugar parishes. Thus, an Iberville planter complained in early 1868 of Bayou Teche planters trying to woo his workers while a neighbor headed for the Lafourche to hire labor. [12]

However vehemently some planters opposed free labor, they had no choice but to work within it. As competition for labor increased, moreover, a subtle, barely perceptible shift in planters' priorities took place. Whereas planters had previously focused on reestablishing mastery, they now concerned themselves with securing sufficient labor within the capitalist labor market. "Inferior hands in our system of labor will not pay," proclaimed one Iberville planter. "I would rather pay one good man $18 than two inferior ones $10 each." Because his workers "seem to have no idea to stick," another noted in early 1867, "I think our best plan is not to bother any longer with them, and try to get some from elsewhere." Having hired several at the "exorbitant" cost of $18.00 per month, he saw "no better prospect for the future." Planters intensified the search for labor outside the sugar region. An agent of Iberville grandee Edward J. Gay told of recruiters employed by John Burnside, the state's wealthiest antebellum sugar planter, offering wages in Pointe Coupée Parish that were difficult to match. Not to be outdone, Gay sent agents as far as the Carolinas to hire laborers, though with poor results. [13]

11. V. J. Rogers to EJG, Feb. 4, 1867, EJGP; [J. P. Bradley] to "My dear daughter," Apr. 30, 1867, Joseph P. Bradley Papers, New Jersey Historical Society, Newark. See also Frances (Hewitt) Fearn, ed., *Diary of a Refugee* (New York, 1910), 143–4. On planters' adjusting to free labor, see *DP*, Feb. 12, 1867; J. W. Keller to W. H. Sterling, Aug. 31, 1867, vol. 275, pp. 53–5, LS, ser. 1598, Agt & ASAC, Franklin, BRFAL.

12. R. Daigre to EJG, Jan. 5, 1868, and P. O. Daigre to EJG, Jan. 25, 1868, EJGP. See also P. J. Smalley to L. H. Warren, Feb. 20, 1868, vol. 535, pp. 39–40, LS, ser. 1823, ASAC for St. Bernard and Plaquemines Parishes, New Orleans, BRFAL; W. H. Webster to L. H. Warren, Feb. 29, 1868, vol. 284, pp. 69–83, Monthly Reps., ser. 1594, SAC of the 3rd Subdist., Franklin, BRFAL.

13. M. Schlatre to EJG, Sept. 5, 1867, R. Daigre to EJG, Jan. 29, Feb. 6, 1867, A. H. Gay to EJG, Feb. 1867, N. G. Pierson to EJG, Feb. 15, 1867, N. G. Pierson to W. Edwards & Co., Feb. 7, 9, 1867, Certificate of Transportation, Mar. 1, 1867, P. O. Daigre to EJG, Oct. 4, 1867, all in

Because competition for labor revealed divisions among planters, some revived the wartime effort of collaborating to restrict the labor market. Planters in St. Bernard and Plaquemines Parishes agreed in late 1867 to pay monthly wages of $12 with rations and $18 without for the best workers. They also prescribed the hours of labor and pledged not to lease land to freedmen. In early 1868, according to the local Freedmen's Bureau agent, Jefferson Parish planters formed "Secret Societies" and vowed not to pay more than $10 per month. Nonetheless, such attempts at obstruction were fraught with difficulties, as planters were torn between their collective and individual interests. Those willing and able to offer advantageous terms brooked no interference with the running of what they traditionally viewed as personal fiefdoms. Although most planters believed a uniform wage to be necessary, one bureau agent reported, others contended "that each employer should be allowed to regulate his own business." So long as some planters thought this way, freedmen held an advantage.[14]

Planters failed both to impose a uniform wage rate and to lower wages. As freedmen took to the road in search of better terms, monthly wages climbed to between $15 and $20. "The planters are giving more money this year," one bureau agent noted in early 1867. Planters could not afford to haggle during spring planting, since any delay could jeopardize their crops—a vulnerability freedmen were quick to exploit. Reporting a strike for higher wages in May 1868, a bureau agent near New Orleans noted that freedmen had "chosen a time of great importance for their strike. Cane requires now constant attention." The incident was not an isolated one. "[T]he Freedmen are unwilling to go to work for such wages as the Planters can afford to give them, but are insisting for very high wages," the Donaldsonville bureau agent reported, "which as Planters have but barely cleared expenses and many are entirely broken up—cannot be given." Admitting "that it is the right of the freedmen to get the best wages possible," the agent nonetheless contended that "this holding aloof from work, because they cannot get high wages is ruinous to themselves and will eventually bring them to penury and want, and all the consequent results."[15]

EJGP. See also M. Schlatre to EJG, Dec. 8, 1867, and T. Garrett to EJG, Feb. 24, Mar. 12, 1868, EJGP; W. Woods to L. H. Warren, Mar. 10, 1868, vol. 294, pp. 79–81, LS, ser. 1634, Agt & ASAC, Houma, BRFAL; S. W. Purchase to W. H. Sterling, Aug. 1867, vol. 284, pp. 16–27, Monthly Reps., ser. 1594, SAC of the 3rd Subdist., Franklin, BRFAL.

14. *Franklin Planters' Banner,* Dec. 28, 1867; Trimonthly Rep. of G. Bruning, Jan. 20, 1868, and Bruning to J. M. Lee, Jan. 1, 1868, both in Letters & Telegrams Received, ser. 1303, AC, BRFAL; J. W. Keller to J. M. Lee, Dec. 10, 1868, vol. 275, pp. 118–9, LS, ser. 1598, Agt & ASAC, Franklin, BRFAL.

15. A. C. Ellis to W. H. Sterling, Jan. 31, 1867, Narrative Trimonthly Reps. of Operations & Conditions from Subordinate Officers, ser. 1310, AC, BRFAL; P. J. Smalley to W. H. Sterling,

Feeling themselves at the mercy of their workers, planters resorted to various stratagems in an attempt to demonstrate their mastery. Some made pay deductions for trifling reasons or tried to defraud freedmen outright. Others discharged freedmen over petty disputes and denied them back wages on grounds they had violated their contracts. Planters engaged in such practices not simply for financial reasons, a bureau agent near Baton Rouge believed, but from "a disposition to annoy the Freedmen in every way possible." Freedmen protested the fraudulent practices either by refusing to work or by petitioning local Freedmen's Bureau agents, who threatened planters with fines, arrest, and imprisonment. Freedmen even turned the tables by concocting their own schemes. In May 1867, one plantation manager informed the owner that he needed additional cash to meet the April payroll, since "some of the hands pretended to a misunderstanding as to my bargain to pay one half wages." The freedmen evidently believed they were to receive full monthly wages and expressed much discontent upon discovering this was not so. Although the manager was sure they had contrived the dispute, he thought it best, "in order to keep them in good heart," to effect a compromise in which the workers received full pay for April but only half wages thereafter.[16]

Planters felt the labor market's effects most acutely during the rolling season, when labor was at a premium. Considering the demands they placed on their workers, planters found the best way to ensure high morale was by increasing

---

May 5, 1868, vol. 535, pp. 60–1, LS, ser. 1823, ASAC for St. Bernard and Plaquemines Parishes, New Orleans, BRFAL; J. H. Brough to J. M. Lee, Jan. 11, 1868, vol. 263, pp. 185–7, LS, ser. 1577, Agt & ASAC, Donaldsonville, BRFAL. On wage rates, see Contract, Feb. 12, 1867, Séverin Landry Papers, LSU; Jan. 8, 13, 15, 25, Feb. 2, 8, 1867, Erwin Diary, LSU; J. H. Erwin to EJG, Feb. 16, 1867, EJGP. For other instances of freedmen's efforts to secure higher wages, see *Thibodaux Sentinel*, Dec. 14, 1867; L. J. Trudeau to EJG, June 2, 1868, J. V. Duralde to EJG, Aug. 9, 1868, and P. O. Daigre to EJG, Aug. 20, 1868, EJGP.

16. W. H. Webster to J. M. Lee, Sept. 30, 1867, vol. 218, pp. 52–61, LS, ser. 1490, ASAC, Baton Rouge, BRFAL; J. W. Austin to EJG, May 6, 1867, EJGP. On planters' attempts to defraud freedmen, see A. F. Hayden to J. H. Brough, Aug. 15, 1866, vol. 262, p. 118, LS, ser. 1577, Agt & ASAC, Donaldsonville, BRFAL; O. H. Hempstead to L. O. Parker, Aug. 20, 1867, Letters & Telegrams Received, ser. 1303, AC, BRFAL; G. A. Ludlow to L. O. Parker, Aug. 31, 1867, vol. 294, pp. 36–7, LS, ser. 1634, Agt & ASAC, Houma, BRFAL; W. Woods to J. M. Lee, Dec. 20, 1867, vol. 294, pp. 53–4, LS, ser. 1634, Agt & ASAC, Houma, BRFAL. On freedmen's refusal to work until paid, see Mar. 15, 1867, Plant. Diary 2, DeClouet Papers, LSU; J. H. Brough to W. Sterling, Apr. 1, 1867, vol. 262, pp. 91–2, LS, ser. 1577, Agt & ASAC, Donaldsonville, BRFAL. On the efforts of Freedmen's Bureau agents to secure freedmen's wages, see J. H. Brough to W. Sterling, Apr. 1, 1867, vol. 262, pp. 91–2, and Brough to W. W. Tyler, Oct. 1, 1867, vol. 263, pp. 102–6, both in LS, ser. 1577, Agt & ASAC, Donaldsonville, BRFAL; Trimonthly Reps. of R. Folles, June 10–20, 1867, vol. 192, p. 167, and Aug. 1–10, 1867, pp. 224–5, both in Monthly Reps. of Operations, ser. 1454, Agt & ASAC, Algiers, BRFAL.

wages, sometimes even to the point of doubling them. "The rolling season is now coming on," remarked the Freedmen's Bureau agent for Assumption Parish in October 1867, "and many more laborers are needed in this Parish who could get very high wages." In addition to their monthly wages, freedmen earned seventy-five cents per watch at the sugar mill, paid weekly in cash. Some planters had the foresight to agree early in the year to increase harvest wages, while those who did not paid the price. "Sugar planters who had neglected to stipulate the amount of wages during Sugar making, when making agreement last spring," one bureau agent noted, "have had some trouble with the Freedmen before they agreed to work extra hours."[17]

Planters nonetheless found that promising higher wages in advance did not always preclude labor difficulties come rolling season. Attracted by competing wages that reached $1.75 per day, freedmen readily violated their agreements by leaving to work for another planter. They also struck for higher wages. The outcome of these initiatives depended upon planters' determination to hold the line as well as the responses of local bureau agents. When freedmen struck for higher wages in midseason, thereby violating their contracts, bureau agents might threaten them with loss of back wages and arrest, but agents usually visited the plantation and persuaded them of the error of their ways. Even without bureau assistance, some planters risked short-term profitability by assuming an uncompromising position. Freedmen on the Bayou Lafourche estate of M. H. Vergez had agreed to work for $45 per month without rations during the 1867 rolling season. Just as the harvest was to begin, however, they demanded rations as well. Vergez refused to accede, and when the strikers faced the choice of working or leaving, all save the leader returned to work. Vergez risked losing his crop, but he probably reasoned that succumbing to a last-minute demand for higher wages would jeopardize his future crops as well as the present one.[18]

Every planter faced the harsh reality that his workers might leave at any time,

17. Contract, Jan. 1867, Joseph Savoy and Family Papers, LSU; O. H. Hempstead to J. M. Lee, Oct. 10, 1867, Letters & Telegrams Received, ser. 1303, AC, BRFAL; J. W. Keller to J. M. Lee, Nov. 20, 1867, vol. 275, pp. 101–3, LS, ser. 1598, Agt & ASAC, Franklin, BRFAL. See also Contract, 1866, Uncle Sam Plant. Papers, LSU; Contract, 1866, Kleinpeter Papers, LSU; Contract, 1867, Landry Papers, LSU.

18. *Thibodaux Sentinel,* Oct. 19, 1867. See also G. A. Ludlow to L. O. Parker, Aug. 31, 1867, vol. 294, pp. 36–7, LS, ser. 1634, Agt & ASAC, Houma, BRFAL; J. W. Keller to J. M. Lee, Oct. 31, 1867, vol. 275, pp. 90–1, LS, ser. 1598, Agt & ASAC, Franklin, BRFAL; J. W. Keller to J. M. Lee, Nov. 10, 1867, vol. 275, pp. 97–100, LS, ser. 1598, Agt & ASAC, Franklin, BRFAL; J. H. Van Antwerp to B. T. Hutchins, Oct. 10, 1868, vol. 472, p. 130, LS, ser. 1899, Agt & ASAC, Thibodaux, BRFAL; M. W. Morris to B. T. Hutchins, Nov. 10, 1868, vol. 295, pp. 85–9, LS, ser. 1634, Agt & ASAC, Houma, BRFAL; A. LeBoeuf to H. S. Peire, Dec. 1, 1867, Consolidated Association of Planters of Louisiana Papers, LSU.

including during the rolling season. Freedmen's Bureau agents interceded when freedmen violated their contracts, but they could hardly arrest a plantation's entire labor force or compel freedmen to return to work against their will—actions that were not likely to solve a planter's problems anyway. Since a few days' neglect could devastate a sugar crop, a planter whose workers left him, if only temporarily, faced ruin. By bolting in midseason freedmen risked losing their back wages. Nor were they assured of finding employment elsewhere. But these were risks many were willing to take. Much to planters' consternation, freedmen were beginning to master the principles of the labor market.

Planters and freedmen struggled not only over wages but also over the freedmen's working lives. Because centralized plantation regimen prevailed in the sugar region, decision-making authority in the quotidian world of work assumed critical importance to both planters and freedmen. Freedmen's Bureau agents often resolved trivial disputes through tactful intervention, but serious disagreements were not easily settled, arising as they did from the contrasting visions of free labor espoused by planters and freedmen. Even planters who had reconciled themselves to emancipation contended that control of labor was necessary, whereas freedmen refused to submit to work routines that too closely resembled those of slavery. Confrontation over ostensibly trivial aspects of daily labor elucidated the larger issue of power and authority. Such conflicts were intensified by the freedmen's political ascendance.

A seemingly innocuous matter, such as rainy weather, provoked bitter recrimination. In June 1867, for instance, freedman Winfield Branch complained to the local bureau office that his employer, Babylon LeBranch, had discharged him and refused to pay his back wages. As it began to rain one day, Branch left work and was later confronted by LeBranch, who demanded to know why he was not working, since the rain had stopped. Branch responded that it was raining when he left the fields, but LeBranch announced that he would "not honor such work." When the freedman voiced his refusal to work in the rain, LeBranch interpreted his response as insubordination. "[I]f you don't want to work the way I want you to work I want you to leave," he declared, discharging Branch. The bureau agent arranged a settlement in which Branch agreed to leave the plantation, but only after receiving his full back wages. This middle course probably left both parties dissatisfied. While the agent's decision upheld the planter's authority to control matters on his estate and to dismiss workers whom he regarded as recalcitrant, it also sustained the freedman's refusal to toil under objectionable conditions, to obey a harshly dictated order, and to allow an employer to deny him his pay.[19]

19. R. Folles to W. W. Tyler, June 28, 1867, vol. 187, p. 174, LS, ser. 1447, Agt & ASAC, Algiers, BRFAL. See also I. D. McClany to W. W. Tyler, June 10, 1867, vol. 535, pp. 9–11, LS, ser.

A planter's authority also became a point of contention when it was applied to freedwomen, who, by curtailing the time they spent in the fields, significantly altered the labor force's configuration. The skewed sex ratios characteristic of antebellum sugar plantations became even more pronounced after the war, as freedwomen's aversion to field work, which had first surfaced during the war, intensified. "The women are nowhere to be found now in the fields," remarked Louis Bouchereau, who estimated in 1868 that the region's labor force had been cut nearly in half. In truth, freedwomen did not abandon field work altogether, as planters and others routinely noted them working in the fields. Nonetheless, in southern Louisiana they notably reduced the time they spent there. Even when freedwomen were in the fields, planters complained that they did not put in, as a bureau agent noted, "more than half of the time required."[20]

While freedwomen's field work sparked much conflict during and immediately following the war, by 1867 a compromise arose, one shaped by planters' and freedmen's needs and by the demands of sugar production. Labor requirements on a sugar plantation fluctuated seasonally. They were acute during planting and rolling seasons but slackened when the crop was "laid by" in summer. Although the slave labor force had been fixed year round, planters now scaled back the number of workers during slow periods. Eventually, two distinct labor forces evolved: regular, or "monthly," laborers and a supplemental force that planters hired during peak seasons. Freedwomen, usually wives of monthly workers, were an important part of the supplemental force. A Freedmen's Bureau agent noted in 1868 that one planter employed thirty-five freedmen as well as the "same number

---

1823, ASAC for St. Bernard and Plaquemines Parishes, New Orleans, BRFAL; J. H. Brough to W. W. Tyler, July 5, 1867, vol. 263, pp. 42–4, LS, ser. 1577, Agt & ASAC, Donaldsonville, BRFAL; Aug. 6, 1868, Plant. Diary 3, DeClouet Papers, LSU.

20. Louis Bouchereau, *Statement of the Sugar and Rice Crops Made in Louisiana . . . 1868–69*, viii; Rep. of M. Hawke, Aug. 24, 1865, vol. 90, pp. 17, 19, Inspection Reps., ser. 1409, Plant. Dept., AC, BRFAL. The evidence on freedwomen's withdrawal from field labor is mixed. For indications that they withdrew, see J. Barros to AFP, May 17, 1865, Pugh Papers, *RASP,* ser. G; 39th Cong., 1st Sess., HR 30, pt. 4, p. 135; *De Bow's Review* 4 (September 1867): 237; Payrolls, 1868, Manchac Plant., James N. Brown Papers, UT; Payrolls, 1868, Kenmore Plant., Consolidated Assoc. Papers, LSU; Plant. Diary 3, DeClouet Papers, LSU. For instances of persistence of field labor, see May 26, 28, 1865, Plant. Diary, Palfrey Papers, *RASP,* ser. I; Payrolls, Jan. 1866, Nov. 1867, Nov. 1868, Uncle Sam Plant. Papers, LSU; June 26, 1866, Erwin Diary, LSU; Feb. 12, Sept. 27, 1867, Plant. Diary 2, DeClouet Papers, LSU; Jan. 27, Feb. 5, July 9, 29, 1868, Plant. Diary 36, WJMP; Rebecca Fletcher, WPA Ex-Slave Narratives, LSU; R. W. Mullen to W. H. Sterling, May 10, 1868, vol. 276, pp. 92–7, LS, ser. 1598, Agt & ASAC, Franklin, BRFAL; Dennett, *South As It Is,* 325–6, 331. On this question generally in the South, see Ransom and Sutch, *One Kind of Freedom,* 44–7, and Jacqueline Jones, *Labor of Love, Labor of Sorrow: Black Women, Work, and the Family from Slavery to the Present* (New York, 1985), chap. 2.

of females—wives of the laborers," who could be called on when needed. An 1867 labor contract likewise affirmed the planter's right "to call upon any able bodied female of said Freedmen's families whenever he may need them for such work as they can perform." Thus a modus vivendi emerged. Planters employed a skeletal labor force while drawing upon readily available workers when circumstances dictated. Freedwomen escaped full-time field employment while availing themselves of good wages when their labor was needed.[21]

One aspect of plantation labor that freedwomen shunned, however, was maintaining and repairing levees, among the most arduous tasks on a sugar plantation. Levees needed constant attention, but because the work was so backbreaking it proved to be especially contentious. Planters wanted this work incorporated into normal duties, whereas freedmen considered it extra labor for which they wanted supplemental pay. "The negroes of the place refuse to work on the levee for less than 1.50 per day," one planter noted, "and nothing can make them do so." William J. Minor instructed his overseers to have freedmen repair levees as "extra work" at the lowest terms possible, but such terms were not very low. An Iberville planter could not persuade freedmen to repair levees for $20 per month; he even offered $1 per day, all money paid in full, but to no avail. Some planters issued jiggers of liquor in addition to extra wages paid in full weekly. Only with such inducements did freedmen agree to perform this task. Full-time levee work even became for some freedmen an alternative to regular plantation employment, increasing monthly workers' opposition to its being considered part of their normal duties. Although most freedmen probably performed some levee work during the year, doing so was regarded as outside normal plantation routine and thus work for which they received extra compensation.[22]

Freedmen also succeeded at having the cutting, hauling, and storing of wood defined in part as supplemental work. These tasks had been critical to plantation operations during slavery, and since wood remained the sugar mill's main source of fuel after the war, they enabled freedmen to earn good wages. Monthly workers each customarily cut and stored a weekly quota of wood as part of their normal duties, but they received extra pay when they surpassed it. "If the men wish to get extra wood let them do it," one planter instructed his overseers. As was the case with levee work, moreover, small groups of freedmen traveled from plantation to plantation and hired themselves out to chop wood. As rolling season approached,

21. P. J. Smalley to L. H. Warren, Apr. 10, 1868, vol. 535, pp. 51–3, LS, ser. 1823, ASAC for St. Bernard and Plaquemines Parishes, New Orleans, BRFAL; Contract, June 4, 1867, Slack Papers, SHC.

22. A. H. Gay to EJG, Sept. 20, 1867, EJGP; Aug. 1, 1868, Plant. Diary 34, WJMP; A. H. Gay to EJG, Sept. 15, 1867, EJGP; Contract, June 4, 1867, Slack Papers, SHC.

the need for wood increased—a situation freedmen soon exploited. "The Planters are all busy now preparing and putting in order their Sugar mills," a bureau agent noted in 1868, "cutting and getting wood out of the swamp for fuel which makes quite a demand for laborers, wages one dollar ($1.00) per day, rations included."[23]

When it came to such matters as levee work and chopping wood, freedmen built upon the antebellum "slaves' economy" in redefining plantation regimen. They also drew upon traditional privileges under slavery by exploiting the plantation's economic resources to supplement their monthly wages. Freedmen not only enjoyed access to provision grounds and garden plots but also used planters' draft animals and farm implements to cultivate them. Some planters protested these practices, but they could not prevent them. Two freedmen complained in early 1868 that their employer, one Madame Segurd, refused them use of teams and plows and tried to dictate what crops they could grow on their provision grounds. The bureau agent informed her that "it was no matter of hers what the freedmen chose to plant," and that her contract specified the freedmen's use of animals and implements. Freedmen also insisted that their own cows, hogs, chickens, and horses be provisioned at their employer's expense. "Subsistence for some comes out of the Planter," the bureau agent for St. Mary Parish observed, "and in many instances the Planter complains of having to pay them wages, give them land, and then have to keep their hogs and horses, but still they allow it." Freedmen saw no inconsistency in receiving wages for their labor while preserving privileges they had enjoyed as slaves, but planters bristled at this practice.[24]

In recasting sugar plantation regimen, nothing was more potentially explosive than the rolling season, which required freedmen to labor frantically yet with clocklike precision. The season's hectic pace could easily become indistinguishable from modes of behavior by planters that bordered on abuse. Yet not only did freedmen make this distinction but planters themselves also had to take note of it lest their workers become demoralized. Appreciating the efforts that the harvest

23. June 19, 1866, Plant. Diary 34, WJMP; Rep., Aug. 10, 1868, vol. 286, pp. 12–5, Trimonthly Reps., ser. 1604, Agt & ASAC, Franklin, BRFAL. See also Aug. 29, 1868, Plant. Diary 3, DeClouet Papers, LSU; R. W. Mullen to L. H. Warren, July 31, 1868, and Rep., Aug. 20, 1868, vol. 286, pp. 8–11, 15–9, Trimonthly Reps., ser. 1604, Agt & ASAC, Franklin, BRFAL.

24. J. White to L. H. Warren, Feb. 29, 1868, vol. 384, pp. 38–41, Trimonthly Reps., ser. 1789, ASAC, New Iberia, BRFAL; R. W. Mullen to L. H. Warren, July 20, 1868, vol. 286, pp. 4–8, Trimonthly Reps., ser. 1604, Agt & ASAC, Franklin, BRFAL. See also R. C. Martin Jr. to R. C. Martin, Sept. 17, 1865, Martin-Pugh Collection, NSU; S. W. Purchase to J. M. Lee, Nov. 20, 1867, vol. 384, pp. 4–7, Trimonthly Reps., ser. 1789, ASAC, New Iberia, BRFAL.

demanded, freedmen performed their work with a vigor unseen at other times of the year—so long, noted a bureau agent in 1867, as they were treated "in a decent and respectable manner" and were "satisfied about their pay."[25]

One feature of harvest work that freedmen rejected, however, was Sunday work. Planters ignored freedmen's aversion to working on Sunday at their peril, and many of them rearranged the harvest work schedule in such a way as to recognize the freedmen's wish to enjoy Sunday to themselves. Planters who tried to impose Sunday work courted their workers' disaffection. "[O]n plantations where they have commenced grinding there was considerable trouble to induce the Freedmen to work on Sunday," a bureau agent near New Orleans reported in 1867. "In several cases they worked on without saying anything until Saturday evening and then all stopped and said they would not work on Sunday." Some planters responded by threatening to dismiss freedmen who did not return to work. But even then, the agent added, freedmen did not go back to work "cheerfully as the planters would like." Fearing the prospects of demoralization, the agent concluded, most planters "will avoid running on Sunday when it can be possible for them to do so without loss." Planters determined to prove a point might try to impose Sunday work, but in doing so they risked alienating their workers. As every planter knew, a disgruntled, dispirited labor force would not work with the enthusiasm necessary to meet the demands of the rolling season. Consequently, most planters concluded that it was better to give their employees the time off rather than risk losing their cooperation.[26]

Even when planters were mindful of freedmen's wishes, however, the results were not reassuring. Throughout 1867 and 1868 the sugar industry's recovery remained sluggish. Few planters viewed their inability to control labor and their deplorable financial condition as coincidental, and fewer still were encouraged by hope for the future. "Here we are at the end of another year without much change in our favor," Alexandre DeClouet lamented at the end of 1867. "The crops were generally very bad, wages high, & very few managed to cover their expenses." DeClouet tried to maintain a positive outlook, but his language betrayed pessimism and resentment. "[I]n spite of all our humiliations as a conquered people, in spite of our forced economies, in spite of all the trouble it oc-

25. S. W. Purchase to J. M. Lee, Nov. 30, 1867, vol. 284, pp. 42–53, Monthly Reps., ser. 1594, SAC of the 3rd Subdist., Franklin, BRFAL. See also J. H. Brough to A. F. Hayden, Nov. 13, 1866, vol. 262, p. 40, and Brough to J. M. Lee, Nov. 21, 1867, vol. 263, pp. 135–7, both in LS, ser. 1577, Agt & ASAC, Donaldsonville, BRFAL.

26. I. D. McClany to J. H. Hastings, Nov. 20, 1867, vol. 535, pp. 27–8, LS, ser. 1823, ASAC for St. Bernard and Plaquemines Parishes, New Orleans, BRFAL. See also Oct.–Dec. 1868, Plant. Notebook, John H. Randolph Papers, LSU; Nov. 1868, Plant. Diary 4, DeClouet Papers, LSU.

casions, & all the patience which is required to manage a lot of free negro brutes I must not complain too much, for many others are worse off than I am."[27]

As though their labor problems were not enough, planters would soon reap an equally bitter political harvest. On November 23, 1867, the constitutional convention—elected mostly by black votes and itself half black—met in New Orleans to frame a new state constitution. What might result from this convention no one could tell, but for planters the prospects were depressing. In addition to disrupting daily plantation routine, black political activity also jeopardized planters' hopes for using the state to regain control over labor. As Radical Reconstruction came to fruition in 1868, planters resolved to do whatever was necessary to defeat it.

For planters determined to stop black political power, 1868 started inauspiciously. They devoted most of January to settling freedmen's accounts for 1867 and negotiating terms for the new year. Such difficulties had become familiar enough, but 1868 was different and the reason was clear. "Politics have crazed the negro here as elsewhere," one planter proclaimed, "and it may be some time in January before they could be procured & set to work." The bureau agent for Iberville Parish similarly remarked that freedmen "show but little energy or ambition to go to work by the month during the coming year. As a general thing they do not want to bring themselves to any one at present." Instead, "they seem to think that the convention and next Election will give them all an office or a living without hard work. And I fear that such ideas will greatly demoralize the labor the coming season." Most freedmen realized that the true significance of their gaining political power was not that they would receive sinecures but that they were about to become American citizens.[28]

Toward that end, freedmen in early 1868 built upon the previous year's efforts at grassroots mobilization. They continued to organize political clubs and followed closely the New Orleans convention's deliberations. That group completed its work by early March, giving Louisiana a constitution that provided for black manhood suffrage and included a state bill of rights. In accordance with the congressional mandate, the electorate now had to ratify the constitution and elect a state government. April 16 and 17, 1868, were set as the dates for elections that would accomplish these goals.

As had been the case the previous spring when the convention delegates were

27. Dec. 31, 1867, Plant. Diary 2, DeClouet Papers, LSU. For similarly dire assessments of planters' prospects, see M. Gay to A. M. Turner, Nov. 8, 1867, Andrew Hynes Gay and Family Papers, LSU, and *Plaquemine Iberville South,* Dec. 28, 1867.

28. M. Schlatre Jr. to EJG, Oct. 5, 1867, EJGP; C. E. Merrill to L. H. Warren, Jan. 31, 1868, vol. 427, pp. 24–6, LS, ser. 1842, Agt & ASAC, Plaquemine, BRFAL.

elected, the outcome of the plebiscite on the constitution itself was never in doubt. Nonetheless, the brief campaign to win ratification and to bring the Republican Party to power intensified the freedmen's political activities, further disrupting plantation routine. "The feeling at present between the employers and employed, especially on plantations where a large number of hands are employed, is not so harmonious as it has been before this Political campaign," the Freedmen's Bureau agent for St. Mary Parish noted in early April. "The Freedmen seem to be a little unsettled and uneasy." Black Republican leaders like John J. Moore organized "radical clubs" on plantations and conducted weekly meetings during which they implored freedmen to ratify the constitution. "We organized those clubs with the intention of teaching the people what they were to vote for and what the constitution meant," Moore later testified. "They all believed that the constitution was something which gave them equal rights before the law. Ignorant as they [were], they got that idea. They believed it was something which would give them the right to be equal with all voters, and to be better off than they were in former times."[29]

Convinced more than ever that politics demoralized labor, planters objected to the freedmen's political activities. "There is some excitement among the Freedmen in regard to the *coming election*," the bureau agent for St. Mary Parish remarked, "and some *complaints* are made by planters that they quit their work too often or do not work well in consequence of this." Planters in Assumption Parish also protested that freedmen were devoting "a little too much time to politics and a little too little to work." Planters backed up their complaints with action. Maintaining that by missing work freedmen violated their contracts, planters once again dismissed them for attending club meetings and engaging in other political activities. "The most persistent & energetic efforts are being made by the Planters of this Parish to defeat a reconstruction of their state in the coming elections," the Lafourche bureau agent reported. "Instances are daily and hourly coming to my notice, in which Planters are discharging laborers merely for visiting political clubs." Whereas freedmen reinforced their political efforts in order to ratify the constitution, planters likewise stepped up their strong-arm tactics in hopes of defeating it.[30]

29. R. W. Mullen to L. H. Warren, Apr. 10, 1868, vol. 276, pp. 65–71, LS, ser. 1598, Agt & ASAC, Franklin, BRFAL; 41st Cong., 2nd Sess., HMD 154, pt. 1, pp. 637, 641–2. See also Trimonthly Rep. of G. Bruning, Mar. 20, 1868, Letters & Telegrams Received, ser. 1303, AC, BRFAL; W. H. Webster to W. H. Sterling, Apr. 30, 1868, vol. 284, pp. 94–105, Monthly Reps., ser. 1594, SAC of the 3rd Subdist., Franklin, BRFAL; Apr. 15, 1868, Erwin Diary, LSU; I. Len to Warmoth, Feb. 15, 1868, Warmoth Papers, SHC.

30. W. H. Webster to L. H. Warren, Mar. 31, 1868, vol. 284, pp. 83–93, Monthly Reps., ser. 1594, SAC of the 3rd Subdist., Franklin, BRFAL; F. Sternberg to L. H. Warren, Mar. 24, 31,

Confronted with planters' threats and intimidation, Republican leaders strove to maintain unity. One party organizer told a meeting of eight hundred freedmen in St. Mary Parish that the two election days "were their own, *not the Planters',*" and that "they were expected to devote those two days time at the Polls." When a candidate for office directed one freedman to attend the polls both days, the freedman replied that his contract did not permit him to lose so much time from work. The candidate nonetheless ordered him to "pay no attention to your contract but go." However necessary they may have seemed, such efforts to preserve solidarity also exacerbated divisions within the black community. Some freedmen, especially those with families, could ill afford to have their wages docked for time lost, nor would they have welcomed risking dismissal. Thus not every confrontation between freedmen and planters indicated black unity. Although freedmen tried to present a united front, tensions and strains, poverty and anxiety, and sometimes even ambition divided them, as did disputes over strategy.[31]

Even when freedmen disagreed among themselves, however, their political organizations usually imposed discipline and ensured unity. Such was the case on a St. Mary Parish plantation in April 1868. The planter had become embroiled in a dispute with workers who demanded their wages before he was able to pay. One evening, according to the local Freedmen's Bureau agent, freedmen held a "club meeting" and decided "on no more work till they were paid." Despite this decision, all but two of the laborers went to their jobs the following day, but when they tried to cross the bayou they were confronted by the two strikers, "armed with Shot gun and Revolver, threatening to shoot the first man who would attempt to cross." The incident, which ended with the strikers' arrest, was not an isolated one. Many planters, observed another bureau agent, complained that whenever they tried to discharge one worker for violating his contract or engaging in misconduct, the rest "would immediately quit work & threaten to leave the place." The agent often found that freedmen were advised to pursue this course by their "club leaders." He also discovered, however, that the vast majority in most cases were willing to remain at work but were "prevented from doing so by a few of the leaders among the freedmen threatening

1868, vol. 472, pp. 5–7, 14–7, LS, ser. 1899, Agt & ASAC, Thibodaux, BRFAL. See also J. White to L. H. Warren, Apr. [20], 1868, and White to [?], Apr. [30], 1868, vol. 384, pp. 54–60, Trimonthly Reps., ser. 1789, ASAC, New Iberia, BRFAL; W. H. Webster to W. H. Sterling, Apr. 30, 1868, vol. 284, pp. 94–105, Monthly Reps., ser. 1594, SAC of the 3rd Subdist., Franklin, BRFAL.

31. R. W. Mullen to L. H. Warren, Apr. 10, 1868, vol. 276, pp. 65–71, LS, ser. 1598, Agt & ASAC, Franklin, BRFAL.

personal violence to those who should go to the fields to work. In some cases standing guard with loaded arms, and threatening to shoot any who attempted to go to work."[32]

The internal divisions that occasionally rent the freed community—and that brought freedmen to the point of violence—should be neither overlooked nor overstated. The sugar plantation's centralized regimen provided freedmen a measure of unity, but their living and working in a manner that resembled their former condition also had its inevitable frustrations. They were beset by the same quarrels and jealousies that plague any people brought into regular and close contact, and their ranks included individuals unwilling to challenge authority or to risk their economic well-being, as well as those more than willing to do so. To assume that ex-slaves always acted in unison, or ought to have, is to deny the black community an internal dimension. That freedmen disagreed, sometimes vehemently, over how best to defend themselves against violence and intimidation does not diminish the significance of their external struggle. They knew what they were up against; they also knew that banding together offered the only hope of weathering the storm that surrounded them. Decisions made at club meetings were not trifling affairs, to be ignored or forgotten the next day, but were instead essential to the black community's self-preservation. Union Leagues and other political clubs helped to maintain discipline and unity, if not harmony, in the face of a common adversary.

The unity that freedmen achieved through their political clubs is illustrated by an episode that occurred on a plantation in St. Mary Parish in late April 1868. One evening some sixty freedmen appeared before the local bureau agent, R. W. Mullen, complaining that the overseer had dismissed laborer Henry Harris for violating what they considered to be an unfair work rule. Upon Harris's dismissal, the freedmen struck. They had previously agreed, according to Mullen, "that if one hand was discharged for anything, every one were to signify their disapprobation and quit in a body." After considerable discussion, Mullen convinced the freedmen to return to the plantation, but only after having promised to visit next morning to settle the matter. The freedmen insisted that they would not work until then, and they demanded that both the plantation manager, one Mr. Sickles, and the overseer be replaced. Arriving early the following day, Mullen found the freedmen still unwilling to work. After much negotiation, Mullen effected a settlement in which Sickles rehired Harris and agreed to change the work rule in

32. R. W. Mullen to W. H. Sterling, Apr. 30, May 10, 1868, vol. 276, pp. 82–92, 92–97, LS, ser. 1598, Agt. & ASAC, Franklin, BRFAL; W. H. Webster to W. H. Sterling, Apr. 30, 1868, vol. 284, pp. 94–105, Monthly Reps. ser. 1594, SAC of the 3rd Subdistrict, Franklin, BRFAL.

question, while the freedmen dropped their demand that Sickles and the overseer be dismissed.

The episode appeared to have been yet another mundane dispute over plantation work rules, but there was more to it than that. In conversing with some of the freedmen, Mullen discovered that they had formed a political club, before which Republican speakers advised them to act together. He also found that the freedmen "are instructed or ordered . . . at their clubs, to act as one man on all plantations, [and] that whenever a man is discharged, for all to immediately strike, unless they can make the planter yield to them." Mullen discussed the matter with Sickles, who believed the incident would repeat itself if he tried to enforce discipline. Sickles was not alone, Mullen thought, and similar incidents throughout the sugar region made all planters fearful lest unified and determined freedmen elude their control. Mullen may have somewhat overstated the threat to planters, but there was no denying the effect of black political mobilization.[33]

The freedmen's unity of purpose was also evident in the April 1868 vote on the constitution. Louisianians ratified the constitution by a majority of 66,152 to 48,739 (58 percent to 42 percent), while voters in the sugar parishes (excluding Orleans Parish) approved it by 20,864 to 8,326, with the black vote overwhelmingly for and the white vote overwhelmingly against (table 5). Republican gubernatorial candidate Henry Clay Warmoth won handily, garnering 63 percent of the vote statewide and substantially more in the sugar parishes. He won more than 93 percent of the vote in St. James and St. Charles Parishes and 98 percent in Ascension Parish. Likewise, Republicans easily captured the state legislature. With Republican control secure and the state's ratification of the Fourteenth Amendment imminent, Louisiana was readmitted to the Union in June 1868.[34]

Republican control increased the significance of the November 1868 presidential election, the first since the war's end. Desperate to regain political power, Democratic (or Conservative) Louisianians, like their counterparts elsewhere in the South, embarked upon a crusade of intimidation and violence—which came to be known as "bulldozing"—designed to capture the presidency and end Reconstruction. As leaders of their communities, planters played an important role in this campaign of terror. Cognizant that bulldozing would demoralize labor on the

33. R. W. Mullen to W. H. Sterling, Apr. 30, 1868, vol. 276, pp. 82–92, LS, ser. 1598, Agt & ASAC, Franklin, BRFAL. For a similar episode, see Mullen to L. H. Warren, Mar. 31, 1868, ibid., 57–61.

34. Donald W. Davis, "Ratification of the Constitution of 1868—Record of Votes," *LH* 6 (summer 1965): 301–5; Perry H. Howard, *Political Tendencies in Louisiana*, rev. and exp. ed. (Baton Rouge, 1971), 425, 446–7; F. Wayne Binning, "Carpetbaggers' Triumph: The Louisiana State Election of 1868," *LH* 14 (winter 1973): 21–39; Taylor, *Louisiana Reconstructed*, 158–61.

TABLE 5

Vote on Louisiana's 1868 State Constitution by Race

PARISH	For			Against		
	White	Black	Total	White	Black	Total
Ascension	53	1,791	1,844	425	50	475
Assumption	52	1,555	1,607	643	10	653
Iberville	39	2,111	2,150	329	7	336
Jefferson	75	2,722	2,797	1,578	635	2,213
Lafourche	54	1,576	1,630	1,166	41	1,207
Plaquemines	12	1,505	1,517	336	2	338
St. Bernard	9	498	507	264	150	414
St. Charles	12	1,266	1,278	122	8	130
St. James	53	2,105	2,158	220	3	223
St. John the Baptist	39	1,256	1,295	394	5	399
St. Mary	23	1,925	1,948	739	89	828
Terrebonne	62	1,562	1,624	591	48	639
West Baton Rouge	4	505	509	295	176	471
Totals	487	20,377	20,864	7,102	1,224	8,326
State Totals			66,152			48,739

Source: Donald W. Davis, "Ratification of the Constitution of 1868—Record of Votes," *LH* 6 (summer 1965): 301–5.

eve of the harvest, they nonetheless dismissed laborers for the slightest infraction of plantation rules in hopes of intimidating them. When planters found that freedmen did not scare so easily, they discharged them explicitly for their political activities. A Unionist planter in St. Bernard Parish told of freedmen applying for work after their previous employers had dismissed them for attending a Republican meeting. A freedman in Terrebonne Parish complained that his overseer had ordered away all those who did not pledge to vote Democratic. When summoned to the bureau office, the overseer claimed he had said: "Boy why don't you vote the Democratic ticket and live all right with us."[35]

Freedmen did not miss the message. Concern for their own safety and that of their families prompted some to support the Democratic Party. Others attended Democratic barbecues out of curiosity or because their employers encouraged them to do so. When planters sponsored Democratic meetings on their own plantations, resident freedmen found it difficult to avoid attending. Planters also offered other inducements. Laborers who pledged to vote Democratic, for in-

35. 41st Cong., 2nd Sess., HMD 154, pt. 1, p. 107; W. M. Morris to B. T. Hutchins, Oct. 31, 1868, vol. 295, pp. 71–4, LS, ser. 1634, Agt & ASAC, Houma, BRFAL. See also N. Bronson to L. H. Warren, July 31, 1868, vol. 472, pp. 99–100, LS, ser. 1899, Agt & ASAC, Thibodaux, BRFAL; C. E. Merrill to J. C. Adamson, Aug. 3, 1868, and Merrill to H. Ware, Aug. 9, 1868, vol. 428, pp. 21–3, both in LS, ser. 1842, Agt & ASAC, Plaquemine, BRFAL.

stance, received protection passes, which planters could demand to see before hiring them for the harvest or next crop season. Passes also ensured freedmen some measure of protection should violence befall them—assuming marauders would take time to read them. One planter admitted to this practice but insisted that no efforts at suasion occurred before the election. Only after it, he contended, did freedmen receive certificates "stating that they had voted the democratic ticket, and that they were entitled to the confidence and protection of the democratic party." Whether planters distributed protection certificates before or after the election, their intent was the same: to prevent freedmen from casting free and fair ballots.[36]

When intimidation failed, as it often did, planters and other white Louisianans resorted to stronger methods. It would be difficult to exaggerate the violence that wracked Louisiana during the fall presidential campaign. Even by standards of the day, the campaign witnessed unparalleled brutality. Such organized gangs as the Knights of the White Camellia—Louisiana's version of the Ku Klux Klan—terrorized freedmen and white Republicans. The sugar country did not suffer the ferocity that tore apart other sections of the state, but fear, punctuated by sporadic violence, was rife. "Much bitterness is existing at the present time between the whites and freed people arising out of political causes," reported the Freedmen's Bureau agent at Thibodaux. "Some threats have been made in case any negro dared to take the office to which he had been elected." The Donaldsonville bureau agent similarly noted that "politically a mutual animosity exists, which may break out on the slightest aggression offered by either party." While hoping for a peaceful election, he admitted that "a vague feeling of impending danger is felt by many." Such feelings, however vague, were not imagined. In St. Mary Parish, Republican organizer John J. Moore overheard a white man caution freedmen to refrain from politics since it was "white people's business," whereas "the business of negroes is to go into the fields and work." If freedmen insisted upon "voting against our interests and sinking the country," the man warned, "we will kill the last one of you."[37]

The most violent episode that befell southern Louisiana during the 1868 campaign season—the riot in St. Bernard Parish, just downriver from New Orleans,

36. 41st Cong., 2nd Sess., HMD 154, pt. 2, p. 311. See also L. Gay to EJG, July 22, 1868, EJGP; Aug. 27, 30, 1868, Plant. Diary 36, WJMP; R. C. Martin Jr. to M. Martin, Sept. 7, 1868, Martin-Pugh Collection, NSU; R. W. Mullen to L. H. Warren, Sept. 20, 1868, vol. 286, pp. 26–30, Trimonthly Reps., ser. 1604, Agt & ASAC, Franklin, BRFAL; 41st Cong., 2nd Sess., HMD 154, pt. 2, pp. 378–9.

37. N. Bronson to L. H. Warren, July 31, 1868, vol. 472, pp. 99–100, LS, ser. 1899, Agt. & ASAC, Thibodaux, BRFAL; V. Benthien to B. T. Hutchins, Oct. 20, 1868, vol. 264, pp. 153–4, LS, ser. 1577, Agt & ASAC, Donaldsonville, BRFAL; 41st Cong., 2nd Sess., HMD 154, pt. 1, p. 636. On the 1868 presidential election in Louisiana, see Carolyn E. Delatte, "The St. Landry

in late October—underscored the fragility of the Republicans' cause. The incident began when a freedman was shot dead following a heated argument with local Democrats. To avenge their slain compatriot, a number of freedmen attacked the establishment of an Italian storekeeper of avowedly anti-Republican sentiments, murdering him and two family members. These slayings provoked retaliation by a group of Sicilian toughs from New Orleans, known as the "Innocents," who rampaged throughout St. Bernard. Federal troops restored order in the parish, but when Governor Warmoth appealed to the military district commander for more troops to ensure a safe election, his request was denied. Realizing that he could not guarantee their safety, Warmoth told potential Republican voters to stay home, virtually abandoning the campaign. In the weeks before the election, some sixty people, mostly freedmen, died in politically motivated violence in the countryside surrounding New Orleans.[38]

Bulldozing and other forms of violence verified not only planters' opposition to black political power but also the freedmen's tenacious defense of their rights. Despite fear that the tiniest spark could ignite a firestorm of terror, freedmen nonetheless campaigned, attended political gatherings, and registered to vote. Such activities compelled many planters to postpone commencement of the rolling season until after the election in early November, much to their consternation. "I suppose after the election we will be wiser and know if these inf[ernal?] negroes will work or not," remarked a New Orleans merchant. A journalist reported that labor was in high demand since freedmen were "too much absorbed in politics to work." "Barbecues elections etc has caused me to progress slowly with all plantation work," one planter noted a few days after the election, "but I hope it is all over now & hope to be able soon to hire more laborers." Their employers' annoyance, however, could not prevent freedmen from exercising their hard-won rights. "The freedmen have the stamina to maintain their views politically," the

Riot: A Forgotten Incident of Reconstruction Violence," *LH* 17 (winter 1976): 41–9; Melinda Meek Hennessey, "Race and Violence in Reconstruction New Orleans: The 1868 Riot," *LH* 20 (winter 1979): 77–91; Taylor, *Louisiana Reconstructed,* 161–73; Allen W. Trelease, *White Terror: The Ku Klux Klan Conspiracy and Southern Reconstruction* (New York, 1971), 127–36; Tunnell, *Crucible of Reconstruction,* 153–9; Frank J. Wetta, "'Bulldozing the Scalawags': Some Examples of the Persecution of Southern White Republicans in Louisiana during Reconstruction," *LH* 21 (winter 1980): 43–58.

38. Various accounts of the riot contradict one another, but the attack upon the Italian storekeeper and the subsequent deaths of several freedmen seem beyond doubt. See *DP,* Oct. 27, 28, 31, 1868; H. M. Whitterman to B. T. Hutchins, Oct. 27, 31, and Nov. 28, 1868, vol. 536, pp. 17–22, LS, ser. 1823, ASAC for St. Bernard and Plaquemines Parishes, New Orleans, BRFAL; 41st Cong., 1st Sess., HMD 13, pt. 1, pp. 26–40; 41st Cong., 2nd Sess., HMD 154, pt. 2, pp. 76–98, 254–71, 376–84, 465–9; and Taylor, *Louisiana Reconstructed,* 169–72. See Tunnell, *Crucible of Reconstruction,* 155, for the number of deaths.

Freedmen's Bureau agent at Donaldsonville noted, "and defend the principles they advocate, which as a matter of course the planter contends against, and tries to run them to the belief of his creed."[39]

Freedmen had the stamina to maintain their political views, but the election results showed that without federal protection they could do little to combat terror. Election day in Louisiana passed relatively quietly, and Republican candidate and Civil War hero Ulysses S. Grant won the presidency without Louisiana's electoral votes. But the hardly credible tally of 33,263 votes for Grant against 80,325 for Democrat Horatio Seymour, in a state with a black majority, confirmed bulldozing's effectiveness. The results in the sugar region were more ambiguous, but they also corroborated the partial success of political terror. Grant received 15,623 votes, compared to Seymour's 13,111 (54.4 percent to 45.6 percent), yet Grant's share of the vote declined markedly from Warmoth's lopsided totals in April, despite the fact that the total number of votes cast remained about the same. Even before the election, one Freedmen's Bureau agent had correctly predicted that many freedmen would vote Democratic out of fear. "[T]he white people now say," he reported afterwards, "that the colored man has very good sense, and know[s] how to *vote.*" Bulldozing jeopardized planters' short-term profits by further disrupting labor on the eve of the rolling season, but, convinced that they had no choice, planters deemed it a necessary step in ending Reconstruction. Republicans captured the presidency in 1868, but white terror carried the day in Louisiana.[40]

However disappointing the results for Louisiana Republicans, the presidential election proved to be only a temporary setback. Despite the violence of 1868 and the Freedmen's Bureau's plan to discontinue its involvement in labor affairs at

39. A. Miltenberger to T. O. Moore, Oct. 23, 1868, Thomas Overton Moore Papers, LSU; *DP,* Oct. 30, 1868; B. Stevens to EJG, Nov. 11, 1868, EJGP; J. H. Brough to L. H. Warren, Sept. 11, 1868, vol. 264, pp. 119–20, LS, ser. 1577, Agt & ASAC, Donaldsonville, BRFAL. For similar observations about freedmen's political activities during the 1868 presidential campaign, see Aug. 16, Oct. 22, Nov. 3, 1868, Erwin Diary, LSU; Sept. 20, 1868, Plant. Diary 3, Oct. 10, 12, 1868, Plant. Diary 4, DeClouet Papers, LSU; Oct. 15, 1868, Plant. Diary 36, WJMP; L. Bouchereau, *Statement . . . 1868–69;* N. Bronson to L. H. Warren, Aug. 31, 1868, vol. 472, pp. 110–1, LS, ser. 1899, Agt & ASAC, Thibodaux, BRFAL; C. E. Merrill to B. T. Hutchins, Oct. 16, 1868, vol. 428, pp. 53–5, LS, ser. 1842, Agt & ASAC, Plaquemine, BRFAL; V. Benthien to B. T. Hutchins, Oct. 19, 1868, vol. 264, pp. 150–1, LS, ser. 1577, Agt & ASAC, Donaldsonville, BRFAL; J. H. Van Antwerp to B. T. Hutchins, Oct. 20, 1868, vol. 472, pp. 134–6, LS, ser. 1899, Agt & ASAC, Thibodaux, BRFAL; R. W. Mullen to B. T. Hutchins, Oct. 21, 1868, vol. 286, pp. 37–41, Trimonthly Reps., ser. 1604, Agt & ASAC, Franklin, BRFAL.

40. W. F. Loan to B. T. Hutchins, Nov. 1, 10, 1868, vol. 286, pp. 41–6, Trimonthly Reps., ser. 1604, Agt & ASAC, Franklin, BRFAL. While almost 29,000 ballots were cast in both April and November in the sugar region, the Republican vote declined and the Democratic vote in-

year's end, freedmen of the sugar region had reason for optimism. Although it was clear that Reconstruction depended upon federal support, such backing appeared to be increasing as president-elect Grant prepared to replace Andrew Johnson. The Republican Party also governed Louisiana at the state and local levels. Republican rule rested squarely on the black vote in Louisiana, but those black voters had exhibited firm resolve, and grassroots political mobilization swept the sugar region in 1867 and 1868. The white counterattack did not bode well for the prospects of black political power were Conservatives to succeed in ending Reconstruction in Louisiana, but by no means was such an outcome foreordained during what was only the opening phase of Radical Reconstruction.[41]

Although neither political mobilization nor its effects on the freedmen's working lives was unique to the sugar region, this intersecting of politics and labor had consequences specific to southern Louisiana. The centralized organization of labor on sugar plantations enabled freedmen to defend their political rights both during and after Radical Reconstruction. In the cotton South, by contrast, the political mobilization of 1867 and 1868 eventuated in sharecropping, which, in dispersing individual households throughout the plantation, gradually undermined the black community's ability to mobilize for collective self-defense once Radical Reconstruction came under attack in the 1870s. Thus the events of 1868 did not end the struggle over labor in the sugar fields, nor did they settle the battle for control of parish courthouses and statehouse. Instead, these two interrelated contests were about to enter upon a new phase.[42]

---

creased by about 5,000. Thus, either many freedmen were coerced in November into voting Democratic or many of them stayed home on election day while more white voters turned out than in April. In some parishes the Republican vote dropped significantly: in Ascension, Warmoth won 98 percent of the vote but Grant only 57 percent; in St. Mary, the corresponding figures were 71.3 percent and 38.6 percent. In St. Bernard, where Warmoth had won 65.5 percent of the vote, Seymour received 473 votes against Grant's 1. W. Dean Burnham, *Presidential Ballots, 1836–1892* (Baltimore, 1955), 486–501; Howard, *Political Tendencies*, 425, 446–7.

41. After 1868, the Freedmen's Bureau was limited to education and securing black veterans' bounty claims.

42. Michael W. Fitzgerald notes how sharecropping in the cotton South undermined the freedmen's ability to mobilize collectively in *Union League Movement*, 213–33, 248–52. "Ironically," he writes, "the freedmen's success in renting land dispersed them widely throughout the countryside, making them more vulnerable to attack" (215). He also observes: "The dispersal of freedmen from the old slave quarters also tended to inhibit collective action. Social demobilization on a large scale ensued, the balkanization of the labor force throughout the countryside" (230). The different ways in which politics and labor intersected in cotton and sugar will be explored further in chapter 8.

ॐ5ॐ

PERSISTENCE AND PROGRESS

The efeminate and effete will have to give place to more competent and energetic men, and capital will find its reward in assisting them.

—Samuel Cranwill to Edward J. Gay, May 13, 1873

Emancipation did not merely transform relations between those who purchased labor power and those who provided it; it effectively remade these two social classes. Redefining masters and slaves as employers and employees was tantamount to turning the world upside down, and the planter elite's metamorphosis was further complicated by the failure of many members to survive war, emancipation, and economic devastation and by the subsequent appearance of new men. Moreover, even as planters struggled with their former slaves over the new labor system, and even as they experienced convulsions attendant upon their own reconstitution as a social class, they also confronted the challenge of survival within both a stagnating regional economy and a rapidly changing international sugar market. Enduring these many travails required a combination of arduous and stringent financial measures, profound psychological and ideological transformation, and no small amount of good fortune. Surviving the new order, in short, depended upon a convergence of factors both within and outside an individual's control. Those who possessed resources, ability, and luck to persist, be they members of the old elite or newcomers, rebuilt the sugar industry and led it into the modern world.

* * *

The sugar industry recovered steadily but slowly after the Civil War. Sugar production averaged an abysmal 54,000 hogsheads during the late 1860s but more than doubled during the early 1870s (table 6). Production continued to improve, reaching a respectable 197,000 hogsheads by the early 1880s. Even this figure did not match the five-year average of more than 300,000 hogsheads before the federal invasion in 1862. Not until 1894 did Louisiana surpass the record 1861 crop of almost 460,000 hogsheads. And any solace planters derived from improved production was partially nullified by a dramatic drop in sugar's price. From its height of eighteen cents per pound in 1864, Louisiana sugar plummeted to about six cents by 1880. "Truly the outlook for sugar planters is a gloomy one," remarked one planter's business partner in 1879; "there is no money in sugar & molasses at present prices."[1]

After the war, planters also found themselves relegated to the periphery of the U.S. sugar market. While production had plunged since antebellum times, domestic sugar consumption increased 62 percent between 1860 and 1875, as sugar was undergoing its nineteenth-century transformation from luxury item to dietary staple. The combination of decreased production and increased demand meant that Louisiana fulfilled a declining proportion of American sugar consumption, from 27 percent in 1860 to a mere 8 percent in 1875. Since more than 90 percent of sugar consumed in the United States by the mid-1870s was imported

TABLE 6

Sugar Production: Five-Year Averages, 1857–1884 (in Hogsheads)

Years	Number
1857–1861	310,408
1862–1864*	58,134
1865–1869	53,611
1870–1874	117,645
1875–1879	164,904
1880–1884	196,892

Sources: Joe Gray Taylor, *Louisiana Reconstructed, 1863–1877* (Baton Rouge, 1974), 370; Alcée Bouchereau, *Statement of the Sugar and Rice Crops Made in Louisiana . . . 1887–88.*

*Being anomalous, the war years have been categorized separately.

1. J. M. Howell to AFP, Jan. 21, 1879, Pugh Papers, UT. For equally pessimistic observations, see Dec. 30, 1870, AFP Diary, S. Dwyer to AFP, Dec. 27, 1877, A. Littlejohn to AFP, Sept. 7, 1877, and R. Beltran to AFP, June 8, 1878, all in Pugh Papers, UT; M. Martin to W. Littlejohn, Feb. 14, 1875, Martin-Pugh Collection, NSU; A. Pugh to T. Pugh, Nov. 23, 1876, W. W. Pugh Papers, LSU; H. Robichaux to P. Butler, Aug. 6, 1878, Thomas Butler and Family Papers, LSU.

and thus subject to the protective tariff, Americans paid artificially inflated prices for any commodity that contained sugar, intensifying public animosity toward both the tariff and Louisiana planters.[2]

As though these difficulties were not enough, planters faced upheaval in the world sugar market after 1860, due mostly to the rise of European beet sugar. Beet sugar accounted for only 20 percent of world sugar production in 1860 but more than half by 1882. Increases in cane sugar output elsewhere also affected the U.S. domestic sugar market. Cuba, which was the United States's main source of sugar after the war, almost doubled its output during the 1860s. Worldwide, cane and beet sugar production doubled between 1860 and 1880, while Louisiana's share of world output decreased from 5.9 percent to 2.9 percent. Louisiana planters had traditionally exerted little influence over the international sugar market, but by the early 1880s they had been reduced to virtual inconsequence. Had they stopped making sugar altogether, few people outside Louisiana might have noticed.[3]

Determining whether or not planters could operate profitably under such circumstances is complicated by variations in yearly production costs, individual experience, and idiosyncratic accounting procedures. Whereas sugar making was ordinarily profitable before the war, when planters could expect returns of as much as 10 percent on investment, it became generally unprofitable for years afterward. During the 1850s, sugar's price ranged from five to ten cents per pound while direct operating costs were as low as 1.5 cents per pound. Direct operating expenses soared to as much as seven cents per pound by the early 1870s, however, and they ranged from five to nine cents during the second half of the decade. Increased labor costs and high interest rates on short-term credit largely accounted for the rise in expenses. Oddly, planters who revived their operations immediately after the war were buoyed by the high price of sugar, but once the price began to level off during the early 1870s, a number of them failed. Certainly, they would have disputed an observation in the mid-1870s that "large sugar planters will always Make Money."[4]

2. Sidney W. Mintz, *Sweetness and Power: The Place of Sugar in Modern History* (New York, 1985), esp. 140, 143–4, 147–50. On the tariff after the war, see Sitterson, *Sugar Country*, 324–42.

3. On the international sugar economy during the late nineteenth century, see introduction to Bill Albert and Adrian Graves, eds., *Crisis and Change in the International Sugar Economy, 1860–1914* (Norwich, U.K., 1984), 1–7. On the rise of the European beet sugar industry and its implications for Louisiana, see Heitmann, *Modernization*, 49–67. Figures in this and the preceding paragraphs have been calculated from Alcée Bouchereau, *Statement of the Sugar and Rice Crops Made in Louisiana . . . 1879–80, 1880–81, 1887–88;* Heitmann, *Modernization*, 57–8; U.S. Dept. of Agriculture, "The Cane-Sugar Industry," in *Report of the Commissioner for the Year 1877* (Washington, D.C., 1878); and Taylor, *Louisiana Reconstructed,* 370.

4. John D. Barnhart, ed., "Reconstruction on the Lower Mississippi," *Mississippi Valley Historical Review* 21 (December 1934): 395. For sugar planting's profitability under slavery and

Few planters, it seems, made money. Even the relatively successful John Burnside reported losses of more than $130,000 in 1869 alone. Burnside possessed resources to absorb this loss, but others were not so lucky. A visitor to St. Mary Parish the same year estimated that fewer than one in six antebellum estates had been in operation since the war. Plantations could be purchased cheaply, he added, so long as a prospective buyer was willing to invest at least $100,000 before realizing a profit. Investment capital was a rare commodity in the postwar South, however, and with long-term credit largely unavailable, planters depended upon short-term loans—at interest rates of as much as 25 percent—to meet operating expenses. As some planters sank more deeply into debt, creditors faced the choice of foreclosing or continuing to throw good money after bad. Although one factor decided in 1871 to stop extending credit to planters who had no hope of meeting expenses, two years later clients continued to besiege him for funds. "The attacks of needy and delinquent Planters today was enough to worry you out of all patience," he informed his business partner in 1873, "they were like a swarm of hornets."[5]

From there matters worsened. A poor 1873 crop, combined with that year's national financial crisis, dealt a crushing blow to an industry still reeling from the devastation of war. Factors complained of debt-ridden planters, who lamented their own inability to obtain funds to pay workers. The sugar industry hit bottom during winter 1873–74, as scores of planters either abandoned their estates or lost them to foreclosure. When asked to estimate the value of his property in 1874, one planter responded that "it would be impossible to sell a sugar-plantation for money. I don't know how I would get at the valuation." New Orleans factor Samuel Cranwill during that winter expressed his frustration with planters, who, he noted, were "playing a strong game against their Factors." Anticipating a small harvest, many set aside an unduly large part of the crop for spring planting while refusing to ship their sugar until they received funds to pay workers. Cranwill had reached his wit's end in "dealing with men in whom all confidence has long since been lost." Now was not time, he announced in late 1873, "to pay out money on uncertainty: as far as the Factor is concerned it is a fight for life in many cases and he who does so is lost."[6]

---

free labor, see Sitterson, *Sugar Country*, chaps. 8 and 14. For an examination of one planter family's finances under slavery and free labor, see Thomas A. H. Scarborough, "The Bislands of Natchez: Sugar, Secession, and Strategies for Survival," *Journal of Mississippi History* 58 (spring 1996): 23–62.

5. John Burnside's tax return, Mar. 1, 1870, James Amédée Gaudet Papers, SHC; *Franklin Planters' Banner*, Jan. 26, 1870; S. Cranwill to EJG, Mar. 13, 1871, Jan. 18, 1873, EJGP. See also L. A. Bringier to S. Bringier, Feb. 24, 1870, Louis Amédée Bringier and Family Papers, LSU; M. Martin to W. Littlejohn, Jan. 27, 1871, Martin-Pugh Collection, NSU.

6. 43rd Cong., 2nd Sess., HR 261, pt. 3, pp. 600–5; S. Cranwill to EJG, Dec. 9, 1873, EJGP. See also A. Robertson to T. Pugh, Feb. 4, 1874, W. W. Pugh Papers, LSU.

Planters were squeezed between factors calling for greater economy of operations and laborers clamorous for high wages and indisposed to perform work for which they might not be paid. "We appreciate the situation that planters are placed in," remarked A. F. Pugh's factors in late 1873, "& regret that the negro laborers cannot be brought to understand the difficulties of the present situation of monetary affairs." Pugh's experiences throughout 1874 illustrate planters' predicaments. He spent much of January in New Orleans pleading with his factors for a loan. Only after mortgaging his property over to them did he succeed in obtaining funds to begin operations for the new year.[7]

Pugh hobbled through the 1874 crop season, but by late summer his factors were imploring him to cut costs. His expenses already outpaced what they had agreed to advance for the whole year. They also urged him to induce freedmen to wait until year's end for their wages, something he knew would amount to an exercise in futility. Indebted as he was, Pugh had no choice but to listen to his factors lecture him on running his affairs. "As regards the anticipated trouble in the event of the hands not being paid . . . we regret to hear such a desponding conclusion," they noted. "Those hands must know that there are plenty ready & willing to take their places at even lower rates." Insisting that "[w]e do not seek to make you feel yourself at the mercy of the laborers you have employed," they added, "we have also to tell you plainly that we cannot go much deeper." Nonetheless, as rolling season commenced, Pugh appealed again for funds, aware that his employees would not work if not paid. Despite his dire prediction, Pugh harvested his crop without the anticipated labor stoppage, but this did not prevent him from prophesying future difficulties. "The troubles of the next three months look as if they would be intolerable but they are inevitable," he noted in late November 1874, "& I have made up my mind to endure them—be they as they may."[8]

But Pugh's travails were not inevitable. His factors might have foreclosed on the mortgage and seized his plantation. That they did not pursue this course was due to Pugh's stature as an important public figure before the war, his personal influence with them, and the resources upon which he could draw as a member of a wealthy and influential family. Such was not the case for many others.

Had Pugh considered sugar planters' general ability to weather the Civil War, emancipation, and economic readjustment, he might have counted his blessings. Among antebellum elite planters (owners of at least fifty slaves and five hundred improved acres) in Ascension, Assumption, Iberville, and Lafourche Parishes,

7. Foley, Conger & Co. to AFP, Nov. 3, 1873, H. J. Boatner to AFP, Jan. [?], 1874, and Jan. 19–21, 1874, AFP Diary, Pugh Papers, UT.

8. Conger & Kelly to AFP, Aug. 18, 29, Sept. 12, 21, 1874; Sept. 25, Nov. 20, 1874, AFP Diary, Pugh Papers, UT.

TABLE 7

Planter Persistence, 1860–1873 and 1860–1880

PARISH	# of Elite Planters, 1860	# and % of 1860 Elite in 1873 Elite	# and % of 1860 Elite in 1880 Elite
Ascension	28	9 (32.1)	8 (28.6)
Assumption	31	19 (61.3)	18 (58.1)
Iberville	63	29 (46.0)	12 (19.1)
Lafourche	32	14 (43.8)	11 (34.8)
Totals	154	71 (46.1)	49 (31.8)

Sources: Karl Joseph Menn, *The Large Slaveholders of Louisiana—1860* (New Orleans, 1964); Tax Assessment Rolls, Ascension, Assumption, Iberville, and Lafourche Parishes, 1873, 1880.

slightly less than half survived by the early 1870s, and fewer than one-third did so by 1880 (table 7). Persistence rates of about one in three among sugar planters paled against those among Mississippi River cotton planters, more than half of whom in 1880 belonged to the old elite. Sugar planters who survived the war and its immediate consequences actually stood a good chance of enduring, since only about one-third of antebellum planters who still belonged to the 1873 elite subsequently dropped out. Nonetheless, by 1874 Pugh was among the minority of antebellum elite planters still in business.[9]

Despite the havoc wreaked on the planter elite by the Civil War, the plantation system itself was not threatened in the sugar region. The concentration of landholding that characterized sugar production before the war remained intact after it. Though no longer slaveholders, planters who persisted still dominated landholding. In none of the aforementioned parishes did the planter elite suffer a loss in the percentage of land it owned between 1860 and 1880 (tables 8–11). The elite underwent marked change after the Civil War, but the proportion of land it held did not.

That a third of the old elite persisted to 1880 does not mean that newcomers made up two-thirds of postwar elite, since those who failed were not necessarily

9. Wayne, *Reshaping Plantation Society,* 75–109; Davis, *Good and Faithful Labor,* 138–43. In his study of Alabama, Jonathan M. Wiener also found persistence rates of about 50 percent between 1860 and 1870. Wiener, *Social Origins,* 3–34. Such persistence rates compare favorably to those in the antebellum Pennsylvania iron industry, for instance, where the rate between 1832 (the charcoal era) and 1850 (charcoal and anthracite) was only 26 percent. Paul F. Paskoff, *Industrial Evolution: Organization, Structure, and Growth of the Pennsylvania Iron Industry, 1750–1860* (Baltimore, 1983), 83–7. For discussion of the methodology used in analyzing planter persistence and postbellum landholding, see the appendix.

TABLE 8

Distribution of Landholders and Acreage: Ascension Parish, 1860, 1873, and 1880

| | SIZE OF HOLDING, IN ACRES | | | | | | |
| | 1–99 | | 100–499 | | 500+ | | Total |
	N	%	N	%	N	%	N
Landholders, 1860	186	79.2	23	9.7	26	11.1	235
Acres, 1860	4,050	9.3	5,103	11.7	34,501	79.0	43,654
Landholders, 1873	147	67.4	39	17.9	32	14.7	218
Acres, 1873	3,000	5.2	9,232	15.9	45,701	78.9	57,933
Landholders, 1880	260	77.8	39	11.7	35	10.5	334
Acres, 1880	4,406	5.9	9,474	12.7	60,590	81.4	74,470

Sources: U.S. Bureau of the Census, manuscript agricultural schedules, 1860 census; Tax Assessment Rolls, 1873, 1880, Ascension Parish.

TABLE 9

Distribution of Landholders and Acreage: Assumption Parish, 1860, 1873, and 1880

| | SIZE OF HOLDING, IN ACRES | | | | | | |
| | 1–99 | | 100–499 | | 500+ | | Total |
	N	%	N	%	N	%	N
Landholders, 1860	355	74.6	84	17.6	37	7.8	476
Acres, 1860	9,697	16.9	19,111	33.3	28,540	49.8	57,348
Landholders, 1873	526	68.7	155	20.2	85	11.1	766
Acres, 1873	18,308	11.8	33,835	21.8	102,895	66.4	155,036
Landholders, 1880	801	74.6	189	17.6	84	7.8	1,074
Acres, 1880	26,009	15.6	8,353	24.1	100,947	60.3	167,309

Sources: U.S. Bureau of the Census, manuscript agricultural schedules, 1860 census; Tax Assessment Rolls, 1873, 1880, Assumption Parish.

replaced. Rather, the less efficient were swept away as the industry underwent consolidation. Under these circumstances, an individual's persistence depended upon good luck, economic resources, and the ability to shift ideologically from owner to employer of labor. In the uncompromising postwar environment, two out of three of these factors were not enough. The new elite, moreover, derived from diverse origins: it included antebellum planters and their families who survived, native southerners who had not been planters before the war, and a small

TABLE 10

Distribution of Landholders and Acreage: Iberville Parish, 1860, 1873, and 1880

	SIZE OF HOLDING, IN ACRES						
	1–99		100–499		500+		Total
	N	%	N	%	N	%	N
Landholders, 1860	147	53.1	82	29.6	48	17.3	277
Acres, 1860	4,885	7.8	19,217	30.9	38,189	61.3	62,291
Landholders, 1873	212	35.0	245	40.4	149	24.6	606
Acres, 1873	9,593	3.7	58,456	22.7	189,688	73.6	257,737
Landholders, 1880	293	38.9	294	39.1	166	22.0	753
Acres, 1880	11,458	4.3	69,515	25.9	186,704	69.8	267,677

Sources: U.S. Bureau of the Census, manuscript agricultural schedules, 1860 census; Tax Assessment Rolls, 1873, 1880, Iberville Parish.

TABLE 11

Distribution of Landholders and Acreage: Lafourche Parish, 1860, 1873, and 1880

	SIZE OF HOLDING, IN ACRES						
	1–99		100–499		500+		Total
	N	%	N	%	N	%	N
Landholders, 1860	212	75.5	38	13.5	31	11.0	281
Acres, 1860	5,261	12.8	9,142	22.2	26,808	65.1	41,211
Landholders, 1873	706	64.0	304	27.6	93	8.4	1,103
Acres, 1873	33,043	13.0	60,354	23.6	161,747	63.4	255,144
Landholders, 1880	793	64.1	340	27.5	104	8.4	1,237
Acres, 1880	38,484	12.4	65,827	20.1	207,205	66.5	311,516

Sources: U.S. Bureau of the Census, manuscript agricultural schedules, 1860 census; Tax Assessment Rolls, 1873, 1880, Lafourche Parish.

but conspicuous group of northerners who came south during and after the war. Less important than each cohort's numerical significance are the qualities they all shared in forming a new social class.

Northerners who purchased plantations were notable more for their success than their numbers. They knew little about sugar making at first but learned quickly, usually after entering into partnerships with indebted planters. Northerners were not racial egalitarians, nor did their familiarity with free labor preclude conflict with their workers. Nonetheless, in undertaking sugar planting, they were not saddled with slavery's cultural and ideological baggage. Preeminent among them was Henry Clay Warmoth. The quintessential carpetbagger, the Illinois-born Warmoth served in the Union army in Louisiana during the war and helped found the state's Republican Party before winning election as governor in 1868. When his controversial term ended in 1872, he invested in a Plaquemines Parish plantation, eventually becoming sole proprietor and creating a vast, technologically advanced sugar empire. Warmoth was joined by others, including John Dymond, a New York merchant who invested in sugar plantations in the 1860s, and John B. Lyon, a Chicago businessman who led a group of midwestern investors in Bayou Teche plantations in the 1870s. Northerners never dominated the industry as contemporaries and later historians alleged, but by infusing new ideas and capital into the sugar industry at a critical time, they were in the vanguard of its modernization during the late nineteenth century.[10]

John N. Pharr and Leon Godchaux typified southerners who had not owned slaves or plantations before the war. Pharr operated a steamboat on Bayou Teche before he began acquiring plantations in 1876; by his death in 1903 he owned eight estates. Godchaux, founder of the future sugar conglomerate, immigrated to New Orleans from France in the 1830s and became a merchant. He purchased his first plantation in 1862 and by century's end owned twelve plantations that comprised more than thirty thousand acres. The upheaval of war gave men like Pharr and Godchaux, who possessed the talent and business acumen to succeed, entry into the planter class, something that had been denied them during the late antebellum period. As products of slave society, they undoubtedly harbored racial prejudices consistent with their backgrounds. Nonetheless, in addition to possessing the necessary financial resources they were also unhampered by the experience of having commanded slaves.[11]

Iberville Parish grandee Edward J. Gay exemplified antebellum planters who possessed both means and ability to face the challenge of economic readjustment. The keys to Gay's success were his entrepreneurial spirit, diversified holdings, and adeptness at adjusting to new circumstances. In addition to his planting interests, Gay owned mercantile firms in his adopted St. Louis and New Orleans. He had started out as a merchant in the former city and undertook sugar making after inheriting an Iberville plantation in the 1850s. The estate, christened "St. Louis," be-

10. Heitmann, *Modernization*, 68–90. Roger W. Shugg was the first historian to claim, with little evidence, that northerners took over the sugar industry after the war; this assertion has unfortunately been repeated by others. Shugg, *Origins of Class Struggle*, 248–9.

11. Sitterson, *Sugar Country*, 312.

came Gay's principal residence, but he divided his time between agricultural and mercantile interests. A shrewd businessman, Gay assumed the mortgages of one broken planter after another following the war, eventually possessing some dozen estates and incorporating his holdings as "Edward J. Gay & Co."

The Gay business records offer a unique window onto the postwar sugar industry from perspectives of both planter and merchant. Managers of Gay's plantations documented the labor difficulties that plagued them, while Samuel Cranwill, Gay's business partner and manager of the New Orleans firm, attested to problems of dealing with indebted planters. Edward Gay successfully overcame these challenges not only because of his extensive financial resources, which were formidable, but also because of his realistic and unsentimental approach to sugar planting. In dealing with other planters, managers, and even laborers, Gay could be a tough negotiator, yet he did not allow prejudice as a former slaveholder to blind him to the demands of what was in essence a business. His background as an enterprising merchant endowed him with an outlook well suited to making sugar with free labor. By no means typical of antebellum planters after the war, Gay personified the qualities needed to survive under the new order.

Determining why some planters survived the vagaries of the capitalist market and the tumult of emancipation while others failed may ultimately be impossible. At a minimum, a planter had to keep operating costs, especially those associated with labor, as low as possible in addition to marshaling the necessary financial resources. Equally important for survival was his coming to terms with the concept of free labor and reconciling it with sugar production. Any planter—whether newcomer or member of the old elite—who tried to browbeat, cajole, or bully his workers into making sugar soon found that he had either to change his ways or to suffer constant labor strife. No amount of money or good fortune could overcome a planter's refusal to think of former slaves as free people. In this one essential feature of plantation life, the old order was dead.

For some, it could not expire quickly enough. Samuel Cranwill's 1873 observation, "The efeminate and effete will have to give place to more competent and energetic men, and capital will find its reward in assisting them," outlined the vision for the industry's future as seen by this uncompromising spokesman of the new order. "[G]radually the extravagant, inattentive, and incompetent owners and managers of plantations are going down—are being set aside—as unequal to the circumstances which surround them," he insisted. "I only wish all such were set aside, and had been long ago, to give place to new and more powerful characters." These new men would not be handicapped by irrational allegiance to slavery, Cranwill believed. Under the new system, labor required "proper direction, proper management, and proper treatment," he asserted, "which many of the *pro slavery idea planters* do not understand how to apply."[12]

Cranwill's cold, hard logic could not be denied, even by those swept into the dustbin of history. "[T]he emancipation of the slaves was a death blow to wealth, culture and refinement," remarked W. W. Pugh, who epitomized the old elite, in 1872. "A very different race of people must succeed those who were so noted for their hospitality and intelligence." Northern journalist Edward King, no defender of slavery, echoed these sentiments in 1873. "A grand and lordly life" was how King described antebellum sugar planting, one "filled with culture, pleasure, and the refinements of living;—but now!"[13]

The ancien régime's bittersweet passing, however, did not tell the whole story. In the early 1880s, Jared Sanders of St. Mary Parish described his situation to a South Carolina friend with both sadness and hope. "I have a vivid remembrance of your old homestead, the kindly face of your father & mother, of your sisters, indeed, of everything that surrounded your hospitable home," he reminisced. "I frequently think how things must look in the hands of strangers, as I suppose the Mannings, Guilliams & Richardsons have fared as sadly as the gentry of our section, sad to see strangers possessing their lands." Turning to his own affairs, Sanders noted: "I own the plantation & lands owned by my father when I was at college. This is exceptional." Despite many problems, Sanders was doing well. "I am still a sugar planter," he noted, "& have been so far successful."[14]

Exceptional antebellum survivors like Sanders were joined by northerners and other newcomers in spearheading the sugar industry's modernization in the decades after the war. Characterized by the abandonment of traditional sugar-making methods and the use of science and technology to improve production, the modernization of the sugar industry was inextricably linked to the labor question. Technological advances, especially at the sugar mill, enabled planters to produce more and better sugar from a given quantity of cane, recompensing them, at least in part, for their lack of labor control. Technological change had occurred before the Civil War, but afterwards it became a way for planters to bypass the apparently insolvable labor problem.[15]

12. S. Cranwill to EJG, May 13, 1873, EJGP.

13. W. W. Pugh to T. Pugh, Nov. 25, 1872, W. W. Pugh Papers, LSU; Edward King, *The Great South: A Record of Journeys in Louisiana, Texas, The Indian Territory, Missouri, Arkansas, Mississippi, Alabama, Georgia, Florida, South Carolina, North Carolina, Kentucky, Tennessee, Virginia, West Virginia, and Maryland,* ed. W. Magruder Drake and Robert R. Jones (1879; reprint, Baton Rouge, 1972), 81.

14. J. Sanders to "Dear John," Sept. 11, 1881, Jared Young Sanders and Family Papers, LSU.

15. My understanding of the modernization of the sugar industry rests upon the following

Although antebellum sugar planters, unlike other southern slaveholders, had embraced many features of the industrial world, they had also adhered to traditional methods and established practices. For years after the war, many continued to regard change suspiciously. "All very complete. Systematical," complained Alexandre DeClouet upon visiting Evan Hall plantation in 1880. "Planting & Sugar making reduced to a science!" Such skepticism, however, could not last forever. Emancipation and changes in the world market compelled planters to alter their views. Technological development came unevenly: slow during the 1860s and early 1870s, it picked up steam by the later 1870s and was in full throttle after 1880. The industry was no monolith; change resulted from countless decisions made over decades. Even those who committed themselves to scientific agriculture and technological development faced a time lag, as new techniques sometimes required years of testing before resulting in increased production.[16]

In order to further the process of adaptation, planters created the Louisiana Sugar Planters Association (LSPA). Founded in 1877, the LSPA focused its initial efforts on lobbying to preserve the tariff. By the early 1880s, it began to shift its attention toward scientific research, holding frequent meetings during which planters exchanged information and reported on their experiments. It also published a journal, the *Louisiana Sugar Planter,* and worked with such governmental and educational institutions as the U.S. Department of Agriculture, Tulane University, Louisiana State University, and the Audubon Park Sugar School in promoting agricultural research. During the late nineteenth and early twentieth centuries, the LSPA was the organization through which planters identified common concerns, fostered research and development, and promoted their own interests as well as those of the industry at large.[17]

Spurred on by the LSPA, planters embraced an array of technological improvements during the last quarter of the nineteenth century. They adopted new

---

works: Geoff Burrows and Ralph Shlomowitz, "The Lag in the Mechanization of the Sugarcane Harvest: Some Comparative Perspectives," *AH* 66 (summer 1992): 61–75; Stanley L. Engerman, "Contract Labor, Sugar, and Technology in the Nineteenth Century," *Journal of Economic History* 43 (September 1983): 635–59; Ferleger, "Productivity Change"; Louis Ferleger, "Farm Mechanization in the Southern Sugar Sector after the Civil War," *LH* 23 (winter 1982): 21–34, and "Cutting the Cane: Harvesting in the Louisiana Sugar Industry," *Southern Studies* 23 (spring 1984): 42–59; Heitmann, *Modernization,* and "Organization As Power: The Louisiana Sugar Planters' Association and the Creation of Scientific and Technical Institutions, 1877–1910," *LH* 27 (summer 1986): 281–94; Joseph P. Reidy, "Mules and Machines and Men: Field Labor on Louisiana Sugar Plantations, 1887–1915," *AH* 72 (spring 1998): 183–96; Sitterson, *Sugar Country,* 269–90; and Schmitz, "Transformation of the Southern Cane Sugar Sector."

16. Feb. 5, 1880, Plant. Diary 6, DeClouet Papers, LSU; Schmitz, "Transformation of the Southern Cane Sugar Sector," 275; Heitmann, *Modernization,* chap. 5.

17. Heitmann, "Organization As Power."

planting techniques, improved methods of cultivation, experimented with fertilizers and agricultural implements, and tested scientifically enhanced varieties of cane. Workers transported harvested cane to steam-powered sugar mills, where the juice was converted to sugar in vacuum pans rather than in open kettles. New mills were more powerful than the older ones, and they processed a greater amount of cane. Because the capital necessary to build large mills often lay beyond the means of individual planters, sugar operations increasingly became corporate enterprises.[18]

The mills' increased capacity also accelerated the emergence of central mills and the separation of sugar production's agricultural and industrial phases. Sugar mills became so powerful that they processed more cane than planters could grow on their own estates. To keep their businesses running efficiently, central mill owners purchased supplemental cane at a set price per ton from outside sources, including planters who no longer processed cane and an increasing number of white farmers who grew cane. Starting in the early 1870s, agricultural reformers proposed a form of tenancy in which white tenant farmers would grow cane for central mills. Planters initially opposed the plan, but such opposition gave way during the 1880s. The most successful and progressive planters—men such as John Dymond, Henry McCall, Edward Gay, Henry Clay Warmoth, and John Burnside—employed white tenant farmers in addition to black wage workers while also purchasing cane from other planters.[19]

With an unstable labor situation and a changing world sugar market cutting at their economic well-being, forward-thinking planters started looking to technology as their salvation. Because they were unable to establish control over labor in the fields, planters focused their efforts at improving efficiency in the processing phase of sugar production—that is, at the sugar mill. More efficient mills recovered a greater percentage of juice from the cane and produced a higher grade of sugar, enabling planters to increase profitability while circumventing the labor problem. The industry's dramatic rise in productivity during the latter part of the

18. Ferleger, "Cutting the Cane," and "Farm Mechanization"; Sitterson, *Sugar Country,* 269–79; Heitmann, *Modernization,* chaps. 3 and 5.

19. For positive comments on the trend toward central mills and the separation of cane growing and milling operations, see B. Caffery to D. Caffery, Aug. 20, 1877, Letterbook 4, Donelson Caffery and Family Papers, LSU; William H. Harris, *Louisiana Products, Resources and Attractions, with a Sketch of the Parishes* (New Orleans, 1881), 217; U.S. Dept. of Agriculture, "The Cane-Sugar Industry," 32; Charles Nordhoff, *The Cotton States in the Spring and Summer of 1875* (New York, 1876), 71; *NILSB,* June 28, 1877. See also Sitterson, *Sugar Country,* 257–66. Sitterson notes, "With the rise in cane production in the years 1880–1910, increased grinding and sugar making capacity was necessary. Larger mills required more cane, and more cane led to larger mills" (262).

TABLE 12

Output per Worker: Five-Year Averages, 1875–1904 (in Hogsheads)

YEARS	NUMBER
1875–1879	2.54
1880–1884	2.96
1885–1889	3.44
1890–1894	5.86
1895–1899	5.60
1900–1904	6.32

Source: Louis Ferleger, "Productivity Change in the Post-Bellum Louisiana Sugar Industry," in *Time Series Analysis*, ed. O. D. Anderson and M. R. Perryman (New York, 1981), 147–61.

TABLE 13

Sources of Productivity Change, 1877–1901 (in Hogsheads)

YEARS	Net Change in Production	Change in Mill Operations	Change in Field Operations
1877–1881	46,002	39,372	6,630
1882–1886	39,054	39,392	−338
1887–1891	188,500	136,852	51,648
1892–1896	26,012	50,952	−24,940
1897–1901	36,534	46,398	−9,864

Source: Louis Ferleger, "Productivity Change in the Post-Bellum Louisiana Sugar Industry," in *Time Series Analysis*, ed. O. D. Anderson and M. R. Perryman (New York, 1981), 147–61.

nineteenth century resulted largely from improvements in capital-intensive milling operations—over which planters exercised ample control—rather than to advances in labor-intensive field operations—over which they exercised little.

It would be difficult to compare labor productivity under slavery and free labor with any degree of reliability. Freedmen continued to toil diligently after emancipation, but because they worked fewer hours, and because many freedwomen withdrew from full-time labor, productivity inevitably declined. Less important than comparing labor productivity before and after emancipation, however, is the dramatic increase in productivity between the mid-1870s and the early twentieth century. Output per worker for the period 1875–1879 was 2.54 hogsheads. That figure swelled to 6.32 hogsheads for 1900–1904—nearly a 150 percent increase (table 12). This increase resulted mostly from improvements at the sugar mill. In three of the five five-year periods between 1877 and 1904, output for field operations decreased while output for milling operations rose significantly (table 13). The two

TABLE 14

Number of Sugar Mills: Open Kettles and Vacuum Pans, 1875–1905

YEAR	Open Kettles	Vacuum Pans	Total
1875	684	48	732
1880	742	99	841
1885	593	122	715
1890	315	164	479
1895	150	199	349
1900	72	204	276
1905	34	171	205

Source: Louis Ferleger, "Productivity Change in the Post-Bellum Louisiana Sugar Industry," in *Time Series Analysis*, ed. O. D. Anderson and M. R. Perryman (New York, 1981), 147–61.

phases of sugar production contributed unevenly to labor's increased productivity during the last quarter of the nineteenth century: improvements in field operations were negligible compared to those at the mill.[20]

The sugar mills' enhanced efficiency is evidenced by the steady rise in output during this period even as the number of mills dwindled. Between 1875 and 1905, sugar production in Louisiana mushroomed from 114,146 to more than 650,000 hogsheads while the number of mills declined from 732 to 205. Not only were fewer mills in use, but they also operated on a qualitatively different technological basis, as the industry shifted from the open kettle method of processing sugar to the almost exclusive use of vacuum pans. Although kettles dominated the industry as late as 1880, they declined thereafter while the number of vacuum pans steadily increased (table 14). Expanding production also resulted from advances in vacuum-pan technology itself. In 1875, sugar mills using vacuum pans produced on average just under 500 hogsheads. This figure multiplied sevenfold during the next thirty years, reaching almost 3,500 hogsheads in 1905—output that would have astounded antebellum planters (table 15). By the turn of the century, the sugar industry had undergone a revolutionary transformation. Not only had planters discarded centuries-old technology, but Big Sugar had been born.

The sugar industry's road to recovery thus progressed through the mill rather than the cane fields, and recovery hinged upon adopting new technology rather than ending planters' labor woes. Technological improvements accorded planters an indirect solution to the labor problem, but the labor problem did not, of and by itself, inevitably cause the sugar industry's modernization. And while planters never achieved the labor control they believed essential to sugar production, they did not entirely lack control, since none who genuinely felt threatened by labor

20. Ferleger, "Productivity Change," 151–2.

TABLE 15

Average Output per Sugar Mill Using Vacuum Pans, 1875–1905 (in Hogsheads)

YEAR	NUMBER
1875	496
1880	736
1885	924
1890	1,228
1895	1,876
1900	2,252
1905	3,438

Source: Louis Ferleger, "Productivity Change in the Post-Bellum Louisiana Sugar Industry," in *Time Series Analysis,* ed. O. D. Anderson and M. R. Perryman (New York, 1981), 147–61.

would have risked investing the capital necessary to modernize operations. Though unable to avoid difficulties with their workers or to exploit them as they had under slavery, planters eventually increased their workers' productivity by extracting more sugar from the cane they raised.

The story of the sugar industry's modernization anticipates somewhat that of free labor's progress during the 1870s. Central to both developments was the planter elite's reconfiguration after the war. Survival under the new order required not only ideological transformation but also economic resources and good fortune. Meeting all three conditions did not ensure success, but not meeting any one of them virtually assured failure, as the sugar industry sorted itself out with what one scholar has called "Darwinian efficiency."[21]

The planters' accommodation to the new labor system did not preclude conflict during the 1870s, as their continuing determination to control their workers clashed with the freedmen's efforts to achieve autonomy within the industry. This conflict centered on labor's mobility and on wages. With freedmen often gaining advantageous terms on economic issues, planters looked once again to politics as a means of establishing labor control. But because Radical Reconstruction ensured black involvement in government, planters and other members of Louisiana's white community would increasingly resort during the 1870s to attacking the Reconstruction state itself.

21. Scarborough, "Bislands of Natchez," 62.

§6§

"OF A MOVE ABOUT DISPOSITION"

Allen says . . . the negroes on the place refuse to work unless
paid for the time they worked in February. . . . He said that the
men are good men and have been on the place, some of them
with families, for two years. . . . It might be better to pay them
than to lose time trying to get other men, which would cost as
much if not more than the amount to be paid to those already
there; and who are known to be good men. . . . There is no time
to be lost getting the cane planted.
—Samuel Cranwill to Edward J. Gay, March 11, 1872

Of the many circumstances to which planters had to adjust under the new
order, one of the most challenging proved to be their workers' ability to
move about. The free-labor market that came into being with slavery's
abolition matured during the 1870s, redounding to the freedmen's benefit. No
longer bound against their will, former slaves left particular plantations over specific grievances or simply because they were free to do so. This geographic mobility—which manifested itself usually at the end of the crop season but sometimes
during it—caused planters much consternation by forcing them to compete for
the services of workers whom they had once controlled. Planters responded am-
bivalently to the labor market—working mostly within it to secure labor but also
trying to shape it to their advantage. Such efforts to alter the free market indicate
that there was nothing natural about how it operated, despite the preachings of
northern reformers and other nineteenth-century liberals. The planters' failure to

obstruct the market or to limit labor's mobility, however, illustrates their diminished economic and political power as well as their inability to impose labor arrangements upon freedmen who resolutely opposed them.

In addition to exposing the planters' vulnerability, the sugar region's labor market benefitted freedmen in other ways. It impacted upon both wage rates and payment methods, and it gave rise to and was consequently shaped by a variety of alternatives to monthly wage labor. During the 1870s, many former slaves—especially young, single men—availed themselves of the opportunity to engage in economic activities on the plantation system's periphery. In doing so, they ensured themselves regular income while avoiding the rigors of steady gang labor under close white supervision. Although the large majority of freedmen continued to toil in a manner that harked back to slavery, they were at least free to move about from year to year, if they chose, and some could even pursue different working arrangements. Freedmen's options were limited, but the mere fact that they had any facilitated their acceptance of wage labor.

Describing his southern travels in 1870–71, Scottish journalist Robert Somers remarked that neither planters nor freedmen in the sugar region seemed to comprehend how a free-labor market was supposed to function. "The great law of demand and supply in the matter of labour operates here under curious difficulties," he noted, "the supply neither knowing what it is worth nor what it wants, and the demand, having no other shift, forced to try all kinds of dodges, offering sometimes less or more indifferently, in order to get the supply to begin, which is the main thing for both." Freedmen and planters, to be sure, often betrayed a poor understanding of market relations, yet both eventually grasped such relations, though from different perspectives. The labor market enabled freedmen to harmonize their desire for autonomy with the demands of sugar production, and it compelled planters to meet freedmen's terms on wages, working conditions, and other matters. Planters countered that labor's mobility spawned a ruinous competition for workers, who exploited employers' dependence on their labor to gain an unfair advantage over them. Unfortunately for the planters, however, labor's mobility remained a disturbing fact of life. Unable during Radical Reconstruction to regulate the labor market through state action, they instead offered incentives in hiring and retaining workers—an experience few found satisfying.[1]

Planters and plantation managers noted with resignation and frustration the freedmen's comings and goings at the beginning of the year as well as their own efforts to hire them. "The Hollidays as usual is our greatest uneasyness, our hands

1. Robert Somers, *The Southern States since the War, 1870–71* ([1871]; reprint, with an introduction and index by Malcolm C. McMillan, University, Ala., 1965), 222.

seem to want to move," observed one manager in late 1871. "I am afraid most of mine will leave me for the river, I hardly know where to stryke to replace them." A planter who successfully hired several "well disposed men" in early 1872 was determined to do what it took to keep them. "[L]ike all travelling darkies," he remarked, they needed "to be kept on the safe side." Keeping freedmen satisfied became a primary concern for employers, especially between crop seasons. "Please send me one hundred Dollars to pay hands," requested one of Edward J. Gay's managers in late 1876. "I wish to satisfy the hands as nearly as possible now as I fear difficulty in getting enough hands after the first Jan." Planters sighed with relief upon completing one crop, but now came the task of negotiating with workers before starting the next.[2]

Freedmen customarily took to the road early in the year, before they had accumulated back wages. The practice of holding half wages in reserve until year's end restricted mobility during the crop season, but it provided no guarantee. If unhappy enough, freedmen could make every planter's worst nightmare come true by leaving in midseason, even if doing so meant forfeiting half their earnings. Threatening to depart in midseason, however, involved some risk. Seeking work elsewhere after the season's start was not necessarily an attractive alternative, especially for freedmen with families. If they failed to find a new employer, they might not be permitted to return to their previous jobs. Most planters did not let matters go so far. A little "grumbling" ordinarily sufficed for them to understand that something was wrong. Planters hardly catered to their workers' whims, but when freedmen complained about wages, working conditions, or other matters, planters had to listen lest they risk losing them. Unsatisfied freedmen might not leave immediately, but come January they would seek an employer more ready to oblige them.[3]

Although planters could not keep freedmen who were determined to go, they could not afford to ignore those who expressed particular grievances. In early 1874, for instance, freedmen on a Gay plantation threatened to leave because the new manager had not yet arrived. Not knowing under whose direction they were to work, they hesitated committing themselves. "The negroes there were always of a move about disposition," Gay's son Andrew explained, "and they are now very much unsettled and a great many of them talking of leaving the place." Andrew Gay convinced them to stay, but he believed the matter could have been avoided

2. R. Daigre to EJG, Dec. 26, 1871, L. L. Butler to EJG, Feb. 10, 1872, and J. W. Austin to EJG, Dec. 25, 1876, EJGP. See also J. T. Nolan to EJG, Jan. 31, 1869, and B. Deblieux to EJG, Oct. 30, 1877, ibid.

3. On withholding wages and its affect on mobility in the postwar South, see Jaynes, *Branches without Roots*, 224–49.

had the manager arrived on time. "I do not think there would have been half the trouble," he concluded, "and they would have been much better satisfied as they would like to see who is going to manage them."[4]

No issue, it seemed, was too trivial to warrant attention. Plantation manager Roman Daigre advised Edward Gay in early 1869 to provide freedmen with high-quality pork. "[T]he last lot you sent," Daigre noted, gave "very poor satisfaction to the hands, they grumbled very much, and as it is yet the first of the year, and would take very little to make them leave, espeacially so many are offering inducement, I think it would be well for us to give them good meat." Edward Gay Jr. faced the potentially disastrous consequences of his workers' dissatisfaction over a similar matter in early April 1872. One Sunday morning only half the freedmen responded to the plantation bell signaling weekly distribution of rations, "and they in no good humor," Gay noted, "and said the rest were going to leave that they couldn't stand my rules." The freedmen objected to Gay's practice of charging them for rations on nonworking days. Although he promised to "fix things to suit them," the workers were about to carry through with their threatened departure when Gay, with no choice, agreed to reduce the cost of rations and to discontinue charging for them on Saturdays. This compromise, he concluded, "seems to be satisfactory."[5]

Planters and managers recognized that the best way to secure reliable workers was to hire men with families. While it stands to reason that employers concerned about the stability of their work forces would prefer men with dependents over unattached bachelors, who could leave on a moment's notice, the challenges were finding such workers and then keeping them content. When Edward Gay's business partner Samuel Cranwill informed Gay of a wage dispute on one of Gay's estates in March 1872, he made sure to note that the workers "are good men and have been on the place, some of them with families, for two years." Cranwill thought it better to settle the matter quickly than to risk losing workers who had demonstrated their reliability. Similarly, in June 1877 David Weeks's plantation manager advised making improvements to the workers' cabins in order to attract "good reliable negro labor in the future." Because freedmen were demanding better accommodations and neighboring planters were providing them, he added, following suit "will enable me to get good reliable married men for laborers to locate here, who will stay here for years."[6]

4. A. H. Gay to EJG, Jan. 7, 1874, EJGP.

5. R. Daigre to EJG, Feb. 16, 1869, and EJG Jr. to EJG, Apr. 2, 1872, EJGP. See also T. Garrett to EJG, Feb. 21, 1869, and W. F. J. Davis to EJG, May 6, 1869, ibid.

6. S. Cranwill to EJG, March 11, 1872, EJGP; [Unsigned] to [Weeks], June 17, 1877, Weeks Papers, LSU.

In trying to secure freedmen's services within the free-labor market, some planters continued to exhibit a visceral aversion to engaging them as equals. Most, however, worried about more rational, pragmatic considerations. In addition to seeking married workers, whom they thought less likely to leave, planters also concerned themselves with hiring a quality labor force. Although planting, cultivating, and harvesting sugarcane were highly regimented, repetitive tasks that did not require a great deal of skill, not all freedmen were good cane workers. Planters who employed reliable workers were wary of losing them. The demands of sugar production also influenced planters' thinking: if they did not secure sufficient labor by late January, they could fall seriously behind in planting cane. This vulnerability translated into bargaining power for freedmen. Race was never far from planters' minds, but their critique of free labor increasingly rested on what they saw as labor's excessive mobility, which they believed gave freedmen undue leverage, rather than on their having to negotiate with them as equals.

While planters might have been expected to exaggerate their workers' moving about, their complaints were not just self-serving bombast. The records of Uncle Sam plantation in St. James Parish during the late 1860s and 1870s, for example, demonstrate moderate but consistent annual turnover among regular, or monthly, workers in the sugar region. They also document a substantial pool of what was sometimes referred to as "floating" labor. This fluid, mobile work force paralleled the North's industrial working class that so worried Gilded Age America's propertied classes. Planters found it convenient to draw upon these workers during peak seasons, but labor's mobility also compelled them to assemble a new work force each year.[7]

Between 1865 and 1878, Uncle Sam's regular labor force exhibited both steady turnover as well as a degree of stability. The percentage of regular workers who were new each year varied from a low of 11.1 percent in 1873 to a high of 52 percent in 1868, with the average for the entire period being 25.2 percent (table 16). Even as Uncle Sam underwent consistent turnover, however, a core group of a dozen 1865 freedmen were still on the plantation in 1878. Most of these workers were undoubtedly plowmen, around whom planters assembled their operations and who

---

7. This analysis of labor turnover and mobility is based upon monthly payrolls from the Uncle Sam Plantation Papers, LSU. Uncle Sam was a representative sugar plantation before the Civil War, with more than a hundred slaves and about a thousand improved acres. Menn, *Large Slaveholders of Louisiana,* 353–4. Uncle Sam has left the most complete run of payrolls with which to view labor mobility. Payrolls usually included a laborer's name, rate of wages, and amount of money earned, paid, and due. Poor handwriting and irregular and idiosyncratic spelling made identifying individuals difficult; also, there was no way of accounting for mortality. Figures presented here reveal general trends, not precise calculations.

TABLE 16

Annual Turnover among Regular Labor Force: Uncle Sam Plantation, 1865–1878

YEAR	# of Workers	# (and %) from Previous Year	# (and %) New
1865	42	—	—
1866	49	39 (79.6)	10 (20.4)
1867	40	34 (85.0)	6 (15.0)
1868	50	24 (48.0)	26 (52.0)
1869	46	38 (82.6)	8 (17.4)
1870	39	29 (74.4)	10 (25.6)
1871	41	30 (73.2)	11 (26.8)
1872	38	30 (79.0)	8 (21.0)
1873	36	32 (88.9)	4 (11.1)
1874	33	27 (81.8)	6 (18.2)
1875	43	27 (62.8)	16 (37.2)
1876	42	35 (83.3)	7 (16.7)
1877	42	35 (83.3)	7 (16.7)
1878	54	27 (50.0)	27 (50.0)

Source: Monthly Payrolls, 1865–1878, Uncle Sam Plantation Papers, LSU.

came to constitute the backbone of the plantation's labor force. Like all sugar plantations under free labor, Uncle Sam had a revolving door through which workers came and went from one year to the next, but it was also home to a number of freedmen who gave the labor force a measure of continuity and stability.[8]

At the same time, the Uncle Sam records indicate that a large number of former slaves in the sugar region eschewed regular plantation employment during the year but came onto plantations when demand for their labor was at a premium. During the 1865–1878 period, the number of workers employed for the rolling season on Uncle Sam usually doubled and sometimes even tripled the number of regular workers (table 17). Many of these temporary workers were family members of regular workers, usually wives and children, but they also included a large number of freedmen who appeared on the plantation for the harvest and then left. Each year, a significant proportion of the additional workers hired for the rolling season—usually well over 50 percent—were new to the plantation (table 18).

Although freedmen in the sugar region exercised a degree of mobility that affirmed planters' perceptions, their moving about was not unique. Freedmen throughout the postwar South were highly mobile. Nonetheless, different components of the sugar region's labor force experienced varying degrees of movement. The labor force included regular workers, mostly men with families, who labored on the plantation for the entire crop season; they exercised some mobility

8. On plowmen, see Reidy, "Mules and Men and Machines," 185, 191.

TABLE 17

Increase from Regular to Rolling Season Labor Force: Uncle Sam Plantation, 1866–1878

YEAR	Regular Workers	Rolling Workers	% Increase
1866	49	73	49.0
1867	40	90	125.0
1868	50	78	56.0
1869	46	98	113.0
1870	39	74	89.7
1871	41	88	114.6
1872	38	101	165.8
1873	36	99	175.0
1874	33	99	200.0
1875	43	94	118.6
1876	42	189	350.0
1877	42	205	388.1
1878	54	143	164.8

Source: Monthly Payrolls, 1866–1878, Uncle Sam Plantation Papers, LSU.

TABLE 18

Annual Turnover among Rolling Season Labor Force: Uncle Sam Plantation, 1866–1878

YEAR	# of Extra Workers	# (and %) from Previous Year	# (and %) New
1866	26	—	—
1867	52	14 (26.9)	38 (73.1)
1868	39	13 (33.3)	26 (66.7)
1869	56	17 (30.4)	39 (69.6)
1870	44	23 (52.3)	21 (47.7)
1871	51	19 (55.5)	32 (62.7)
1872	68	23 (33.8)	45 (66.2)
1873	68	38 (55.9)	30 (44.1)
1874	73	35 (47.9)	38 (52.1)
1875	58	32 (55.2)	26 (44.8)
1876	152	28 (18.4)	124 (81.6)
1877	174	64 (36.8)	110 (63.2)
1878	100	53 (53.0)	47 (47.0)

Source: Monthly Payrolls, 1866–1878, Uncle Sam Plantation Papers, LSU.

but also sometimes remained for several years. It also included supplemental workers, mostly dependents of regular workers, who resided on the plantation but worked only at peak seasons and whose mobility matched that of their husbands and fathers. Finally, it included a group of highly mobile workers who avoided regular plantation labor for most of the year but were attracted by high wages paid during the rolling season. These laborers—who tended to be young, single men with no familial obligations—rarely worked on the same plantation for more than one harvest. It is difficult to know why some freedmen left while others stayed from year to year. Leaving probably reflected unhappiness, but staying did not necessarily imply contentment. What the freedmen's remaining did connote, however, was choice and not legal compulsion.[9]

However distasteful they may have found it, employers had no choice but to become accustomed to their workers' freedom to come and go. "Most of my single men have gone away," reported one manager soon after completing his 1873 harvest. Most undoubtedly would have preferred workers who were, as a labor recruiter put it, "not to young, but good settled men," but few could afford that luxury, especially during rolling season. "We do not hear very serious complaints about the supply of labor; but from the readiness with which parties seeking work are employed we infer that there is still room for a much heavier number of hands," observed an Assumption Parish newspaper editor as the 1880 harvest approached. "All the chronic loafers and idlers, with which our small towns and villages are infested, tempted by high rolling wages, begin to grow perceptibly thinner. These fellows will accumulate in a prosperous two-month rolling sufficient means to support them, after their style of living, until next rolling."[10]

In complaining about "chronic loafers and idlers," the editor not only revealed his own racial and class biases but also identified an important feature of the sugar region's new labor system. Although many freedmen abandoned the plantations and "infested" southern Louisiana's towns and villages after emancipation, a significant number remained within the orbit of the plantation system although they were not employed as regular field hands. Instead, they occupied the plantation economy's interstices by engaging in various alternatives to monthly wage labor.

9. The most comprehensive work on mobility in the postwar South is William Cohen, *At Freedom's Edge: Black Mobility and the Southern White Quest for Racial Control, 1861–1915* (Baton Rouge, 1991). See also Pete Daniel, *The Shadow of Slavery: Peonage in the South, 1901–1969* (Urbana, Ill., 1972); Jacqueline Jones, *The Dispossessed: America's Underclasses from the Civil War to the Present* (New York, 1992), chap. 4; Mandle, *Roots of Black Poverty*; Daniel A. Novak, *The Wheel of Servitude: Black Forced Labor after Slavery* (Lexington, Ky., 1978); Ransom and Sutch, *One Kind of Freedom*, chap. 8; Wayne, *Reshaping Plantation Society*, 110–49, 208–9; and Wiener, *Social Origins*. For a reassessment of the question of labor mobility, see Gavin Wright, "Postbellum Southern Labor Markets," in *Quantity & Quiddity: Essays in U.S. Economic History*, ed. Peter Kilby (Middletown, Conn., 1987), 98–134. The migration to Kansas of 1879–1880 had little impact in the sugar region. See Nell Irvin Painter, *Exodusters: Black Migration to Kansas after Reconstruction* (New York, 1976), esp. chaps. 13–5, and Robert G. Athearn, *In Search of Canaan: Black Migration to Kansas, 1879–80* (Lawrence, Kans., 1978).

10. R. Daigre to EJG, Jan. 1, 1874, and C. C. Neally to R. Daigre, Sept. 15, 1873, EJGP; *Napoleonville Pioneer of Assumption*, Oct. 16, 1880. On the importance of temporary workers during the rolling season in the twentieth century, see Reidy, "Mules and Men and Machines," 195.

In doing so, they enjoyed wage labor's benefits while escaping the regimentation of plantation employment.

The most common arrangement outside regular plantation work was task labor, or, as it became known, "jobbing." Jobbers performed ancillary chores essential to sugar plantation operations: maintaining ditches and roads, repairing levees, and especially chopping wood. Hundreds of freedmen listed their occupation as "wood chopper" in the 1870 federal census. Since these were strenuous tasks, they attracted young, strong, single men, who moved from place to place earning cash wages up front. Planters found it easier to hire jobbers than to induce their regular hands to perform this work. Freedmen sometimes planted cane and then jobbed until rolling season. In 1876, for instance, W. W. Pugh hired freedmen to plant cane for monthly wages "& afterward to ditch by task."[11]

Because planters could never have enough wood, they always needed choppers. Individuals hired themselves out, or squads contracted with labor recruiters who provided choppers to planters. Recruiting wood choppers, however, created as many problems as it solved: choppers often arrived late and seldom in the numbers planters had requested; they had often been rounded up in New Orleans and were unreliable. Choppers themselves were often disappointed when a broker's promises of lucrative wages proved unfounded. Consequently, planters patronized brokers as a last resort, preferring instead to hire choppers themselves, but demand for their services made hiring them troublesome, especially during summer. "We seem to have some difficulty in getting wood choppers," David Barrow remarked in 1876. "Have had to agree to pay every two weeks."[12]

Hiring jobbers satisfied the short-term needs of individual planters, but many considered it detrimental to their collective, long-term interests. One planter complained in 1877 that "this very jobbing in wood has tended more to demoralize labor than any other one thing." Jobbers, he insisted, "should be under some obligation to remain [on plantations] the whole year." A journalist noted employers' difficulties hiring labor because of jobbing. "[T]he negroes everywhere seem to avoid the field as much as possible, and find lucrative employment as wood choppers, ditchers and general jobbers," he contended, "holding themselves in readiness for the sugar-making season, with the extra high wages to be obtained in that period." So bad had the problem become that St. Mary planters in 1878

---

11. Jan. 10, 1876, W. W. Pugh Diary, Pugh Papers, UT. See also Whittlesey to [Warmoth], July 5, 1878, Warmoth Papers, SHC; 43rd Cong., 2nd Sess., HR 101, pt. 2, p. 256; 44th Cong., 2nd Sess., HMD 34, pt. 5, p. 352; *Plaquemine Iberville South,* Feb. 3, 1877; *NILSB,* Feb. 26, 1880; A. Bouchereau, *Statement . . . 1880–81,* xxv.

12. D. Barrow to EJG, Aug. 15, 1876, EJGP. See also contract between EJG and C. H. LaPierre, July 27, 1870, and A. H. Gay to EJG, Aug. 5, 1873, ibid.

tried dictating, though unsuccessfully, that jobbers agree "to go to the field whenever the crop requires it and to help in sugar making."[13]

Such criticism pointed to planters' failure to restrict jobbing. "So long as planters employ colored men to cut wood and ditch by the job, dissatisfaction and shirking will be found among their monthly hands," one planter maintained in 1878. "These jobbers, who idle away much of their time, do more harm than good on any plantation where employed." Lafourche district planter Thomas Harang echoed these sentiments in late 1879. "The [freedman] becomes more and more tired of field work. He wants to be independent, and more than all, he wants to see his money at the end of his day's work. He is always ready to spend it as fast as he can get it, sometimes faster, and foolishly," Harang insisted. "He wants to go to meeting; to political gatherings; to the nearest store or coffee-house. He does not wish to be hindered, bothered and brought into the traces by that regular and, to him, dismal sound the plantation bell or horn." Thus, Harang concluded, "the negro will chop wood, cut ditches and canals; he will undertake any job work; he will do anything which may require no strain on his brains, and no regular hours of work from sun to sun." It appears not to have occurred to Harang and other critics of jobbing that digging ditches and chopping wood in the heat and humidity of a south Louisiana summer were hardly enviable tasks. Nonetheless, Harang's vituperation affirmed jobbing's pervasiveness as well as planters' increasing frustration over their inability to do anything about it.[14]

In addition to jobbing, many freedmen hired themselves out on a daily or monthly basis. The practice of signing annual contracts had ended by the early 1870s, as planters and freedmen entered into less formal agreements. Instead of pledging to work on a plantation for an entire year, some freedmen lived on or near it and worked by the week or month, as the planter needed. This practice was common in January, when planters prepared for planting while freedmen enjoyed the year-end holiday. "I find that I will have to hire hands by the day to plant my cane," one manager noted in early 1870. "I have a few hands by the month and have the promise today of some more, but cannot depend on them." Employers also hired daily laborers in midseason, although doing so was less desirable. Not only were temporary workers unreliable, since they could leave, but they also had to be paid in full. Although most employers frowned upon hiring on a daily or monthly basis, the practice constituted something of a compromise. Freedmen could work for a time on a plantation before deciding whether they would remain; planters could commence spring planting while getting a sense of the quality of

13. *NILSB*, Oct. 4, July 26, 1877; *DP*, Dec. 21, 1877.

14. *NILSB*, Sept. 12, 1878; *Thibodaux Sentinel*, Dec. 27, 1879.

their labor force. Planters preferred regular hands, but the choice was not exclusively theirs.[15]

The freedmen's desire to work on a daily basis, combined with the plantation's spatial geography and the fact that many estates remained undercultivated into the 1870s, led to a form of squatting. Sugar plantations generally "fronted" waterways, and behind them stretched considerable swampland or unimproved acreage. Planters permitted freedmen to reside on these lands, in return for which squatters drained, cleared, and improved them. Squatters also provided additional labor. "Some planters like to have these settlements of negroes on the rear of their plantations," one observer noted, "because they are always convenient when extra hands are needed." Since squatting also removed many freedmen from the labor force, he was quick to add, "allow[ing] negroes to squat about is a ruinous practice, which demoralizes all other laborers, and eventually injures even those who are temporarily benefitted by it." Freedmen did not see squatting as ruinous, however, since it enabled them to escape regular plantation labor while also affording them a way to earn extra income. By the early 1870s, hundreds of freedmen were said to be squatting in Terrebonne Parish, and similar arrangements were common throughout the region. With so many freedmen squatting, a journalist complained, "it is almost impossible to get one of them to work, unless it is by the job, and that at prices exceeding any paid before."[16]

While some planters saw squatters as a convenience, others considered them a nuisance. An 1877 episode in Lafourche Parish involving three adjoining plantations—the Nelson estate that Edward J. Gay had recently acquired, that of his neighbor George Taylor, and a third estate—offers a case in point. Several cabins located in a wooded area at the rear of Gay's place were occupied, Taylor informed Gay, by "non-working negroes among whom were some noted as thieves." Two cabins in particular were "especially favorably situated for carrying on thieving & rascality between the three plantations." Taylor urged Gay to clear out this chronic trouble spot. "If you continue to cultivate the Nelson place I trust you will break this whole nest up," Taylor entreated, "at least so far as to allow no one to occupy one of these cabins unless in your constant employ." Evidently speaking from experience, Taylor predicted "that your first applicants for the *nest* of these hands will be the very ones who will be a nuisance to the adjoining plantations."

15. W. P. McMillan to EJG, Feb. 7, 1870, EJGP. See also P. O. Daigre to EJG, Mar. 13, 1869, T. Garrett to EJG, Jan. 22, 1872, and J. O. Robichaux to EJG, July 6, 1876, ibid.; R. C. Martin Jr. to R. C. Martin, July 15, 1870, Martin-Pugh Collection, NSU; Feb. 20, 1873, Daybook 1873–1877, Frederick D. Robertson Account Books, LSU.

16. *NILSB*, Aug. 10, 1871; *Franklin Planters' Banner*, June 23, 1869. See also A. H. Gay to EJG, Jan. 7, 1874, EJGP; L. Bouchereau, *Statement . . . 1869–70*, x; 45th Cong., 1st Sess., HMD 5, pp. 216–7.

Squatters were a source of labor for planters on whose places they resided, but their neighbors viewed them differently.[17]

If jobbing, day labor, and squatting reflected a desire among certain freedmen to avoid monthly wage labor, this desire also manifested itself in renewed interest in sharecropping and tenancy during the early 1870s. After the war, planters and freedmen had experimented with various share-wage arrangements, but unlike the situation in the cotton South, these did not evolve into sharecropping. Nonetheless, with more freedmen pushing for access to land, many planters felt they had no choice but to accede to their wishes. "I cannot tell how many of the old Hands will contract for next year," plantation manager Thomas Garrett informed Edward Gay in late 1871. Observing a disposition among freedmen to rent land, Garrett noted that "quite a number of them will not work for wages next year." Andrew Gay likewise complained in early 1874 of being short of labor, since several of his workers had "moved down below on vacant lands to work on shares or are renting land." Although wage labor predominated in the postwar sugar region, planters still had to contend with the freedmen's yearning for land.[18]

Not all planters opposed sharecropping; some even advocated it. Consequently, a public debate over sharecropping's merits took place during the early 1870s, involving not only planters but also merchants, journalists, and other interested parties. Proponents argued that sharecropping released employers from making monthly cash payments, divided risk between planter and cropper, and provided croppers an incentive by giving them an interest in the crop. They also criticized planters' insistence on the indivisibility of field and mill operations as an anachronistic legacy of slavery that slowed the industry's development. Detractors countered that sharecropping might work with white croppers but not with freedmen, who they insisted did not possess the requisite internal motivation. Black sharecroppers, one critic typically noted, "neglect and abuse the mules, destroy the buildings, burn the fencing, and neglect their crops at critical periods, and frequently refuse to help save crops in which they have half interests." Many planters also resented unsolicited advice on how to run their affairs, especially when it came from those who did not have to put their money where their mouths were.

---

17. G. C. Taylor to EJG, Jan. 12, 1877, EJGP.

18. T. Garrett to EJG, Dec. 25, 1871, and A. H. Gay to EJG, Jan. 7, 1874, EJGP. See also R. Daigre to EJG, Jan. 4, 1869, C. H. Dickinson to EJG, Feb. 3, 1869, R. Daigre to EJG, Jan. 3, 1870, and S. Cranwill to EJG, Dec. 16, 1871, ibid. There are important distinctions between share-wage systems, sharecropping, and tenancy. For the sake of convenience, however, and unless otherwise indicated, all arrangements in which planters and freedmen divided the crop as an alternative to monthly wages will be referred to as sharecropping. On this point, see Woodman, "Post–Civil War Southern Agriculture and the Law."

"Planters . . . ought to be allowed to attend to their own business," blustered one who had heard enough about sharecropping.[19]

Nonetheless, planters and freedmen explored a wide array of sharecropping and tenancy agreements in addressing sugar production's many complications. J. M. Howell's 1874 arrangement may be seen as representative. Howell provided plant cane to new tenants, charging for half of it. (The previous year's tenants already had theirs.) Tenants furnished their own teams and implements, and they and Howell shared responsibility for maintaining the plantation's infrastructure. Howell required tenants to furnish at least ten arpents of cane to grind. They grew as much corn as they wished, giving Howell a third, but they were also required to plant peas as fertilizer. Howell and the tenants divided the finished sugar equally, but in cases where Howell supplied seed cane he kept all the molasses, whereas tenants who furnished their own seed cane kept half of it. Howell incurred any extra expense harvesting the crop, and he assumed responsibility for marketing it. If a tenant remained the next year, the contract was automatically renewed; but if a tenant decided to leave, Howell paid for half or all seed cane left behind, depending upon whether the tenant had originally supplied seed cane. Howell retained the right to subsequent crops yielded by a single planting. As this situation demonstrates, working a sugar plantation on a sharecropping or tenancy basis was not impossible, but it posed many complex problems that planters preferred to avoid.[20]

The vast majority of planters, it seems, wished to skirt sharecropping's complications. For instance, almost all working plantations along Bayou Black in Terrebonne Parish and Bayous Salé and Cypremort in St. Mary Parish employed monthly wage labor in 1871. Only three of twenty-four Bayou Black estates did not operate on a wage-labor basis, while twenty-seven of thirty-three plantations along Bayous Salé and Cypremort employed wage labor. Moreover, plantations worked on shares cultivated on average a mere 40.2 arpents of cane and 24.7 arpents of corn and employed only 4.5 hands, whereas plantations worked by wage

19. For positive comments, see A. Ferry to S. Cranwill, July 24, 1871, and Ferry to EJG, May 4, 1874, EJGP; *DP,* Jan. 14, June 5, 1872; *NILSB,* July 17, 1873, Jan. 22, Mar. 5, Dec. 24, 1874; *Thibodaux Sentinel,* Jan. 25, Mar.–Apr. 1873; L. Bouchereau, *Statement . . . 1871–72,* xii, and *1873–74,* x–xi; and King, *Great South,* 83–4. For negative opinions, see *DP,* Dec. 14, 1870, and Aug. 13, 1873 (quotations). See also *NILSB,* Apr. 21, 1871, Feb. 20, June 19, 1873.

20. J. M. Howell to AFP, Sept. 4, 1874, Pugh Papers, UT. An arpent was an old French unit of land area commonly used in Louisiana; it equaled about .85 acre. For other examples of sharecropping arrangements, see V. P. N. Winder to EJG & Co., Sept. 20, 1871, C. D. Erwin to EJG & Co., Oct. 22, 1872, S. Cranwill to EJG, Dec. 6, 1873, and G. C. Taylor to EJG, Feb. 6, 1874, EJGP; R. C. Martin to R. C. Martin Jr. Oct. 27, 1873, and R. C. Martin to Messrs. Foley, Conger & Co., May 30, 1873, Martin-Pugh Collection, NSU; W. B. Flower to T. Pugh, Feb. 24, 1874, W. W. Pugh Papers, LSU; *Franklin Planters' Banner,* Dec. 7, 1870; *NILSB,* Aug. 24, 1871.

labor cultivated on average almost 150 arpents of cane and 100 arpents of corn and employed nearly 20 hands. Two years later, few plantations in these areas were worked on shares. Although many freedmen found ways to elude monthly wage labor during the 1870s, sharecropping was not one of them.[21]

The ability of so many freedmen to avoid regular plantation employment, combined with labor's geographic mobility, intensified competition among planters for labor. Mobility and competition reinforced each other, creating a vicious circle that planters could not break. As freedmen moved about, planters tried to outbid one another for their services, prompting freedmen, in turn, to seek better situations. Leading a migratory lifestyle may not have been desirable, but freedmen could hardly resist the benefits of a functioning labor market. Planters, individually and collectively, reacted to the market in contradictory ways. Some continued to accommodate themselves to it, though they never ceased protesting what they saw as labor's unfair advantage. Others undertook deliberate steps at intervention in order to correct these supposed inequities. In either case, planters believed the free-labor system as it had evolved was inadequate to the demands of sugar production.

Planters' complaints about the labor market during the 1870s took on the sound of cant: labor supply was inadequate, freedmen did not work diligently, high wages "demoralized" labor, and workers exercised too much mobility. Labor, in short, kept capital subordinate to its whims, rendering planters helpless without state regulation. Competition among employers for labor was not indicative of a functioning market, according to most planters, but was instead "the great trouble," as one noted. "There are too few laborers for the demand, and planters have had to submit to injustice."[22]

Such injustice as planters suffered was largely of their own making. By outbidding one another, and by enticing one another's workers, planters placed themselves, one admonished his colleagues, "at the mercy and in the power of their agricultural servants." Freedmen performed their work indifferently, he added, knowing that if dismissed they would be "welcomed with eager arms by the first planter they will apply to for employment." A journalist in St. Mary Parish insisted in 1880 that freedmen were becoming "more and more unmanageable" and were "bringing the planter to their way of thinking, in regard to how they should work." There was no telling "at what moment there will be a serious move on their

21. *NILSB*, Apr. 27, July 20, 1871, and July–Sept. 1873.

22. 43rd Cong., 2nd Sess., HR 261, pt. 3, pp. 626–7. For a summary of these views, see *De Bow's Review* 6–7 (January 1869): 85–6. Louis Ferleger notes that planters sounded these complaints into the twentieth century. "The Problem of 'Labor' in the Post-Reconstruction Louisiana Sugar Industry," *AH* 72 (spring 1998): 140–58.

part, to compel the planter to still further comply with any request they may make." Freedmen may not have recognized the scenario planters depicted, but such protests, if not unbiased, revealed an important truth: planters were compelled to engage workers through the labor market.[23]

No matter how distasteful planters and managers found competing with one another for workers, they eagerly sought them near and far, thus demonstrating their halting yet persistent adjustment to free labor. A Gay plantation manager, C. M. Gillis, told of one Bayou Lafourche freedman who expressed a desire to move to Iberville Parish. "I think it would be a good idea to let him come up here," Gillis advised Gay, "as it would be a kind of foundation for the other Lafourche hands to come here in case you should need them this year, or in the future." Planters were fully aware that enticing workers exacerbated the "labor problem" and was inimical to their long-term interests, but they also realized that if they wanted labor they had little choice. Nonetheless, enticement was a breach of etiquette that produced bitterness. William J. Minor fumed that a neighbor who hired away several workers in 1869 was "guilty of a dirty low lived trick." Louis Bouchereau likewise observed that competition among planters for labor bred hostility, which "precludes the exchange of social courtesy and neighborly kindness."[24]

Neither social courtesy nor neighborly kindness was much in evidence when two of Louisiana's most influential sugar planters, John Burnside and Edward J. Gay, vied in early 1875 for some of the same workers. After several of Burnside's agents were found to be enticing freedmen employed by Gay, Edward Gay Jr. paid Burnside a visit. "I have just called on Mr. Burnside," Gay informed his father, and "he declares his astonishment that his agents are working on your hands as he says it has been a special instruction . . . that no hands should be got from your place." Burnside promised to put a halt to these actions, but he declined to dismiss those freedmen who had been enticed away from Gay, evidently needing their services too badly to make amends.[25]

Especially rankling to planters accustomed to controlling every aspect of plantation life was the influence of others' practices on their work forces, as the labor market steadily corroded the fragile interdependence among them. Planters in St. Mary Parish, for example, agreed in early 1878 to pay monthly wages of $15 plus rations, withholding only one-third. Soon, however, some were offering better

23. *NILSB*, Aug. 10, 1871, July 15, 1880. See also letters from "S. M.," Oct. 4, 1877, and "Spectator," June 24, 1880, ibid.; and C. L. Marquette, ed., "Letters of a Yankee Sugar Planter," *JSH* 6 (November 1940): 535.

24. C. M. Gillis to EJG, May 20, 1874, EJGP; June 18, 1869, Plant. Diary 37, WJMP; L. Bouchereau, *Statement . . . 1869–70*, ix–x. See also R. Daigre to EJG, Jan. 15, 1871, EJGP.

25. EJG Jr. to EJG, Jan. 19, 1875, EJGP.

wages and even paying in full monthly, prompting one planter to complain that everyone else would be forced to follow suit or risk not having sufficient labor. Was it right for a few individuals, he asked, to ignore the "expressed wish of a majority of those engaged in agriculture" by raising wages "to such a figure as will place it out of the means of the great majority to hire labor at all?" This was not a mere rhetorical question but spoke directly to planters' dilemma under the new order. Slaveholders' individualism, though strong, had always been tempered by class solidarity, which itself was never threatened by competition for labor. Now the need to secure workers undermined planters' reliance on one another.[26]

Such divisions as the labor market spawned among planters did not preclude them from trying to unite in confronting the "labor problem." Throughout the 1870s, planters repeatedly urged unity of action as the only way to reestablish labor control. Since these efforts were designed as much to regulate each other's actions as to present a united front against labor, they quickly fell apart. Each call to organize attested to the failure of previous attempts. Responding to the economic depression that began in 1873, planters achieved temporary unity in driving down wages for 1874, but this consensus was short-lived. St. Mary planters met to frame a labor policy for 1875, agreeing to pay $13 per month plus rations. While pledging not to entice freedmen already under contract within the parish, they tellingly added that this provision did not include workers "coming from another parish or any great distance." Planters wanted to prevent competition among neighbors while preserving the right to hire workers from elsewhere. Even the Louisiana Sugar Planters Association, formed in 1877, did not formulate a labor policy to which planters had to subscribe. By competing for one another's workers even as they deplored the practice, planters revealed the gap between what they wanted and what they could achieve.[27]

Whereas planters were unable to regulate their side of the market's "great law of demand and supply," they attempted to alter the supply by recruiting workers from outside the sugar region. In doing so, they hoped to increase the labor pool and force workers to compete for jobs, transforming a seller's into a buyer's market. "Now, the only competition we have is between planters bidding for labor," one noted in 1877. Although planters' attempts to increase the labor supply might be seen as interfering with the market's "natural" workings, such efforts also connoted acceptance of the principle of supply and demand upon which the labor market rested. The planters' problem was not that a market existed at all but that

---

26. Letter from "Brutus," *NILSB*, Feb. 14, 1878. For a similar complaint, see Apr. 5, 1877, ibid.

27. On calls for planter unity, see *Franklin Planters' Banner*, Feb. 13, June 23, 1869, and Nov. 23, 1870; *DP*, Dec. 28, 1874. The LSPA minute books for the late 1870s and early 1880s are virtually silent about labor. Minute Books, Louisiana Sugar Planters Association Papers, LSU.

it was skewed in labor's favor. Increasing the supply would return the market to its normal condition, planters believed, but they never clearly defined their views of a normal labor market. They simply interpreted their difficulties hiring workers as prima facie evidence that the labor market was broken and must be fixed.[28]

One way planters tried repairing the labor market during the late 1860s and early 1870s involved recruiting freedmen from Virginia and the Carolinas. Perhaps recalling how the slave trade had transplanted thousands of slaves from the Southeast to the Old Southwest, planters looked again to this source of labor. Most knew better than to believe that these freedmen would be more tractable than their own former slaves. Increasing the labor supply, they reasoned, would diminish the freedmen's bargaining power. Planters at first hired their own agents to induce freedmen to come to Louisiana, but they soon contracted with independent labor recruiters, giving rise to a brokerage trade in which planters customarily paid all moving expenses plus a commission fee.[29]

Soon, planters and others expressed discontent with labor recruiters as well as with the workers they recruited. "Very little dependence can be placed in men engaged in such traffic," noted one New Orleans merchant. "Some of my last Va. hands are very much dissatisfied," reported Thomas Garrett, "no cause but they are too Lazy to work." Louis Bouchereau likewise contended that eastern laborers became demoralized when they "got within the influence of a dollar a day." Insisting that former slaves from the east were just as undependable as those from Louisiana, planters resolved that bringing more into the region compounded rather than settled their problems. "[T]he sooner the planter quits paying out money for the importation of such unreliable hands," observed one journalist, "the better it will be for him and the community." Nor did it go unnoticed that planters were also importing Republican votes. By 1872, the movement to recruit freedmen from the East was dead.[30]

Equally futile was an effort to replace freedmen with Chinese immigrants. During the early 1870s, John Burnside, Edward J. Gay, and others imported several hundred Chinese workers, either through independent labor recruiters or by sending their own agents to California and even to China. Believing that Chinese

28. *NILSB*, Apr. 5, 1877.

29. On securing labor from the eastern seaboard states, see E. Hall & Co. to Miltenberger & Pollack, Oct. 22, 1869, Moore Papers, LSU; S. Cranwill to EJG, Oct. 11, 1870, EJG & Co. to L. L. Butler, Sept. 2, 1870, T. Garrett to EJG, Feb. 14, 1870, Jan. 8, 1872, EJGP; J. Selby to C. Mathews, June 4, 1872, Mathews Papers, LSU; *Franklin Planters' Banner*, Feb. 9, 1870. On planters' dealings with independent recruiters, see T. A. Lyon to T. O. Moore, Sept. 11, 1869, Moore Papers, LSU; [S. Cranwill] to EJG, Dec. 14, 1869, EJGP.

30. A. Miltenberger to T. O. Moore, Aug. 28, 1869, Moore Papers, LSU; T. Garrett to EJG, May 28, 1871, EJGP; L. Bouchereau, *Statement . . . 1870–71*, xviii–xx; *DP*, June 16, 1871.

immigrants would be more controllable than freedmen, planters at first roundly praised them. Competition for their services intensified, however, until most planters became convinced that securing Chinese immigrants was more trouble than it was worth. Nor were the Chinese more amenable to working in a slavelike manner than had been freedmen, and they resisted planters' efforts to lower wages and impose discipline. They eventually left the plantations for New Orleans or southern Louisiana's towns. By 1873, planters' dreams of replacing freedmen with Chinese workers also lay in shambles.[31]

Drawing upon an idea that enjoyed public support throughout the postwar South, planters encouraged European immigration into the sugar region. The Louisiana legislature created a state bureau of immigration as early as 1866, and private ventures rode the wave of New South boosterism in the years following. The Louisiana Immigration Company, for instance, organized in 1871, was underwritten by several prominent planters. Edward J. Gay contracted with a number of Scandinavian immigrants in 1870 and 1871. Planters also sought Germans. "A plantation with fifty Germans would give less trouble than twenty negroes," remarked one planter. Another, however, maintained that while Germans were indeed excellent workers, "like all others, [they] are apt to break their contracts and go to others who offered higher wages." At various times during the 1870s and 1880s, individual planters also employed Dutch, Irish, Spanish, Portuguese, and even black convict labor. Starting in the 1880s, they brought in thousands of Italian workers in a venture that enjoyed only slightly better success than had their previous ones.[32]

For the remainder of the century, planters continued to harbor the notion that outside immigration would solve their labor problem. Their failed search for al-

31. The EJGP are replete with discussions of Chinese labor during the early 1870s. The experience of the Chinese in the sugar region is discussed in Lucy M. Cohen, *Chinese in the Post–Civil War South: A People without a History* (Baton Rouge, 1984), 95–101, 107–32. On labor immigration in the postwar South in general, see Eric Foner, *Nothing but Freedom: Emancipation and Its Legacy* (Baton Rouge, 1983), 46–9.

32. On the Louisiana Immigration Company, see *Thibodaux Sentinel,* June 3, 1871. On Edward Gay's efforts to bring in Scandinavians, see [Mary Gay?] to Mother, Oct. 29, 1870, L. L. Butler to EJG, Aug. 20, 1871, and contract, Oct. 16, 1871, EJGP. On the Germans, see L. Bouchereau, *Statement . . . 1870–71,* ix, xviii–xx; *NILSB,* Nov. 24, 1870. For references to "Dutchmen," see Oct. 30, 31, 1870, Plant. Diary 37, WJMP. On Irish laborers, see Apr. 16, 1870, Frank Webb Plant. Diary, SHC. On Spanish and Portuguese workers, see T. C. Porteous to E. Bourbon, July 27, 1880, Thomas C. Porteous Letterbook, LSU. On convict labor, see W. T. Gay to EJG, Jan. 16, 1872, W. C. Murray to EJG, Sept. 11, 1877, and H. D. Hart to EJG, Sept. 29, 1877, EJGP. On Italian workers, see Jean Ann Scarpaci, *Italian Immigrants in Louisiana's Sugar Parishes: Recruitment, Labor Conditions, and Community Relations, 1880–1910* (New York, 1980), and "Immigrants in the New South: Italians in Louisiana's Sugar Parishes, 1880–1910," *Labor*

ternatives proved how dependent they were upon the labor of former slaves and their descendants—a situation that many feared boded ill for the future. "Who will cultivate the lands when the negroes who now work are dead?" wondered New Orleans factor Samuel Cranwill. This was "a serious consideration," he insisted, "and emigration to supply the required labor is not to be expected."[33]

Although he expressed a legitimate concern, Cranwill need not have worried so much. Despite planters' unrelenting search for new workers, black labor fueled sugar plantations for decades after the former slaves had passed on, just as plantation labor overshadowed black peoples' lives in the sugar region until well into the twentieth century. Nonetheless, while the freedmen's options were limited after emancipation, they hastened to exploit what choices they had—either by moving about from year to year or by working on the perimeter of the plantation economy. The ability to leave the plantation was a boon to a people who had once been deprived of that basic right, and labor mobility was a reality that all planters had to face. Planters' diverse and often contradictory responses to their workers' mobility spoke volumes of its effectiveness.

Some historians of emancipation have argued that former slaves saw more to freedom than simply the right to sell their labor for wages within the capitalist marketplace. Others have contended that planters used their formidable economic and political power to prevent a legitimate labor market from taking shape, thereby gaining control over their former slaves. In the sugar region, however, planters were far from omnipotent in dealing with freedmen. Moreover, not only did a functioning labor market exist during the 1870s, but it continued to bedevil planters in the decades following. Freedmen may not have aspired to living as transients, nor did they necessarily wish to emulate the experiences of wage workers in the industrial North. Nonetheless, they were not about to turn their backs on the advantages they derived from the labor market or on the leverage it gave them in confronting planters. Freedmen who could ascribe larger meaning to their ability to move about were likewise capable of attributing greater importance to the wages they earned for their labor.[34]

History 16 (spring 1975): 165–83. On immigration into Louisiana during and after Reconstruction, see E. Russ Williams Jr., "Louisiana's Public and Private Immigration Endeavors: 1866–1893," *LH* 15 (spring 1974): 153–73.

33. S. Cranwill to EJG, July 26, 1873, EJGP.

34. The freedmen's aversion to market relations is forcefully argued in Saville, *Work of Reconstruction.* Works that emphasize, from very different perspectives, planters' ability to forestall development of a labor market include Wiener, *Social Origins,* and Wayne, *Reshaping Plantation Society.* See also Schmidt, *Free to Work,* 166–9. Ferleger, in "Problem of 'Labor,'" argues that the sugar region's labor market persisted into the twentieth century.

Despite emancipation, most former slaves in the sugar country, men and women alike, continued to work under the watchful eyes of overseers, managers, and planters.

Historic New Orleans Collection, Acc. No. 1959.159.41

The closely organized manner in which this work gang, composed mostly of women, returns from hoeing the fields reflects the continued regimentation of sugar plantation routine many years after slavery.

Historic New Orleans Collection, Acc. No. 1974.25.26.224

The Chinese were but one of a number of ethnic peoples whose labor sugar planters hoped would supplement—or even replace—that of former slaves in the decades after emancipation.

Historic New Orleans Collection, Acc. No. 1953-73

Women cutting cane.
Louisiana State Museum, New Orleans

Men cutting cane.
Louisiana State Museum, New Orleans

Workers load cut cane onto carts on Southdown plantation in Terrebonne Parish.
Historic New Orleans Collection, Acc. No. 1974.25.13.264

Laborers at the cane shed load cane onto the carrier en route to the sugar mill.
Louisiana Collection, State Library of Louisiana, Baton Rouge

The sugar mill crushing cane.
Harper's Weekly, Vol. 31 (1887)

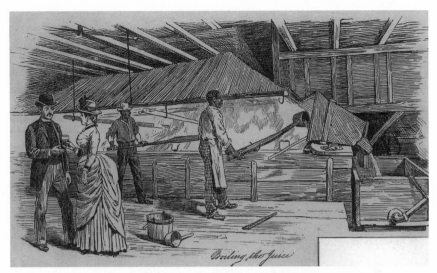

Skilled workers endure the heat of the kettle fires while boiling cane juice and converting it into sugar.

Louisiana Collection, State Library of Louisiana, Baton Rouge

The sugar house at Evan Hall plantation in Ascension Parish, one of the most technologically advanced operations of the time, in the late 1880s.

Picture Collection, Evan Hall Plantation Photographs, Mss. 1061, Louisiana and Lower Mississippi Valley Collections, LSU Libraries, Baton Rouge

Iberville Parish planter Edward J. Gay not only
survived but prospered under free labor.
Courtesy of the Gay Family

Planters like William Whitmell Pugh of Bayou
Lafourche experienced greater difficulties during
the transition to free labor.
William Littlejohn Martin Collection, Allen J. Ellender
Archives, Nicholls State University, Thibodaux, La.

The elegant grandeur of Houmas House, the Ascension Parish estate of John Burnside shown in this early-twentieth-century photograph, continued to reflect Burnside's postwar financial success long after his death in 1881.

Andrew D. Lytle Collection, Mss. 893, 1254, Louisiana and Lower Mississippi Valley Collections, LSU Libraries, Baton Rouge

As depicted in this late-nineteenth-century (circa 1890) photograph, the ramshackle condition of Shadows-on-the-Teche plantation house in St. Mary Parish symbolizes the economic downfall that many planters suffered after the war. The house has since been restored.

Andrew D. Lytle Collection, Mss. 893, 1254, Louisiana and Lower Mississippi Valley Collections, LSU Libraries, Baton Rouge

Laborers and others in front of the store on Belle Grove plantation.

The quarters on Evan Hall plantation.

Historic New Orleans Collection, Acc. No. 1978.26.56

Workers and other residents pose on the main road of Smithfield plantation.
Louisiana State Museum, New Orleans

This twentieth-century photograph of the abandoned quarters of Hester plantation in
St. James Parish portrays the ultimate fate of many once-prosperous sugar estates.
Louisiana Collection, State Library of Louisiana, Baton Rouge

§7§

THE REWARDS OF WAGE LABOR

Some [freedmen] spend their wages as soon as received, this is particularly the case with those who are paid up in full, whereas those who leave a portion of their wages on deposit, gradually accumulate a fund which they use when opportunity presents itself, for purchasing a small tract of land.

—*Napoleonville Pioneer of Assumption*, May 31, 1879

The most telling consequence of the labor market in the postbellum sugar region was its effect on wages. Issues over which freedmen and planters negotiated—and often came into conflict—involved not only the amount of wages but also their timely payment and the proportion held in reserve until year's end. During the 1870s, freedmen successfully prevented planters from significantly reducing wages and from imposing uniform rates. They also compelled planters by decade's end to reduce from one-half to one-third the proportion of monthly wages withheld, and in certain localities to end entirely the despised practice of reserving wages. Competition for labor forced planters to offer good wages and to pay freedmen more of their earnings every month.

Of equal importance to the question of how much freedmen earned is that of what they did with their money. If the freedmen's engaging the labor market to influence wages connoted acceptance and internalization of the capitalist marketplace's values, so too did their spending habits. Freedmen used their wages to obtain basic necessities and to expand the horizon of consumption by purchasing the wide array of commodities that a monied economy made available to them.

They also used their discretionary incomes to help solidify the black community's cultural and institutional foundations. Perhaps most importantly, certain freedmen accumulated enough money to acquire small amounts of property. Thus, while geographic mobility helped reconcile freedmen to wage labor, so too did a limited degree of social mobility. Although most freedmen continued to work in a manner reminiscent of slavery, they nonetheless ascribed a larger meaning to the money they earned. The rewards of wage labor included a measure of individual autonomy and the black community's collective self-determination.

By the late 1860s, wage labor had assumed a distinctive shape. Freedmen customarily earned a stipulated monthly wage, half of which planters held in reserve until completing the crop. Initiated under wartime free labor, this practice enabled planters to limit, if only partly, labor's midseason mobility. During the crop season, freedmen were paid half their wages in cash the first Saturday of each month for the previous month's work. Planters also withheld half wages during the rolling season, but they raised rates to compensate for the increased work load. Freedmen surrendered some independence by having wages withheld, but they enjoyed regular cash payments and could often anticipate substantial disbursements at year's end.

Generalizations about wage rates during the 1870s are difficult to make. A uniform rate never applied to the entire region, despite planters' efforts to impose one, and rates often varied widely in a given year. During the early part of the decade, wages ranged from $15 for "ordinary field hands" to $25 or more for the best workers, in addition to rations and housing. "Expenses are literally eating us up," one planter complained in 1873. "Labor is too high. $15 per month, with rations and house rent, is . . . more than our most successful planters can afford." The 1873 economic depression prompted planters to reduce wages to $13 for 1874, but they allowed wages to rebound to the $15–25 range by 1875. Pay rates fluctuated considerably for the rest of the decade. "In the Teche country we pay from $15 to $25 per month for men," noted one planter in 1877, "and provide them house, garden, fire-wood, rations, half an acre of land in field, and team and half Saturday to work the same." Such rates, planters insisted, demoralized labor. "[T]he higher the wages the less the work performed," griped one planter in 1873.[1]

1. *Franklin Planters' Banner,* Dec. 22, 1869; *DP,* Aug. 17, 1873; U.S. Dept. of Agriculture, *Report of the Commissioner, 1877,* "The Cane-Sugar Industry," 34–5; *DP,* Aug. 24, 1873. See also *DP,* Mar. 9, 1869, Apr. 6, 1870, July 29, 1873, Sept. 1, 1875, Oct. 3, 1877, Jan. 6, 1878; R. C. Martin to R. C. Martin Jr., Jan. 20, 1870, Martin-Pugh Collection, NSU; Payroll, Kenmore plant., June 1870, Consolidated Assoc. Papers, LSU; S. Cranwill to EJG, Mar. 13, 1871, EJG to J. S. Shepherd or Shepherd & Johnson, Apr. 11, 1878, EJGP; Jan. 7, 1873, Daybook 1873–1877, Robertson

Just as labor mobility manifested itself during the period between crop seasons, bargaining over wage rates occurred in late December and January. The reserved wages freedmen received at year's end gave them considerable leverage in negotiating with planters and emboldened some to demand better terms. Others simply transformed most of January into an extended furlough, causing planters to bemoan what one called the "great trouble of the Hollidays." "As to labor, after the frolics of New Year's day & Christmas, Negroes will have spent all their money & will work," insisted a New Orleans factor in late 1869. "Of course the hands will want some holiday and time to spend their money before beginning another year," noted Lavinia Gay in early 1871. "We cannot tell what changes there will be among them but of course there will be some, and planters all dread the worry & trouble of beginning a new year." Alcée Bouchereau reported that "Hands were backward" in contracting for 1878, "as they yet held on to some of their last year's money." Racial and class biases caused white observers to overstate the freedmen's frivolousness with their earnings but not their negotiating leverage.[2]

Completing the contracting process began rather than ended planters' difficulties, for they knew that any delay in paying freedmen would cause trouble. The Louisiana legislature in 1867 made laborers' wages a privileged lien, so planters could not legally escape their financial obligations. Such responsibilities paled next to their anxiety over the potential demoralization of workers who were not paid as expected. Thomas Garrett, manager of a Gay plantation, advised Gay in 1872 to send payroll money lest the workers become dissatisfied. "I have been very tight on the hands lately, forcing them up to their contract," he noted, "and I must not fail to come up to my part." Not all planters acted so conscientiously. In 1873, a New Orleans merchant told of a planter-client who "refused to pay the *Hands* their 1st July wages" and encountered "a great deal of trouble with them in *consequence*." Most planters viewed such a policy as shortsighted. "If there is anything [planters] are more honorable about than another, it is in regard to paying their laborers, and if for no other reason, because their interest prompts them to do so," insisted one who overstated planters' scrupulousness but nonetheless pinpointed

Account Books, LSU; Somers, *Southern States*, 222; Braxton Bragg to J. N. Fenlong, Feb. 12, 1875, Braxton Bragg Letter, LSU; 43rd Cong., 2nd Sess., HR 101, pt. 2, p. 258; Jan. 10, 1876, W. W. Pugh Diary, Pugh Papers, UT; Jan. 19, Feb. 2, 1879, Frellsen Plant. Diary, LSU; Payroll ledger, 1880, Randolph Papers, LSU.

2. R. Daigre to EJG, Dec. 21, 1873, EJGP; A. Miltenberger to T. O. Moore, Dec. 18, 1869, Moore Papers, LSU; L. Gay to J. Gay, Jan. 15, 1871, EJGP; A. Bouchereau, *Statement . . . 1878–79*, ix. See also *Thibodaux Sentinel*, Jan. 15, 1870; M. Martin to W. Littlejohn, Jan. 27, 1871, Martin-Pugh Collection, NSU; O. Hacket to EJG, Mar. 4, 1877, EJGP; Nordhoff, *Cotton States*, 70.

their main concern. "We have learned long ago that it won't do to defraud the laborer, so that if we were not honest from higher motives we would be for self-interest." The manager of a Pugh plantation told his employer in 1876, "I would advise the payment of hands to day if possible because there will be a great deal of dissatisfaction if not paid, as you said the payment will be on the 1st Saturday of the month."[3]

No planter could afford to ignore his workers' worries about their pay. In October 1874, Edward J. Gay commissioned an agent, Samuel Hollingsworth, to tour his plantations and report on the freedmen's morale. Hollingsworth's reports have not survived, but Gay's instructions illustrate his concern. "It would be well to know that the hands are satisfied and work well," he informed Hollingsworth, "and that no difficulty has taken place during the season with them." Gay expressed special interest in the freedmen's being paid, since it was upon this that their esprit de corps rested. "Everything you can learn . . . on the matter of the general satisfaction of the laborers is important," he instructed, "because we may thereby learn privately how they have been regularly paid each month." Gay was not averse to taking a tough stance against what he deemed workers' unreasonable demands, but he also knew a little solicitude went a long way.[4]

It was no coincidence that Gay ordered this inquiry just before rolling season, when the increased work demands and heightened competition for labor intensified the wage conflicts and prompted planters to make concessions on both wage rates and the method of payment. In October 1875, David N. Barrow wrote of a neighboring planter who "finds it very hard under the present demand for hands to get laborers and says unless he can get cash to pay them he cannot work to advantage." "There is some scarcity of hands for cane cutting," echoed a St. Charles Parish journalist. "The planters, their overseers and representatives, all over this parish and many from St. John and St. James, have been to Hahnville and engaged all the colored people . . . to work during the grinding season and are offering good wages." Planters in St. Mary Parish met in October 1877 to discuss securing additional labor for the rolling season but derived no solutions. By 1880, the planters' situation had not improved. "In regards to my work on Plantation I cant say that I have made very great head way," noted one manager as rolling sea-

---

3. T. Garrett to EJG, May 27, 1872, EJGP; R. Flower to Mrs. P. Mathews, July 5, 1873, Mathews Papers, LSU; 43rd Cong., 2nd Sess., HR 261, pt. 3, pp. 626–7; U. Componeau to [Mrs. F. W. Pugh?], Mar. 4, 1876, Pugh Papers, UT. See also A. H. Gay to EJG, Dec. 2, 1877, W. Martin to EJG, Dec. 4, 1877; A. J. Donelson to EJG, May 7, 1878, EJGP; U.S. Dept. of Agriculture, *Report of the Commissioner, 1877*, "The Cane-Sugar Industry," 40; *Napoleonville Pioneer of Assumption*, Mar. 13, 1880. On the law giving laborers a privileged lien, see Woodman, *New South—New Law*, 54.

4. EJG & Co. to S. Hollingsworth, Oct. 31, 1874 (copy), EJGP.

son approached. "Labor is very scarce more so than I have ever seen it." A journalist likewise remarked that sugar mills could not "do half their usual amount of work, as labor is so scarce that, although high wages are offered, it is difficult to get hands on any terms."[5]

With labor at a premium, rolling season wages skyrocketed during the early 1870s. "I think it will be very difficult to get any extra labour about here for taking of the crop and they will demand high wages," Andrew H. Gay informed his father in fall 1870. "I am told that people are offering $50. & $60. per month and feeding them." The manager of a Gay plantation confirmed this report, complaining that "it is impossible to hire hands here under $50. or $60 per mo for grinding season." The 1873 economic depression forced planters to lower wages, but rolling-season wages for the best workers ranged from seventy-five cents to $1 per day, plus rations, and from $1 to $1.25 without rations—in addition to between fifty and seventy-five cents per night watch. With the 1880 rolling season nearing, Lafourche and Terrebonne Parish workers "demanded" $1 per day, plus rations; planters, it was reported, "acceded to the request of their employees."[6]

Aware of the value of their labor, freedmen struck for higher wages. Newspaper reports, although usually couched in terms intended to demonstrate the strikes' ineffectiveness, attested to their frequency. Such work stoppages lacked the planning and organization necessary for success, but they perturbed planters to no end. Expressing planters' sentiments, a St. Mary journalist complained in 1870 that freedmen "strike as they commence rolling cane and demand higher wages." From the Lafourche district in 1872, a journalist observed that "frequent strikes for higher wages have occurred on Sugar plantations of late," but he added that planters resisted these demands "in most instances." One planter claimed that laborers' demands for higher wages as rolling season began, combined with the unscrupulousness of planters who enticed their neighbors' workers, left many unable to secure labor. On the eve of the 1873 rolling season, Roman Daigre remarked that freedmen in Iberville Parish were "not disposed to hire themselves to take off crops, only by the day, and their object is to strike for higher wages when we get in a pinch." Daigre thought it best to hire labor from elsewhere. "I have a pretty fair crop to save," he reported, "and don't want to be short of hands."[7]

5. D. N. Barrow to EJG, Oct. 17, 1875, EJGP; *DP,* Nov. 5, 1875, Oct. 21, 1877; W. Knight to J. H. Gay, Sept. 11, 1880, EJGP; *NILSB,* Dec. 2, 1880.

6. A. H. Gay to EJG, Aug. 13, 1870, J. W. Austin to EJG, Aug. 11, and Sept. 4, 1870, R. M. Walsh to EJG, Oct. 16, 1876 (copy), all in EJGP; *NILSB,* July 5, 1877, Aug. 1, 1878, and Oct. 14, 1880 (quotation).

7. *Franklin Planters' Banner,* Nov. 9, 1870; *Thibodaux Sentinel,* Dec. 17, 1870, Nov. 16, 1872; R. Daigre to EJG, Sept. 18, 1873, EJGP. See also J. Nolan to EJG, Oct. 18, 1870, and P. T. Achee to EJG & Co., Oct. 26, 1875, EJGP.

As dependent as planters were on the freedmen's labor, freedmen did not always have to strike to make their demands known. "Negroes are so independent," remarked Andrew H. Gay before the 1871 rolling season, "that there is very little dependence to be placed in them and they are demanding high prices and are not willing to contract except by the day." Freedmen on a Gay plantation near Thibodaux refused to plant cane for $1 per day in November 1877. Although they had not yet begun to harvest the crop, the workers demanded higher wages. The manager at first rejected this demand but suggested to Gay that they accede. "We could commence next week to planting if we had your order to raise wages, as the hands will not work for less than they can get elsewhere," he noted. "The business on the place will drag until you order the wages to be raised." Henry Clay Warmoth's manager informed him in October 1878 that several freedmen visited the plantation seeking work but left "because they could not get a dollar & Board *now*." Rolling was to begin in a matter of days, when wages would have gone to $1 a day plus rations, but confident that their terms would be met elsewhere, the freedmen refused to wait.[8]

So desperate were planters for harvest labor that they began during the mid-1870s to pay cash wages on a weekly basis for watch work. Regular payment, remarked one manager, "is a powerful inducement with negroes." While recruiting workers for Roman Daigre in 1873, labor agent C. C. Neally informed him that "negroes are disposed to wait [back?] for the full wages, & paing them the watch money every week is correct & customary & the Balance at the end of sugar grinding that will satisfy them." Duncan F. Kenner recommended to Benjamin Tureaud in 1875 that, in order to hire extra labor for the rolling season, Tureaud should "try & get them . . . by paying *cash* every Saturday." John H. Gay likewise notified his father in 1876 that he "had to come to their terms so far as paying them every Saturday." Henry Clay Warmoth's plantation manager suggested in October 1878 that the sooner they began rolling operations the better chance they had of procuring "floating hands," adding that "prompt pay in cash also commands the labor." Slowly, a compromise emerged. Planters continued to withhold part of the freedmen's regular monthly wages, but they paid them weekly instead of monthly for watch work during rolling season. This system enabled planters to avoid meeting in full the monthly payroll of a greatly enlarged work force while also ensuring freedmen regular cash payments.[9]

8. A. H. Gay to EJG, Aug. 27, 1871, and A. J. Donelson to EJG, Nov. 17, 1877, EJGP; Whittlesey to H. C. Warmoth, Oct. 14, 1878, Warmoth Papers, SHC. See also J. W. Austin to EJG, Dec. 25, 1876, and W. D. Burton to EJG, Nov. 20, 1877, EJGP.

9. A. Ferry to EJG, Oct. 23, 1875, and C. C. Neilly to R. Daigre, Sept. 15, 1873, EJGP; D. F. Kenner to B. Tureaud, July 16, 1875, Benjamin F. Tureaud Family Papers, LSU; J. H. Gay to EJG, Oct. 3, 1876, EJGP; Whittlesey to Warmoth, Oct. 11, 1878, Warmoth Papers, SHC.

In noting that "prompt pay in cash . . . commands the labor," Warmoth's manager spoke more truth than he realized. If cash commanded labor, workers demanded prompt cash. So sensitive were freedmen about being paid on time during rolling season that they did not hesitate to upset the delicate equilibrium of plantation routine, causing endless worry for planters who failed to meet their obligations. Preparing for the 1871 harvest, Thomas Garrett tried to persuade his workers to await their pay until completing the crop. Once the harvest started, however, there was trouble. "I had thought I would not pay the hands untill the crop was off," he noted in late October, but "I find it has caused considerable dissatisfaction. They say they want some money to purchase such articles they need for rolling." Consequently, Garrett decided to pay his workers the customary half wages for October. This change enabled Garrett to win his workers' cooperation, but by early December they were again "clamorous for some money." To complicate matters, Garrett experienced unrest with the "Missi[ssippi] hands" he had hired for rolling season, who, unhappy over having their wages withheld, quit. "I think the cause of their leaving was they pretended not to know that they were employed for the whole Rolling, and would not be paid in full untill the crop was off," Garrett observed. "They demanded to be paid in full every month."[10]

Garrett was not alone. Freedmen employed by Louis Coppenex, a client of Edward J. Gay's factorage, quit work in December 1871 because they had not been paid as much as expected. They returned to work only after Coppenex promised to obtain additional funds to pay them. The same year, another of Gay's clients, S. Fortier of St. James Parish, requested money to secure his workers' goodwill for the harvest. "If I were to fail paying them," Fortier speculated, "it might put me in a very unfortunate position." A. F. Pugh found himself in a similarly unfortunate position in fall 1874. Having lowered wages earlier that year, Pugh anticipated trouble come rolling season. "Nov. 1, and then what? Then is the hour of much anxiety to me, and I fear will give rise to much trouble & bad feeling." Pugh was right. Only days before the harvest, his workers struck and demanded a return to the previous year's wages, which Pugh felt he had no choice but to pay. Word of this decision did not sit well with Pugh's factors, to whom he was deeply indebted. "We regret to hear that the negroes on the Augustin & Whitmell places are getting incited over the effects of their fancied proprietorship of those places during the past summer & fall," they lamented. "The sheriff's officer will if necessary knock one or two of them over with buck shot, & the balance will quiet down," they confidently predicted, while urging Pugh to resist any further demands. "From our experience a concession to those turbulent negroes would only

10. T. Garrett to EJG, Oct. 20, 27, and Dec. 4, 1871, EJGP.

effect a temporary lull." Pugh no doubt agreed, but he also probably found such advice unhelpful.[11]

Although freedmen did not dictate terms to planters, few planters could risk assuming an uncompromising stand when faced with their workers' wage demands. Those who did flirted with disaster, as evidenced by an 1874 episode involving Samuel Cricklow, manager of a Gay plantation in Lafourche Parish. In early October, as rolling season was about to start, Cricklow's workers struck and demanded seventy-five cents per day plus rations. Cricklow resolved not to give in, and when many of the strikers left, he planned to replace them with day laborers at one dollar per day. "If they don't go to work," Cricklow insisted, "I will have to hire outsiders altogether—*'floating hands'*—& will cost me perhaps a dollar a day. I tell them that they must go to work or leave the place as I will not pay a cent more to *them* & if I have to go up, will pay it to others as day hands." Cricklow preferred to put his, and Gay's, short-term profitability at risk rather than capitulate to strikers and thus surrender long-term labor control.[12]

Cricklow's strategy reassured neither Gay nor Samuel Cranwill. Their response offers a unique insight into planters' thinking under free labor.

> The absolute necessity on your part of a calm and non-committal course with the hands is evident. But action should be taken at once. The crop must not be endangered; and there is propriety in paying $1.00 day to *"floating hands"* while your regular hands offer to work at 75¢.
>
> If there were an honorable understanding amongst planters none of them would on any account hire your laborers guilty of such bad faith.
>
> If you have no hold on the laborers that will secure them your best course is to take matters quietly and make the best compromise you can.
>
> Laborers on other plantations may also demand additional pay during rolling time, finding the hands on the Home Plant. getting it. With this you have nothing to do. They cannot compel such an exaction, as they would forfeit the back wages.
>
> If you let the hands scatter from the plantation serious consequences may result.
>
> You ought to be the best judge of the course to be pursued knowing all the surrounding conditions;—but remember the interest of the plantation and those concerned in it is the first consideration and will of course with you outweigh all personal feeling towards the laborers for their bad faith.
>
> You knew the writer has opposed from the first the system of paying full wages;

11. L. Coppenex to EJG & Co., Dec. 2, 1871, S. Cranwill to EJG, Dec. 7, 1871, S. Fortier to EJG, Dec. 7, 1871, EJGP; Oct. 4, Nov. 2, 1874, AFP Diary, and Conger & Kelly to AFP, Dec. 28, 1874, Pugh Papers, UT. See also EJG Jr. to EJG, Nov. 29, 1873, EJGP; *NILSB*, Aug. 29, 1878.

12. S. P. Cricklow to Messrs. EJG & Co., Oct. 6, 1874, EJGP.

and when on a visit to you four months ago predicted exactly what has happened—that at rolling time the negroes would strike for higher wages, and give great trouble not only to you but to your neighbors.

In a word however, action has to be taken at once—no time to lose. Look squarely at the conditions in existence—remove from your mind all feeling of hostility towards the hands—and let the interest of the place be paramount to every other consideration. It may not do to trust to the uncertainty of "*floating hands*." Make the best possible compromise with the laborers *at once,* if your calm judgment decides that it is the best course—(and we think it undoubtedly is) and don't trouble yourself about what your neighbors think or say.

The trouble has arisen by beginning wrong—and now there is no time to make patch work out of the result by taking uncertain chances of "floating labor."[13]

In this remarkable letter, Gay and Cranwill identify the challenges that planters confronted in vying for workers who were free to go. Cricklow's difficulties arose from his paying in full each month rather than withholding the customary half wages. Gay and Cranwill urged him to abandon this practice, warning that it would create problems during the harvest. Cricklow ignored their advice, thereby placing himself in a position that the freedmen were quick to exploit. Predictably, they struck for higher wages as the harvest approached, and when Cricklow refused to yield, they left and were readily hired by neighboring planters. Although Cricklow felt confident he could replace the strikers with floating hands, Gay and Cranwill objected to this course, owing less to the cost than to their unreliability. They urged Cricklow to compromise. Whether or not Cricklow acted upon this advice, Gay and Cranwill succinctly articulated planters' concerns in reconciling wage labor with sugar production.

Confessing to Gay his uneasiness over Cricklow's handling of the incident, Cranwill suspected an underlying cause that Cricklow neglected to mention: "*Perhaps in regard to their pay for what they have already done.*" Cranwill might have done well to speculate whether the trouble was due more to Cricklow's bad faith than to the freedmen's, since workers who were not paid as promised could not be expected to remain when others were eager to hire them. Whatever the cause of the problem, Cranwill maintained that rolling season was no time for intransigence and that Cricklow's proposal to hire floating hands was absurd. By mid-October, Cricklow had not resolved the crisis, despite Cranwill's insistence that he pay seventy-five cents per day, which had become standard in the neighborhood. As though Cricklow's standing could get any worse, he later asked Cranwill

13. EJG & Co. to S. P. Cricklow, Oct. 7, 1874 (copy), EJGP.

to recruit laborers from New Orleans for the harvest. Cranwill was furious. "[S]uch managers are simply disgusting," he fumed. "He had plenty of warning and advice if he had attended to it."[14]

Gay and Cranwill counseled against paying full wages monthly, but by the mid-1870s many planters began reducing the proportion of wages held in reserve from one-half to one-third, and some even paid in full every month as a way to attract workers. Withholding wages had often occasioned as much conflict as did wage rates. The shift to paying two-thirds monthly, or what one observer called the "new system," offered further proof of planters' accommodation to free labor just as it illustrated the freedmen's ability to exploit the labor market. Receiving full wages proved especially attractive to freedmen, and the practice was correspondingly riskier for planters, as Samuel Cricklow's unhappy experiences demonstrated. By resorting to it, planters once again sacrificed the long-term goal of labor control for the immediate goal of securing workers. Few could afford to think beyond the present, however, and thus conformed to paying freedmen either two-thirds or full wages monthly.[15]

The labor market's logic dictated that once a few planters began offering more attractive payment terms, the rest had to follow suit. Alexis Ferry, who managed a Gay plantation in St. James Parish, informed Gay in 1876 that neighboring planters were paying in full each month. He recommended that they do the same lest they be compelled to hire "perfect trash more costly & good for nothing." By paying in full, he insisted, "we can sellect thirty good men by the inducement," which "will certainly be cheaper in the end." Ferry had "plenty of good field hands" who wanted to remain with him, but because he could not assure them that they would be paid in full "they have been on other plantations." Two years later, J. W. Austin similarly informed Gay that several of his best workers had left him for neighboring planters. "[A]s indications were strong that others were about to leave," he reported, "I felt compelled to offer $15. per mo to no. 1 hands, one third to be reserved and have thus far been able to secure all the laborers I needed."[16]

Even reserving only one-third could not guarantee sufficient labor. Most planters were paying two-thirds by 1877, but freedmen continued to push for full payment, as William A. Shaffer of Terrebonne Parish learned in early 1880. Shaffer had been accustomed to hard bargaining, but in 1880 his workers now demanded "all their wages cash at the end of each month," whereas he was "still holding out for paying 2/3 wages." To Shaffer's misfortune, his neighbors were

14. S. Cranwill to EJG, Oct. 8, 12, 15, 1874, EJGP.
15. *NILSB*, Apr. 26, 1877.
16. A. Ferry to EJG, Jan. 4, 1876, and J. W. Austin to EJG, Apr. 6, 1878, EJGP.

paying in full, and as every planter knew, it was impossible to compete against this practice without conforming to the trend. Shaffer tried to do so, but he relented when half his work force left on January 7. "In view of the urgent necessity of planting the cane immediately I agreed this morning to pay in full," he lamented. "I am convinced it will not work." Shaffer's concession induced several recently departed workers to return, enabling him to start operations for the year. Nevertheless, he remained pessimistic: "Planters can never succeed with such a labour system," he predicted. Plantation affairs settled into a steady routine by early February, but Shaffer still lacked sufficient labor. In early March, he complained of workers still "going and comeing every week."[17]

Despite the experiences of Shaffer and others, paying two-thirds was more common than full payment during the late 1870s. Nonetheless, full payment became frequent enough to spark predictable complaints. Those who could not pay in full charged that doing so demoralized labor and undermined their own individual interests as well as those of the community at large. "From the monthly payment of wages in full and the execrable system of job work," Donelson Caffery contended in 1877, "the labor has been spasmodic, unreliable and on the rise this whole season." A St. Mary newspaper editorial likewise articulated planters' views on the new mode of payment. "[I]n paying full wages to colored laborers, planters have no security whatever for the fulfillment of the contract on the part of his hands." Workers "may strike for higher wages at the approach of the grinding season and thus place the planter completely at their mercy." Not only would labor become scarce during rolling season, but freedmen would also refuse to work efficiently during the entire year: "the colored laborers, as a class, are so improvident that they can with difficulty be induced to work when they have money to spend."[18]

As inevitable as planters' complaints were their efforts to act in unison. A number of St. Mary planters met in October 1877 to establish wage rates for the following year and to end full payment. "It was unanimously resolved," noted the reporter in attendance, "that next year *none should pay full wages monthly*, but that one third should be reserved until the end of the year to make planters secure." Yet this attempt at concerted action ended as futilely as had previous ones. By early 1878 some planters were reneging on their pledges. An editorial entitled "Honor Among Planters" bemoaned the fact that, despite planters' promises not

17. Jan.–Mar., 1880, Plant. Journal 11, William A. Shaffer Papers, SHC (quotations Jan. 1, 6, 7, 8, Feb. 6, Mar. 8). See also A. Bouchereau, *Statement . . . 1878–79*, ix; Jan. 19, Feb. 2, 9, 1879, Frellsen Plant. Diary, LSU; Jan. 10, 11, 12, 1883, Diary 17, William Porcher Miles Papers, SHC.

18. *DP,* Oct. 3, 1877; *NILSB,* Apr. 19, 1877. See also *Napoleonville Pioneer of Assumption,* Mar. 13, 1880; [unsigned] to brother, Sept. 20, 1881, Weeks Papers, LSU.

to pay full wages, "already we hear a repetition of the old story—violation of these pledges by avaricious and unscrupulous planters." One planter's unscrupulousness was another's sound business practice.[19]

By the late 1870s, conflict over wages seemed routine. "There may be dissatisfaction at times both of employee and employer, as to the rate of wages," remarked an Assumption Parish journalist in 1879, "but this state of affairs is found in all countries, and constitutes what is called one of the struggles between labor and capital." If wage disputes were not unusual, however, freedmen raised the stakes by demanding full payment, which they often received, given the realities of the labor market. Conceding this issue exacerbated rather than solved planters' problems, since it freed workers from financial ties to particular plantations. By the early 1880s, paying two-thirds had become the best arrangement planters could hope for. Herein lies a certain paradox. Despite planters' apparent desperation, the matter-of-factness with which they noted their workers' comings and goings suggests a growing confidence in their own ability to attract workers and in wage labor as a whole. A practice once considered inconceivable was becoming, however distastefully, more and more commonplace.[20]

Even as they came to terms with full payment, planters nonetheless found it disconcerting, since they considered the wages they paid to be generous. Daniel Dennett, St. Mary Parish newspaper editor and self-appointed industry spokesman, calculated in 1869 that freedmen earned about $375 per year in wages and other perquisites. "We doubt if there is a spot in the whole South where they are as well paid as in this parish," he insisted. William H. Harris, Louisiana's commissioner of agriculture and immigration, reached a similar conclusion some ten years later. Although such estimates mildly overstated the freedmen's income, they were not entirely inaccurate. The freedmen's gross earnings—including wages, rations, housing, firewood, garden plots, and other benefits—ranged between $325 and $350 per year. This figure was comparable to the earnings of non-agricultural workers nationwide, who made about $380 per year; it also compared favorably with the income of southern black sharecroppers and tenant farmers, who earned less than $200 per year, and with that of wage workers in the cotton South, where monthly wages varied from $10 to $13. Sugar workers' income, itself a boon to people once stripped of the fruits of their toil, thus approximated the earnings of American laborers of similar social status during the 1870s.[21]

19. *NILSB*, Oct. 11, 1877, and Feb. 14, 1878. See also Nov. 8, 1877, ibid., and *Thibodaux Sentinel*, Jan. 5, 1878.

20. *Napoleonville Pioneer of Assumption*, May 31, 1879.

21. *Franklin Planters' Banner*, Mar. 27, 1869; William H. Harris, *Louisiana, Her Resources, Advantages, and Attractions: Being a Description of the State and the Inducements Offered to Those*

Monthly wage labor also enabled freedmen to remain free from debt. Owing to the practice of keeping wages in reserve, many workers actually had substantial balances in their favor at the year-end settlement. Freedmen in the sugar region did not customarily purchase commodities on credit, at highly inflated prices, as was the case in the cotton South. Rather, their purchases were in-kind payments drawn against their accounts. "Where sugar-planters keep no store for their hands, it is customary to pay the hands half their wages at the end of the month and the balance at the close of the year," noted Charles Nordhoff, "and I imagine those who make advances in goods try to keep their men to about the same limit." Not only did sugar workers escape the credit arrangements that ensnared cotton sharecroppers, but withheld wages, like any deferred-payment system, constituted an interest-free loan to planters. Freedmen chafed at this practice, but it had the benefit of forcing them to save money during the year. They could not routinely purchase everything they needed and enjoy large payments at year's end. Instead, freedmen made choices: the more they spent during the year, the smaller the final settlement; the more they economized, the larger the settlement. Freedmen did not live in affluence, but neither did they suffer abject impoverishment.[22]

Freedmen spent their earnings in any number of ways. Some, though not as many as planters contended, squandered their wages by drinking, gambling, and engaging in other vices associated with working-class life. This was especially true of young, single men, especially the floating hands, of whom there were a large number in southern Louisiana. Slavery had hardly served as a school for thrift, frugality, and sobriety, and some freedmen had not internalized these values even years after emancipation. Nor did the infamous 1873 failure of the Freedman's Bank encourage them to use their money wisely. "Not even ten additional years of

---

Seeking New Homes (Austin, Tex., 1881), 12. See also *Napoleonville Pioneer of Assumption*, Jan. 4, 1879; King, *Great South*, 81; Nordhoff, *Cotton States*, 70. At $20 per month for ten months and $1.50 per day for two months (twenty-six days each) during the rolling season, a sugar worker's annual wage earnings amounted to $278. Adding to this figure $48 in rations for the year ($4 difference between monthly wages with and without rations) brings the total to about $326. Rent-free housing, garden plots, and use of teams and farm equipment make Dennett's and Harris's figures plausible. Annual earnings of nonfarm workers are from Stanley Lebergott, *Manpower in Economic Growth: The American Record since 1800* (New York, 1964), 528. On annual incomes of southern tenant farmers and sharecroppers during the late 1870s, see Ransom and Sutch, *One Kind of Freedom*, 214–6. Average monthly earnings, with board, for agricultural wage workers in the Deep South cotton states in 1870 were as follows: South Carolina, $10.33; Georgia, $10.83; Alabama, $10.82; Mississippi, $13.38; and Louisiana, $14.34. Lebergott, *Manpower in Economic Growth*, 539. On cotton South wage workers, see LaWanda F. Cox, "The American Agricultural Wage Earner, 1865–1900," *AH* 22 (April 1948): 95–114; Jones, *The Dispossessed*, chap. 3; Davis, *Good and Faithful Labor*, 204–6.

22. Nordhoff, *Cotton States*, 72.

slavery," wrote W. E. B. Du Bois early in the twentieth century, "could have done as much to throttle the thrift of the freedmen as the mismanagement and bank-ruptcy of the savings bank chartered by the nation for their especial aid." Wage labor gave freedmen a disposable income, and some of them disposed of it as quickly as possible.[23]

Most freedmen did not squander their wages but used them to purchase both basic necessities and luxury items. In doing so, they usually patronized the planta-tion store or commissary, which became a fixture after emancipation. Many of these establishments offered a wide array of commodities and became thriving businesses in themselves. Customs varied in how freedmen were paid and how they purchased merchandise, depending upon the proportion of their wages with-held, whether or not they received rations, and the kinds of goods available in stores. In general, freedmen received half or two-thirds of their wages each month in cash or a combination of cash and merchandise. They might also make pur-chases against the portion of their wages held in reserve, which reduced their final payment. Planters maintained accounts for each household head—recording how much he or she earned, received in cash or merchandise, and was owed at settle-ment. While few of these accounts have survived, the records of Benjamin F. Tureaud's Houmas plantation and store in Ascension Parish offer unparalleled in-sight into the freedmen's spending habits during the 1870s. They show that freed-men not only participated in creating a consumerist economy but also enjoyed a purchasing power that helped accommodate them to wage labor.[24]

Because planters provided rations only to workers, freedmen purchased provi-sions for their families and dependents. Moreover, since the workers' rations con-sisted of the same fare they had received as slaves, pork and corn meal, they sup-plemented their diet by purchasing other foodstuffs, such as beef, meal, rice, flour, cheese, bread, butter, coffee, lard, and starch. Although these items might be con-sidered necessities, they also marked a modest expansion of the freedmen's con-sumption habits since slavery.

Freedmen further supplemented these necessities by acquiring goods that rep-resented new opportunities for consumption and connoted the expanding wants

23. W. E. B. Du Bois, "The Freedmen's Bureau," *Atlantic Monthly* 87 (March 1901): 354–65 (quotation 363). On the failure of the Freedman's Bank, see Carl R. Osthaus, *Freedmen, Philanthropy, and Fraud: A History of the Freedman's Savings Bank* (Urbana, Ill., 1976). On the behavior of young, single, unattached men in historical context, see David T. Courtwright, *Violent Land: Single Men and Social Disorder from the Frontier to the Inner City* (Cambridge, Mass., 1996), chaps. 1–3 and 9.

24. This discussion of the freedmen's spending habits is based upon account books in the Tureaud Papers, LSU, vols. 12–28 and 46–73. Though fairly regular and complete, the records' idiosyncrasies and oversights make entire reconstruction of the freedmen's expenses and spend-ing habits impossible.

of free people. They purchased such consumables as crackers, cakes, soap, tobacco, cigars, tea, whiskey, gin, port wine, brandy, codfish, sardines, sugar, salt, pepper, condensed milk, and candy. The Tureaud store also stocked fancier personal and household items that reflected American society's burgeoning consumerism during the latter part of the nineteenth century. Freedmen regularly bought calico, dresses, shoes, shirts, and handkerchiefs, as well as "ladies fancy hats," "fancy hose," dress shirts, cologne, chignons, wallets, spectacles, tobacco pouches, pocket combs, fiddle strings, necklaces, and jewelry. Household items included mouse and rat traps, padlocks, wash basins, brooms, clothes pins, ax handles, cotton towels, coffee drippers, candlesticks, pie and dinner plates, tea canisters, pens, paper, envelopes, and looking glasses, among other things. Owning such objects was beyond anything slaves might have imagined. Planters obligingly furnished commodities through their plantation stores, which not only provided them additional income but also increased the freedmen's dependence upon the goods planters supplied.[25]

Freedmen spent their wages readily, but they also used them in more long-term, constructive ways. Medical care and supporting the aged, disabled, and other nonproducers were no longer planters' responsibilities but now became the freedmen's. Former slaves also used their earnings to establish schools, churches, mutual aid and benevolent societies, and fraternal orders, and to hold the picnics, excursions, and other activities that were essential functions of these institutions. Seeing the financial resources provided by their earnings used to lay the institutional foundations of the free black community further reconciled freedmen to wage labor.[26]

While the black community's collective needs impelled freedmen to accept

25. In addition to the Tureaud account books, see D. F. Kenner to B. Tureaud, Aug. 27, 1875, Tureaud Papers, LSU; P. T. Achee to EJG & Co., Oct. 26, 1875, EJGP; J. R. Carroll to D. Carroll, Mar. 6, 1877, Daniel R. Carroll and Family Papers, LSU. In his examination of the freedmen's purchasing habits at plantation stores in the cotton South, Lawrence N. Powell shows that northern planters similarly cultivated a consumerist mentality among freedmen. Powell, *New Masters*, 87–93. Lawrence B. Glickman demonstrates how, during the late nineteenth century, American workers and labor leaders reconciled wage labor and consumerism with traditional republican values in redefining the concept of a living wage. Lawrence B. Glickman, *A Living Wage: American Workers and the Making of Consumer Society* (Ithaca, N.Y., 1997). In his study of mid-nineteenth-century Greene County, Georgia, Jonathan M. Bryant discerns a "nascent consumerism" that resulted from increasingly commercialized social relations. Bryant, *How Curious a Land*, 164–5.

26. Glen Lee Greene, *House upon a Rock: About Southern Baptists in Louisiana* (Alexandria, La., 1973), 175–7; William Hicks, *History of Louisiana Negro Baptists from 1804 to 1914* (Nashville, n.d.), 27–9, 46–7, 76–9, 121–2, 204; Walter N. Vernon, *Becoming One People: A History of Louisiana Methodism* (n.p., 1987), chaps. 4 and 5. On the freedmen's institution-building in the South, see Foner, *Reconstruction*, 88–102.

wage labor, so too did the opportunity for individuals to achieve a measure of autonomy through property ownership. By the early 1880s, a small but significant number of freedmen managed to accrue modest amounts of property, including land. Such property did not permit them to escape wage labor entirely, nor was it a stepping stone to economic independence, but it did allow some either to remain on the periphery of the plantation system or to expand their options within it. Property ownership also signified limited but crucial social mobility, which further reconciled freedmen to wage labor.

Among a sample of 238 black laborers in Ascension Parish in 1880, 46, or 19.3 percent, owned taxable property; in 1882, 52, or 21.9 percent, did so.[27] Considering together those laborers who owned property in either or both years, a total of 65, or 27.3 percent, owned property at some point in the early 1880s. Though not rare, property holding was precarious. While 19, or 8 percent of the sample, joined the ranks of property holders between 1880 and 1882, 13 of the 46 property holders in 1880, or 28.3 percent, owned no taxable property in 1882. This apparent downward social mobility may have been due partly to death or geographic mobility, since 9 of the 13 downward sliders do not appear on the poll tax list in 1882, despite the freedmen's propensity to pay the one-dollar poll tax even if they did not own property (71.7 percent of the sample did so in 1880). Nonetheless, 4 of 46 property holders in 1880, or 8.7 percent, still resided in the parish in 1882 and no longer owned property. Freedmen could gain property, but they could also lose it.

Black property holding was small scale. The 46 property holders in 1880 owned on average $61.98 worth of property. The wealthiest owned land and other assets valued at $530; the poorest possessed $8 worth of livestock, which he subsequently lost. Most owned between $25 and $150 worth of property. In the aggregate, 46.8 percent of their holdings were in land or improvements thereto, 50.5 percent in livestock, and 2.7 percent in wagons or carriages. The properties of the 1 laborer who owned land and the 20 others who made taxable improvements to land averaged $63.57. Forty-two laborers owned livestock with an average value of $34.19, and 5 owned carriages or wagons with an average value of $15.40. For freedmen who remained on plantations, owning a wagon or livestock built upon the tradi-

27. For the following discussion, "laborers" refers to black heads of households who gave their occupation as "laborer" in the 1880 federal census; "farmers" refers to those who gave their occupation as "farmer" in the 1880 federal census; "property owners" refers to laborers or farmers who owned property according to the 1880 and 1882 Ascension Parish tax rolls, Louisiana State Archives, Baton Rouge. For discussion of the methods used herein to measure black property holding, and of related problems, see the appendix. On black property owning in the rural Deep South after slavery, see Loren Schweninger, *Black Property Owners in the South, 1790–1915* (Urbana, Ill., 1990), 144–51, 161–6.

tions of the antebellum slaves' economy and affirmed the freedmen's self-worth. "About their cottages they can keep chickens and pigs, if they like," observed Charles Nordhoff, "and often they have a horse, a cow, and even an old carriage of some kind, in which they drive out on Sunday with great satisfaction, crowding in wife and children."[28]

Although the tax-assessment rolls do not itemize the improvements on land for which freedmen were taxed, the information they provide offers insight into the meaning freedmen ascribed to such property. Often residing together in small settlements, many freedmen erected dwellings or other structures on marginal lands at the rear of plantations that fronted the Mississippi River. "Improvements on land at back of Burnsides" and "improvements at rear of Linwood [plantation]" were commonly used to describe black property holders' assets. Making improvements on land that one did not own might seem improvident, yet doing so allowed freedmen a measure of autonomy. Working for wages on a daily basis while also cultivating small plots of land, freedmen who owned taxable property occupied both a social and geographical space between wage laborer and proprietor. "In the sugar country the negro does not aim to buy twenty or forty acres, and plant cane for himself," Charles Nordhoff noted. "But they like to own an acre or two, on which they place a cabin; and the homestead makes them contented." Several freedmen paid taxes for improvements on different estates in 1880 and 1882, indicating that such improvements either were left behind when freedmen moved on or were transportable. In the latter case, such property may have included cabins, which freedmen could disassemble and take elsewhere. Owning their own homes, however ramshackle, gave freedmen a sense of independence that they rarely enjoyed while living in plantation quarters.[29]

The geographic distribution of property among Ascension Parish laborers indicates that the lands behind plantations were especially conducive to black property holding. Lying within the parish's seventh and eighth wards, east of the Mississippi River, these marginal lands adjoined—and were often part of—plantations of the fifth and sixth wards that fronted the river. Many freedmen who technically resided in the seventh and eighth wards actually lived on the periphery of these plantations. Not only were these freedmen more likely to own property than were full-time plantation laborers, but they also owned more of it. Of

28. Nordhoff, *Cotton States*, 70.

29. Ibid., 70–1. In the Caribbean, slaves and later freedmen exhibited a strong sense of proprietorship over their homes and garden plots. McDonald, *Economy and Material Culture of Slaves*, 109–11, 149. Louisiana slaves did not develop quite as strong an attachment to their cabins, but their sense of proprietorship would have grown after emancipation, when they gained the right to own property.

the 30 laborers in the 1880 sample who lived in marginal areas, 18, or 60 percent, owned property, with an average value of $70.39, whereas 28, or only 13.5 percent, of the 208 laborers in plantation wards owned property, with an average holding of $56.57. Although black property owners in plantation wards outnumbered those on the periphery, the percentage of freedmen on the periphery who owned property was much higher than it was for those in plantation wards.

Establishing a causal connection between geography and property holding would be difficult. Having previously acquired productive property, certain freedmen may have gravitated toward the sugar region's marginal lands in order to elude plantation labor. Conversely, access to land on the plantation's periphery may have given ambitious freedmen the opportunity to purchase property and to achieve a degree of upward social mobility. Both tendencies were probably at work. Still, many freedmen at one point or another came to own property, which allowed them either to avoid full-time plantation employment or to supplement their wages. Whether they remained wage laborers or achieved semi-independent proprietorship, they expanded their options.

If few freedmen owned large amounts of property, even fewer rose from wage laborer to farmer. Forty-three black heads of households, representing about 2 percent of black households in Ascension Parish in 1880, identified themselves as farmers. Of these, 35, or 81.4 percent, owned property, with an average value of $229.03. The wealthiest owned forty-four acres of land and improvements valued at $880, livestock worth $41, and a wagon worth $10, for a total of $931; the poorest owned $40 worth of improvements on land. Black farmers owned more property than did laborers, but their holdings were still modest.

One telling feature of Ascension's black farmers was the negligible number who owned land: a mere 10 black farmers, all of whom resided in plantation wards, owned land, with an average holding of 15 acres, while none of the 23 property-holding black farmers in marginal areas did so. (Two farmers in plantation wards held property other than land.) As might be expected, black farmers in plantation wards devoted more of their assets to land and improvements than did those in marginal areas. In the aggregate, they held 86.4 percent of their property in land and improvements, 10.6 percent in livestock, and 3 percent in wagons and other property, while black farmers in wards seven and eight held 46.9 percent of their property in improvements on land, 48.6 percent in livestock, and 4.5 percent in wagons. Black farmers in plantation wards owned an average of $380.83 worth of property, whereas those in marginal areas owned on average $149.83. There was considerable difference between black farmers in plantation wards and those on marginal lands, but little between black farmers and black laborers on marginal lands.

Thus freedmen in Ascension Parish and throughout the sugar region occupied various rungs on the economic ladder. Although the majority of plantation laborers remained without assets, a few acquired small amounts of property. A step above these were black laborers and black farmers who resided in marginal areas, such as Ascension's seventh and eighth wards, and who remained on the plantation's periphery. Most freedmen in this situation labored within the plantation system, but they inhabited a social and geographic world between wage worker and landholder; while black farmers on marginal lands owned more property than did black laborers, the two owned similar kinds of property and conducted like economic activities with them. Finally, an infinitesimal number of freedmen achieved the status of landowning farmer. These were so exceptional that they provided no realistic example for other freedmen to emulate, but that probably did not prevent many from trying to do so.

These categories were not static. Freedmen who acquired property were a small minority, but access to their ranks remained open. Neither privation nor property holding was a permanent condition. Instead, freedmen were socially as well as geographically mobile, experiencing both the rewards and pitfalls of the capitalist market. Few accumulated the capital to escape wage labor, but the system allowed some to pursue alternatives to regular plantation employment or afforded them enough social mobility to make wage labor bearable. An 1879 newspaper editorial, which overstated the freedmen's acquiring land, could nonetheless have described their accruing other forms of property: "Some spend their wages as soon as received, this is particularly the case with those who are paid up in full, whereas those who leave a portion of their wages on deposit, gradually accumulate a fund which they use when opportunity presents itself, for purchasing a small tract of land."[30]

---

30. *Napoleonville Pioneer of Assumption,* May 31, 1879. See also *DP,* Sept. 1, 1875. Sharon Ann Holt similarly contends that former slaves in the tobacco South accumulated small savings or acquired modest amounts of property, enabling individual black households and the black community as a whole to achieve a measure of autonomy. Sharon Ann Holt, *Making Freedom Pay: North Carolina Freedpeople Working for Themselves, 1865–1900* (Athens, Ga., 2000). The argument that limited social mobility and the ability to accumulate savings or acquire property helped reconcile northern wage earners to wage labor has received its classic treatment in Stephan Thernstrom's *Poverty and Progress: Social Mobility in a Nineteenth Century City* (Cambridge, Mass., 1964; reprint, New York, 1969). For a similar argument, see Herbert G. Gutman, "The Reality of the Rags-to-Riches 'Myth': The Case of the Paterson, New Jersey, Locomotive, Iron, and Machinery Manufacturers, 1830–1880," in *Work, Culture, and Society in Industrializing America: Essays in American Working-Class and Social History* (New York, 1976), 211–33. But compare David Montgomery, *Citizen Worker: The Experience of Workers in the United States with Democracy and the Free Market during the Nineteenth Century* (Cambridge, U.K., 1993), and Amy Dru Stanley, *From Bondage to Contract: Wage Labor, Marriage, and the Market in the Age of Slave Emancipation* (Cambridge, U.K., 1998).

* * *

Freedmen of the sugar region put to effective use the lessons they had learned about the operation of the labor market. Despite planters' efforts to lower wages and establish standard rates, wages remained fairly lucrative—especially for people who had once been systematically stripped of the fruits of their labors. Sugar workers were not petit bourgeois, but neither were they degraded, alienated proletarians. Their working lives may still have resembled what they had known as slaves, but wage labor included enough rewards to prevent them from pushing for alternatives, as did their counterparts in the cotton South.

Many planters and their supporters considered the freedmen's rewards under wage labor to be too great. "The existing system may be the best, that could be adopted under the circumstances," remarked an editorial on the labor situation before the 1879 rolling season, "but its many acknowledged short comings ought to prompt those interested to scrutinize it closely." No doubt those interested had already devoted much time to scrutinizing the existing system. If they found it to be the best "under the circumstances," then they were determined to change the circumstances. Having failed to regain labor control through legal means or by employing the ways of the market, from the mid-1870s planters resorted increasingly to intimidation, violence, and other extralegal methods. Only by attacking the Reconstruction state, they reasoned, could they hope to resolve once and for all the labor problem in the sugar fields.[31]

31. *NILSB,* Oct. 16, 1879.

§8§

AMBIGUITIES OF REDEMPTION

Election day. Nothing doing on plantation. . . . The sight at the polls confirms my belief that a so called republican government is a *farce*.

—November 2, 1879, William A. Shaffer Plantation Journal

Although the end of Reconstruction in 1877 was a decisive moment for freedmen and their white Republican allies in Louisiana and throughout the South, it was replete with ambiguities in the sugar region, eradicating neither black political power nor the Republican Party. For reasons that existed elsewhere in the South as well as for those unique to southern Louisiana, the sugar parishes remained a Republican enclave until the Bourbon elite suppressed black political rights in the 1890s. While freedmen sometimes bitterly disagreed among themselves over strategy and tactics, the sugar plantation's centralized regimen and the labor arrangements it spawned afforded them an essential unity of purpose, enabling them to mobilize collectively for self-defense and to maintain internal solidarity and discipline.

But the persistence of black politics beyond 1877 contained its own ambiguities. Although freedmen in the sugar region participated in politics, Redemption was as calamitous for them as it was for freedmen in the cotton South. Not only did it reverse Reconstruction's gains, it also placed the state's coercive power in the hands of white men of property, including sugar planters. Fearing labor's demoralization, especially during rolling season, sugar planters could not systematically prevent freedmen from exercising their legal rights, but they could call upon state power—not to mention extralegal force—in moments of labor crisis. The importance of this coercive power was epitomized by state authorities' contrasting responses to strikes by sugar workers in 1874 and 1880. Although violence was averted in both instances, Republican governor William Pitt Kellogg's hesitation before deploying the state militia in 1874 contrasted starkly with Democratic governor Louis Wiltz's unequivocal decision to call out the militia in 1880. Redemption's meaning was unambiguous for the question whether force would be used against labor.

From the moment they assumed office in spring 1868, Republicans in Louisiana and other southern states faced what one historian has called a "crisis of legitimacy." All but a handful of Louisiana's white citizens considered the government created by the Reconstruction Acts to be an abomination that they were obligated to resist, by force if necessary. White resistance to the administration of Governor Henry Clay Warmoth, who served from 1868 to 1872, had been intense, but such resistance reached a frenzy following the election of Warmoth's successor, William Pitt Kellogg, a Vermont carpetbagger. Although the fall 1872 state elections did not witness the violence of 1868 (owing to the Fifteenth Amendment to the U.S. Constitution and the recently enacted Enforcement Acts), the election's aftermath was chaotic. Both Kellogg and Democratic gubernatorial candidate John McEnery claimed victory, as did rival Republican and Democratic legislatures. Only the decision of Ulysses S. Grant, recently reelected president, to bestow legal recognition upon Kellogg ensured his victory, showing clearly that Republican rule in Louisiana rested upon federal support.[1]

Despite white opposition to Warmoth and vilification of Kellogg, and despite the corruption, factionalism, and racial tensions that eventually doomed Louisiana Republicans, Radical Reconstruction had a profound impact upon the lives of

---

1. Foner, *Reconstruction*, 346. Important works on Louisiana's political history during Reconstruction include Taylor, *Louisiana Reconstructed*; Vincent, *Black Legislators*; Dawson, *Army Generals*; and Tunnell, *Crucible of Reconstruction*. On Warmoth, see Francis Wayne Binning, "Henry Clay Warmoth and Louisiana Reconstruction" (Ph.D. diss., University of North Carolina, 1969); Richard Nelson Current, *Three Carpetbag Governors* (Baton Rouge, 1967), 36–66, and *Those Terrible Carpetbaggers* (New York, 1988); Charles L. Dufour, "The Age of Warmoth," *LH* 6 (fall 1965): 335–64; Althea D. Pitre, "The Collapse of the Warmoth Regime, 1870–1872," *LH* 6 (spring 1965): 161–87. For Warmoth's apologia, see his memoirs, *War, Politics, and Reconstruction: Stormy Days in Louisiana* (New York, 1930). On Kellogg, see John Edmond Gonzales, "William Pitt Kellogg, Reconstruction Governor of Louisiana, 1873–1877," *LHQ* 29 (April 1946): 394–495. On the 1872 state elections and their aftermath, see Taylor, *Louisiana Reconstructed*, 227–49.

freedmen throughout the state. The freedmen's entrance into the polity and their becoming citizens, with rights and privileges worth defending, reinforced their determination not to let planters dominate them as working people as had been the case under slavery. Politics and labor for freedmen were distinct facets of the same struggle, equally integral to the meaning of freedom. More concretely, black majorities in several sugar parishes guaranteed black political power at the local level, giving freedmen a direct say in how the state affected them. In Ascension Parish in 1872, for example, the state legislator, sheriff, coroner, and entire police jury were black men. "In that Parish [Ascension] the negroes and Carpet baggers carried every thing before them," one planter lamented.[2]

Freedmen also influenced lawmaking. Black men never dominated public office to the extent Reconstruction's detractors claimed, but black legislators spearheaded the Republican Party's reform agenda—including public education and other social welfare measures—that transformed the state's role in daily life and improved conditions for freedmen throughout Louisiana. In addition to these affirmative manifestations of black political power, there was a defensive one of no less importance. So long as freedmen exerted some influence over law and public policy, planters could not use the legal system to enact vagrancy, anti-enticement, or contract-enforcement statutes—as they had done during presidential Reconstruction—for restricting the labor market and reestablishing control over their workers. Likewise, planters could not rely upon a Republican governor to employ the state militia's coercive power to quell labor disturbances.[3]

Nevertheless, as averse as William Pitt Kellogg and other southern Republican governors may have been to using force against freedmen, they could not refrain entirely from doing so, especially when freedmen appeared to violate the law. The events surrounding the Terrebonne Parish strike of January 1874—which was precipitated by wage reductions but quickly became politicized—demonstrated how a state government committed to defending the freedmen's rights could also be compelled to mobilize on behalf of private property. Kellogg temporized as long as he could, ordering the militia into Terrebonne only when he believed that freedmen there left him no choice, but the militia's suppression of the strike—the

2. Robert E. Moran, "Local Black Elected Officials in Ascension Parish (1868–1878)," *LH* 27 (summer 1986): 273–80; W. W. Pugh to T. B. Pugh, Nov. 25, 1872, W. W. Pugh Papers, LSU.

3. Until 1890, Louisiana enacted no laws governing labor except the 1869 vagrancy law. Intended to apply only to New Orleans and vicinity, this law sparked protests from black legislators, who unsuccessfully pushed for its repeal in 1870. It was eventually amended to further restrict its applicability. Cohen, *At Freedom's Edge*, 240–1; Vincent, *Black Legislators*, 108–10. On the consequences of black participation in politics throughout the South during Radical Reconstruction, see Foner, *Reconstruction*, 346–79.

first time since presidential Reconstruction that state power came to the planters' defense rather than to the freedmen's—revealed the dilemma of a party committed to preserving the rights of both freedmen and property holders. Planters, for their part, acted not as former slaveholders trying to reassert the old authority but rather as men of property attempting to reestablish order on their estates. In this respect, they shared northern property holders' hostility to organized labor as well as their determination to suppress labor unrest. Despite Kellogg's genuine reluctance to sending in the militia, the strike's resolution boded ill for freedmen were Reconstruction to end.

The strike was triggered when planters, responding to the national economic crisis, reduced 1874 monthly wages from the $15–$20 range to $13—a rate that, as one of them put it, was "in accordance with the present prices of sugar and molasses." Planters had failed miserably on previous occasions to reduce wages, but the economic depression and poor 1873 harvest impelled them finally to act in unison as a matter of self-preservation. Although freedmen throughout the sugar region expressed resentment over this action, those in Terrebonne Parish took the lead in protesting it. Terrebonne freedmen assumed a militant stance, but it was conflict among them, rather than between them and planters, that eventuated in state intervention.[4]

The strike began on January 5, when some two hundred freedmen convened at the Zion Church near Houma to discuss the reductions. They demanded monthly wages of $20, plus rations, with nothing held in reserve; they also proposed forming "sub-associations" that would rent land, perhaps reflecting an inevitable frustration with wage labor in light of recent events. The strikers met again several days later to reaffirm their demands and to hear several orators— including William H. "Hamp" Keyes, the black state representative for Terrebonne— urge them not to work for less than $20 and to take the land by force. After the meeting, a group of strikers marched peacefully through Houma with fife and drum.[5]

Terrebonne freedmen, however, were deeply divided over the strike. They may

4. Letter of H. O. Colomb, in *DP,* Jan. 11, 1874. See also W. P. Flower to T. Pugh, Jan. 8, 1874, W. W. Pugh Papers, LSU. For freedmen's disaffection over the reductions, see Jan. 17, 31, Feb. 1, 1874, AFP Diary, and Jan. 19, 1874, W. W. Pugh Diary, both in Pugh Papers, UT; A. H. Gay to EJG, Jan. 4, 1874, R. Daigre to EJG, Jan. 1, 14, Feb. 2, 1874, C. M. Gillis to EJG, Jan. 14, Feb. 4, 8, 1874, EJGP; 43rd Cong., 2nd Sess., HR 261, pt. 3, pp. 620–6; *DP,* Jan. 7, 1874; *NILSB,* Jan. 8, 1874.

5. The strike's main outline has been gleaned from several sources, primarily the *DP.* See also *NILSB* for January, and *Thibodaux Sentinel,* Jan. 17, 24. Minor inconsistencies occur among and within individual accounts. Although some journalists embellished their reports and may even have fabricated stories of outrages by freedmen, there is no denying that disagreements and violence occurred among freedmen.

have maintained unity in defending their political and legal rights against planters' attacks, but taking the offensive by engaging in a large-scale strike caused many of them to have misgivings. During the next several days, strikers roamed the parish and forcibly disrupted operations on plantations where freedmen had refused to join them, threatening violence toward those who returned to work. But such tactics undermined the strikers' cause and gave planters critical leverage, since the latter now had legal grounds to call upon local and state authorities to suppress unrest. Under the right to contract, individual freedmen were free not to work, but they had no right to interfere with laborers who chose not to strike. Meanwhile, emotions ran high as rumors circulated of strikers threatening violence against citizens. Fear likewise spread among freedmen, who became convinced that planters intended to bring in "the Spaniards"—a group of New Orleans thugs—to put down the strike. Remembering how such bands had prowled the region in 1868, freedmen were no more inclined to view these reports skeptically than were whites who believed everything they heard about strikers intent on unspeakable outrages.

A dramatic confrontation took place on January 13, when some fifty armed strikers, led by Alf Kennedy, descended upon Henry Minor's Southdown plantation and attempted to prevent freedmen from working. When Minor warned that he would brook no such interference, the strikers left to gather "reinforcements" and vowed to burn down Minor's sugar mill. Minor sought assistance from the black parish sheriff, one Lyons, who formed an interracial posse of about twenty-five men. Minor also telegraphed Governor Kellogg and asked him to dispatch the state militia to restore order. Having already received similar requests, Kellogg was loath to do so. Instead, he commissioned W. J. Snow and Peter Joseph of the New Orleans Metropolitan Police to investigate affairs in Terrebonne.[6]

The following morning, a large body of strikers returned to Southdown, where Sheriff Lyons and the posse met them. Realizing that his force could not deter the strikers, Lyons offered to disband the posse if the strikers would also disperse. In the meantime, however, Officers Snow and Joseph arrived and informed the strikers

6. Formed by Henry Clay Warmoth, the Metropolitan Police, or the Metropolitans, were the interracial military arm of the Louisiana Republican Party during Reconstruction. Early in Warmoth's term, federal law forbade the southern states from reorganizing their militias, and even after the law's repeal, Warmoth placed no trust in the state militia. Warmoth had also been prompted to organize the Metropolitans, over which the New Orleans city government had no authority, after the violent 1868 presidential election. Taylor, *Louisiana Reconstructed*, 177–8; Dennis C. Rousey, *Policing the Southern City: New Orleans, 1805–1889* (Baton Rouge, 1996), chap. 5. Sheriff Lyons's given name does not appear in contemporary sources on the strike, nor is Lyons listed in Eric Foner, *Freedom's Lawmakers: A Directory of Black Officeholders during Reconstruction*, rev. ed. (Baton Rouge, 1996).

that state authorities would not countenance their actions. Although the strikers interpreted the Metropolitan officers' presence as an act of "duplicity" by Kellogg and announced themselves ready to fight, Snow and Joseph eventually effected a compromise in which both strikers and posse would disband. A meeting was also scheduled for the following day, to be attended by the Metropolitan officers, strike leaders, and prominent men of the parish, to end the dispute. The situation seemed at this point to have been defused, but for the rest of the day freedmen evidently continued disrupting work on plantations in Terrebonne as well as in neighboring Lafourche Parish. Snow and Joseph notified both Kellogg and militia general A. S. Badger that troops were needed to restore order. With no choice, Kellogg reluctantly ordered forty infantry and one piece of artillery, under command of former Confederate general James Longstreet and William F. Loan, into Terrebonne. He also appointed a special committee, headed by Hamp Keyes, to accompany the militia and to act as intermediary between it and the strikers. The troops arrived in Houma later that evening.

Such mediation as Keyes and the committee might have provided was obviated on the morning of January 15. Upon arrival of a supplemental force of twenty-five cavalry, warrants were issued for the strike's leaders, including Alf Kennedy, who were arrested and incarcerated in the parish jail. Two days later, a mass meeting took place at which Henry Minor, Hamp Keyes, Thomas Cage (the black state senator for Terrebonne), and several parish officials urged compromise. Meanwhile, the imprisoned strike leaders were taken to New Orleans and arraigned. All soon gained their release when Cage and Keyes furnished their bonds, and with the strike broken, legal proceedings against them were dropped. Freedmen went to work for $13 per month, and planters were now, as one newspaper proclaimed, "masters of the situation."[7]

If the strike ended somewhat anticlimactically, it also proved to be only a temporary victory for planters, since within a year or so the realities of the labor market would force them to increase monthly wages to $15–$20. Nonetheless, the events of the strike itself were not without significance. Previously, planters had undertaken extralegal measures while freedmen called upon legitimate state authority for protection. In 1874, however, striking freedmen resorted to tactics beyond the bounds of law and order while planters acted with the force of law behind them. Suppressing the strike did not require actual use of force, but only because freedmen relented before violence became necessary. If a southern Republican governor could be compelled to dispatch the militia on planters' behalf, there was no telling how a Democratic administration would react to labor unrest.

7. *NILSB*, Feb. 5, 1874. See also Jan. 22, 1874 , ibid.

However indecisively state power had been deployed against freedmen, its use during Reconstruction was ominous.

The planters' triumph had other repercussions, for it emboldened them to escalate their attack on the Kellogg administration and on the freedmen's political rights. State power had been wielded on planters' behalf, although only because freedmen had broken the law. So long as freedmen did not resort to illegal tactics, planters could not call upon the state to control them. A long-term settlement of the labor problem thus still hinged upon ending Republican rule and black political power. Moreover, white Louisianians had hoped that either the federal courts or Congress would overturn the disputed 1872 state elections and remove Kellogg from office. As they realized by early 1874 that this was not about to happen, their opposition became increasingly open and violent. Despite the freedmen's determination to stand up for their political rights, white Conservative pressure on the Kellogg government intensified until it culminated in Reconstruction's defeat.

Planters sometimes claimed, not entirely ingenuously, that they and their workers, as one of them noted, "live together in the utmost peace and harmony when not interfered with by politicians." Intent on eliminating such interference, planters revived the tactic begun during the late 1860s of using their power as employers to dissuade freedmen from exercising the right to vote. In June 1874, for instance, James Todd of St. Mary Parish published an open letter pledging not to hire any freedman who voted in the fall and urging others to follow suit. Todd denied trying to force freedmen to vote Democratic, and he insisted that he did not intend to dismiss those he already employed for voting. Rather, he announced that in the future he would not hire "those who will destroy my interests and rights if they are afforded the opportunity." Given their difficulties hiring workers, planters split on the "Todd letter"—believing it impractical, some refused to support it; others thought it a good idea. If freedmen "continue to vote so directly against the interests of the property holder, nothing is easier than to replace them with a class who *will* understand that their employers' interests are theirs," insisted one newspaper editor who articulated many planters' sentiments but also expressed much wishful thinking. "It is *self protection* to the planter, and if the negroes like politics better than their houses and employment on the plantations, let them take their own choices." The Todd letter, like other previous stratagems, would have limited impact in the fall, but it reflected planters' desperation to neutralize the black majority's political power.[8]

8. 43rd Cong., 2nd Sess., HR 261, pt. 2, pp. 26–9. The Todd letter appears in *DP,* June 19, 1874, and *NILSB,* July 2, 1874. For opposition to it, see 43rd Cong., 2nd Sess., HR 261, pt. 3, pp. 600–5. The quotation in support is from *NILSB,* July 2, 1874.

The Todd letter paled against the bulldozing tactics of the paramilitary White League. Founded in spring 1874, the White League unabashedly announced its intentions to destroy Republican rule and restore white Democrats to power. Raising intimidation to an art, the White League forced Republican officeholders to resign and prevented black men from registering to vote. The White League did not stop at threats: it unleashed a reign of terror in the months before the 1874 fall elections so effective that violence at the polls on election day became unnecessary. The White League was responsible for the Coushatta massacre in August, in which five white Republicans were slain, and in the Battle of Liberty Place in September, it defeated Metropolitan police and state militia in a conflict at the foot of Canal Street in New Orleans, leaving thirty-two dead and forcing Kellogg to seek protection under the U.S. flag. Federal troops restored Kellogg to power, but clearly Republicans could not govern even New Orleans, their home base, without federal support. These incidents, however harrowing, merely punctuated an electoral season that was exceptionally violent even by Louisiana standards.[9]

The White League was especially strong in the sugar parishes of St. Mary and Iberia (created in 1868 from parts of St. Mary and St. Martin), where planters routinely threatened to dismiss freedmen who voted Republican. "In my presence," a Republican sheriff testified, "the negroes were told that if they voted the republican ticket they would be discharged immediately by their employers." A black constable stationed at the polls near New Iberia reported that white men had threatened every freedman either to vote Democratic or "be turned out of his employment." Freedmen did not have to experience violence personally to get the message. Months after the election, a number of them told a congressional investigative committee that they had freely voted Democratic and had not suffered intimidation. One freedman maintained that his employer had "asked" him to vote Democratic; another who voted Democratic, when asked if his employer belonged to the White League, responded: "He am the White League."[10]

As community leaders, planters played an important role in the White League by condoning if not actually committing violence. However determined they were to end Republican rule, planters were also of a divided mind on political terror. They believed that politics bore much responsibility for labor's demoralization and therefore must be stopped, but they were realistic enough to see that bulldozing might also cause their workers to become demoralized and thus unwilling to

9. On the White League, see Taylor, *Louisiana Reconstructed,* 297–304; Tunnell, *Crucible of Reconstruction,* 193–218; and H. Oscar Lestage Jr., "The White League in Louisiana and Its Participation in Reconstruction Riots," *LHQ* 18 (July 1935): 617–95.

10. These examples, and others like them, can be found in 43rd Cong., 2nd Sess., HR 101, pt. 2, pp. 119–21, 127–8, 137–8, 182–5, and 43rd Cong., 2nd Sess., HR 261, pt. 3, pp. 344, 347–8.

work with the enthusiasm necessary to harvest the crop. Concern over labor's demoralization, especially during rolling season, caused some to refrain from at least the more extreme forms of bulldozing, enabling freedmen to continue their political activities.

Far from lording it over the workers, some planters seemed helpless against the freedmen's exercising of their political rights. "The negroes quit the plantation to attend clubs and meetings," one Ascension Parish planter complained. "Often in the busiest seasons they will go in a body to an election meeting, or to hear speeches and such things, and it operates greatly against the interests of the planters." F. S. Goode, Terrebonne Parish planter and Democratic candidate for the state senate in 1874, denied trying to influence his workers' votes. To the contrary, despite his urging them to vote Democratic, Goode stood by at the polls, located on his plantation, and watched "every man in my employ, without exception, vote against me, one after another." Such episodes attested not to the emptiness of planters' threats but to the freedmen's resolve in the face of intimidation and violence. Many planters conceded the issue and postponed the rolling season until after the election rather than attempt to harvest their crops during the volatile campaign. "Election day and no work going on," one planter noted in early November.[11]

Concern for their personal financial affairs caused some planters to condemn the White League's methods, which threatened to upset the delicate equilibrium of the plantations and demoralize the workers. Even so staunch an opponent of Reconstruction as A. F. Pugh not only castigated the White League but also blamed it for the prevailing political chaos. "White Leagues are arousing an alarm for the general war of races," Pugh warned in early September, "which will cause the loss of the crops." After the Battle of Liberty Place, Pugh noted disgustedly: "The White Leagues have ruined every thing, and yet do not realize what they have done." "What fools," he lamented. White League violence, in Pugh's and other planters' eyes, brought not stability but disruption of plantation routine and general economic turmoil. Most planters found freedmen's political activities disconcerting, but many of them—fearing labor's demoralization and subsequent loss of crops—looked upon the White League's methods as equally unsettling.[12]

Despite planter ambivalence over all-out political terror, if not over the desire to end Reconstruction, and despite an ill-fated attempt at compromise, or "Fusion," in several sugar parishes in fall 1874, positions on both sides of the political divide hardened after the elections. Having failed to dislodge Kellogg either

11. 43rd Cong., 2nd Sess., HR 261, pt. 3, pp. 26–9, 648–53; Nov. 2, 1874, W. W. Pugh Diary, Pugh Papers, UT. See also L. Bouchereau, *Statement . . . 1874–75,* vi–vii.

12. Sept. 1, 21, 1874, AFP Diary, Pugh Papers, UT.

legally or forcibly, white Conservatives set their sights on the 1876 state and pres-idential elections. In exposing the Louisiana Republicans' crisis of legitimacy, the events of 1874 thus portended what might come after Reconstruction. Yet no mat-ter how formidable the position of Reconstruction's opponents or how precarious that of its supporters, Redemption was not a foregone conclusion. Instead, it required an unprecedented level of bulldozing by white Conservatives. The con-sequences of this crusade, while tragic for Louisiana as a whole, proved to be du-bious in the sugar parishes, where, as the 1876 campaign confirmed, freedmen continued to mobilize for self-defense, and where, consequently, resolution of the labor problem still eluded planters.[13]

The fact that Democrats had redeemed all but three southern states—Louisiana, South Carolina, and Florida—by 1876 did not obviate the significance of that year's elections. Furthermore, while Louisiana's role in the disputed presi-dential election and in the Compromise of 1877 is a familiar one, Reconstruction's demise had as profound an impact upon the state's black population as had the implementation of Radical Reconstruction a decade earlier. It had long been clear that southern Republican governments would not last a day without federal sup-port, and by 1876 the nation was in "retreat from Reconstruction." Disgust with Republican corruption, the worst economic depression the nation had yet seen, and a desire to move beyond the animosities of the Civil War contributed to white Americans' weariness over Reconstruction. This sentiment was painfully exempli-fied by Grant's refusal, for fear of repercussions in upcoming northern elections, to save Mississippi Republicans in 1875 from a Conservative-led firestorm of vio-lence and fraud that ended Reconstruction in that state. Nonetheless, if federal abandonment of Mississippi presaged Reconstruction's collapse before 1876, both sides in southern Louisiana brought to bear all of the resources at their disposal, convinced as they were that they were fighting for their political lives.[14]

In what had by now become a mantra, planters observed with both annoyance and resignation how politics interfered with plantation operations. "Not much work today. Negroes gone to register," one noted. "Expect to start grinding just after the election." The harvest on an estate of Edward Gay commenced a week late because of the workers' political activities. "Would have started on Thursday," a visitor reported, "but political excitement in Thibodaux caused the men to leave

13. On the Fusion movement in 1874, see Taylor, *Louisiana Reconstructed*, 301.

14. The literature on the end of Reconstruction is vast. See especially C. Vann Woodward, *Reunion and Reaction: The Compromise of 1877 and the End of Reconstruction* (Boston, 1951); William Gillette, *Retreat from Reconstruction, 1869–1879* (Baton Rouge, 1979), 300–62; and Michael Perman, *The Road to Redemption: Southern Politics, 1869–1879* (Chapel Hill, N.C., 1984), chaps. 7–9, 12. For a specific treatment of Louisiana, see Taylor, *Louisiana Reconstructed*, chap. 11.

the field in a body on Wednesday and repair to town armed with guns and cane knives." The thoughts of a planter whose freedmen left work to attend political meetings as ripened cane stood in the fields can only be imagined, but planters did not just sit by and watch. Nor did their condemnations of black political campaigning preclude them from trying to influence the black vote. "We dread to get up any excitement among laborers till the other side takes the initiative," insisted one planter, who was sure that "large numbers of negroes can be induced to vote the conservative ticket." A Democratic orator reported speaking before a crowd of some five hundred people, the vast majority of whom were black. "It was in the neighborhood of large plantations," he noted, "where the laborers are principally composed of colored men."[15]

Even when planters used tactics short of outright intimidation, their intent was clear. R. H. Wilkinson, a Democratic planter and federal election marshal in Plaquemines Parish, admitted after the election that he had discussed politics with his workers and had given them Democratic tickets just before the election. They arrived at the polls en masse in Wilkinson's wagons and voted Democratic, despite Republican efforts to change their minds. Wilkinson denied having influenced the freedmen, claiming instead that they had previously expressed disgust with the Republican Party and had instructed their foreman to ask him for Democratic tickets. The freedmen's side of the story is not known, but others told of less subtle attempts to control their votes or to prevent them from voting, including routine threats of dismissal. "When a man is working in a place and votes the republican ticket, and next day he is turned out," as one freedman put it, "you see that is trouble for him." Another who voted Democratic later explained that he had "voted for the men who had given me work and food."[16]

In addition to their well-honed techniques of intimidation, Conservatives resorted to fraud. The highly mobile nature of the labor force, as well as the large influx of workers for the rolling season, created many opportunities to tamper with voter lists and to stuff ballot boxes. When congressional investigators tried to determine the number of voters in Plaquemines Parish in 1876, for instance, Republican election official William Prescott charged that Democrats had tampered with voter lists, since some 2,400 votes had been cast in a parish that usually included no more than 2,000 registered voters. While admitting that it was not unusual for many laborers to enter the sugar parishes for the rolling season, thus increasing the voting population, Prescott nonetheless contended that the 1876 crop, being short, would not have required such a large increase. The vote count,

15. Sept. 12, Oct. 30, Nov. 7, 1876, Plant. Journal 7, Shaffer Papers, SHC; R. M. Walsh to EJG, Nov. 10, 1876, EJGP; *NILSB*, Aug. 24, 1876; 44th Cong., 2nd Sess., HMD 34, pt. 2, pp. 622–31.
16. 44th Cong., 2nd Sess., HMD 34, pt. 5, pp. 313–6, 352; ibid., pt. 2, p. 43.

he insisted, was due to Democratic fraud. Another witness, in noting an equally suspicious rise in Lafourche Parish's vote, remarked that "a fixed number of hands" ordinarily resided on a plantation during the year and that "it is only during the polling season that any great influx of additional labor is brought in." Confusion over whether this witness actually said "polling season" or "rolling season"—since either would have been true—attests not only to the link between politics and labor arrangements in the sugar region but also to the possibilities for electoral fraud with such a transient population.[17]

Conservatives, of course, did not monopolize shady electioneering techniques. Any irritation that planters felt over their workers' political activities was exacerbated by Republican efforts to ensure a large black turnout on election day. Authorized to determine the location of polling places, Republican officials established many of them on plantations, prompting planters' objections on grounds that insurers would raise rates or cancel policies if something so risky as an election took place on their property. Planters also took umbrage at what they saw as violation of their rights as property holders, especially for the purpose of facilitating black voting. "The fixing of polling-booths is another of the prerogatives of the supervisor, which was exercised in rather a new style," noted one journalist whose views planters endorsed. "A majority of the booths were placed in plantation-quarters, this official assuming the power to go into men's plantations and to establish polls in or about sugar-houses, most of which were at work." Conservatives also charged that Republican officials focused their voter registration efforts on plantation districts, obvious Republican bastions, while ignoring areas with white majorities. However self-serving, such complaints underscored Louisiana Republicans' determination to hold onto their power.[18]

As they resorted to such methods, Republican officials tapped into a groundswell of black loyalty that one Democrat likened to "religious faith." Despite instances of freedmen breaking ranks and allying themselves with Democrats, former slaves drew upon their collective ethos—which was fostered by cultural traditions born of slavery as well as by labor arrangements characteristic of sugar production—to preserve unity within the black community. Jefferson Rhodes, a Baptist minister in Lafourche Parish, preached allegiance to the Republican Party, adding that were a member of his congregation to support the Democrats, Rhodes would pray "to make him know better." Conversely, black ministers whose Republican loyalties wavered faced their congregations' disapprobation. Several Methodist ministers, a Lafourche freedman observed, "have been ostracized very

17. 44th Cong., 2nd Sess., HMD 34, pt. 5, p. 291; 45th Cong., 1st Sess., HMD 5, p. 82.
18. 45th Cong., 1st Sess., HMD 5, p. 24; 44th Cong., 2nd Sess., HMD 34, pt. 5, pp. 116, 339.

heavily for having had very liberal opinions and not conforming exactly with the radical leaders."[19]

In speaking of ministers having been ostracized, this freedman identified one of the primary means by which the black community preserved solidarity during the 1870s. Freedmen who joined the Democrats encountered cajoling, verbal abuse, and even the severing of social and personal relations and isolation from the community. As one freedman explained, "a man . . . [who] has a different opinion in his political views . . . will be abused about it and talked about on the streets and chastised, as though he really has no right to exercise his own opinion, and that he must be taught and led by somebody else." Having once scratched out the name of a Republican candidate for office but having otherwise voted the straight party ticket, the speaker had nonetheless been shunned. "[A] man came to me and met me in the court-house, shaking his finger in my face, saying that I had voted for a democrat," he recalled. "I thought that was ostracism."[20]

Wayward black Democrats faced ostracism from their wives and other women of the freed community, whose disfranchisement did not keep them from participating in politics or from influencing the election's outcome. The Republican Party established women's auxiliaries, according to one observer, in order to "drive all the republican voters back—all these men who had thought otherwise or who might attempt to do otherwise than vote the straight Republican ticket." After several freedmen formed a Democratic club in Thibodaux, Republicans organized freedwomen, who, as one witness put it, "went into that club and treated the colored democrats very rudely, and, consequently, they could not vote the democratic ticket." A freedman's wife left him because he promised his employer he would vote Democratic; she returned only after he voted Republican. Several freedmen who tried to vote Democratic were driven from the polls by Republican stalwarts and "abused by some women standing on the levee." But perhaps none matched the women who broke up a Democratic meeting near Thibodaux. "By God, I thought there was going to be a revolution here," exclaimed the Lafourche Parish sheriff. "The democrats are armed, and the women are coming out with cane-knives and hoes and axes."[21]

As the actions of the freedwomen demonstrated, party allegiance was a more serious matter than merely observing social niceties. Freedmen who abandoned the Republican cause in 1876 faced even more aggressive forms of ostracism as the black community mobilized to impose internal discipline. Freedmen who spoke publicly on behalf of the Democratic Party later told of overt threats made against

19. 44th Cong., 2nd Sess., HMD 34, pt. 2, pp. 622–31; ibid., pt. 5, pp. 53, 126–7.
20. Ibid., pt. 5, p. 55.
21. Ibid., 53, 57–8, 99–114, 131, 298.

them. "Any God damn nigger that will vote the democratic ticket ought to be hung; I could cut his heart out right now," one freedman boasted. Another claimed to have overheard several freedmen disparage a black defector: "There goes the damned big democratic nigger. Before long we will get him." A freedman who had broken ranks was simply told: "G-d d—n you, don't you come round here with your speeches in this community of this people, because we don't want any democrats around here."[22]

Freedmen backed up tough talk with action. When one freedman whose political sympathies were in doubt approached the polls, a Republican ticket was thrust into his hand and he was made to vote it. "They said, 'This is a freedom ticket. That is the ticket you have got to vote,'" a witness reported. "He took the straight radical ticket and held it open and put it in the box." Such tactics may not have been standard practice, but they were not isolated incidents. One Democrat claimed that Republican methods in 1876 "consisted of general threatening and intimidation on the part of the republican negroes against the negroes who had voted the democratic ticket, and saying those negroes should be killed." Many freedmen, he insisted, "were prevented from voting the democratic ticket by the intimidation practiced against them," an assertion containing both ulterior motive and more than a grain of truth. Freedmen sometimes disagreed bitterly among themselves over goals, strategies, and tactics. Moreover, it is hardly surprising that the factionalism, corruption, and racial tensions that divided the Louisiana Republican Party's leadership in New Orleans would manifest themselves, in one way or another, in local communities and wreak havoc throughout the countryside. Yet if the black community's internal divisions should not be overlooked, neither should they be overstated. Ostracism, threats, and even violence offered indisputable proof of cleavages within the black community, but they also reflected the freedmen's determination to achieve and maintain unity against external enemies. Freedmen may have become disgruntled with the Republican Party, but the cold, hard reality was that the Democratic alternative was no alternative at all. Understanding this unavoidable fact of political life, many freedmen felt that their compatriots must not be permitted to vote Democratic if there was anything they could do about it.[23]

The victory of Republican presidential candidate Rutherford B. Hayes resulted not from southern black voters' resiliency but from the national party's determination to hold onto the presidency at whatever cost. With the nation seemingly on the verge of civil war over the disputed 1876 election, Republicans won by

22. Ibid., pt. 1, p. 111, 114, and pt. 2, p. 112. Taylor, *Louisiana Reconstructed*, 480–9, also examines intimidation within the black community during the 1876 campaign.

23. Ibid., pt. 5, pp. 290, 298.

agreeing to end Reconstruction. Despite Reconstruction's many shortcomings, its failure was catastrophic for freedmen throughout the South and especially for those in Louisiana, where Republicans' only hope of maintaining power was with federal support. In 1877, Republican control of the presidency hinged not upon defending Reconstruction but upon abandoning it. Thus, Hayes assumed the presidency, the few hundred federal troops stationed in the South were ordered back to their barracks, and in Louisiana—whose gubernatorial contest was yet again disputed—Democrat Francis T. Nicholls was inaugurated, while Republican candidate Stephen B. Packard and his supporters were sacrificed on the national party's altar of power.

Historians have long debated 1877's importance to the story of Reconstruction. Republicans held only three southern states by that date, and the nation as a whole—its attention having turned to other issues—had largely forsaken the former slaves. Moreover, despite black southerners' abandonment by the North and by the federal government, black political and legal rights prevailed in parts of the South after 1877. Until legal segregation and the systematic disfranchisement of the 1890s, many black men routinely cast free and fair ballots, black people enjoyed basic civil and legal rights, and the Republican Party's presence endured even though its candidates had little chance of gaining statewide office. In the history of the South, the years between 1877 and the early 1890s were an uncertain period in which race relations had not yet solidified and alternative solutions to the race question were still possible.[24]

Whatever 1877's significance, the sugar region remained an enclave of black political power and Republican voting strength. This persistence has often been attributed to the sugar planters' tariff-driven dependence on the Republican Party and to their ambivalent role in the Bourbon coalition that ruled Louisiana after Reconstruction. Not only did the sugar planters' support for the tariff make for an uneasy alliance with their Bourbon partners—wealthy cotton planters and the New Orleans business community—but a small number of sugar planters were

24. On the uncertainties of the post-Reconstruction period for southern race relations, see C. Vann Woodward, *The Strange Career of Jim Crow* (New York, 1955). On black and Republican politics in the South after Reconstruction, see J. Morgan Kousser, *The Shaping of Southern Politics: Suffrage Restriction and the Establishment of the One-Party South, 1880–1910* (New Haven, Conn., 1974), and Jerrold G. Rusk and John J. Stucker, "The Effect of the Southern System of Election Laws on Voting Participation: A Reply to V. O. Key, Jr.," in *The History of American Electoral Behavior,* ed. Joel H. Sibley, Allan C. Bogue, and William H. Flanagan (Princeton, N.J., 1978), 198–250. For post-Reconstruction politics in Louisiana, see William Ivy Hair, *Bourbonism and Agrarian Protest: Louisiana Politics, 1877–1900* (Baton Rouge, 1969).

also Republicans and thus contributed to a political climate in which the party was not considered anathema.[25]

The tariff and sugar planters' political proclivities, however important, do not entirely explain why the Republican Party and black political rights endured in the sugar region. Republican planters hardly discouraged black men from voting Republican, to be sure, but most sugar planters actually opposed the party. Nor did sugar planters' reliance on the tariff preclude them from sanctioning the suppression of black rights during the 1890s. The tariff and sugar planters' political leanings therefore account only in part for continuing Republican influence and black political power after 1877. Instead, southern Louisiana's distinct political character was rooted in the process of sugar production as well as in the resulting modes of labor organization. That black men in the sugar region exercised political power when many in the cotton South no longer did so underscores how black grassroots political mobilization and the labor arrangements that sugar production engendered continued to reinforce each other well after Reconstruction.

Many black people continued to exercise political and legal rights where cotton dominated. For every Republican enclave in the cotton South, however, there were many other areas, such as the cotton parishes of the Natchez District, just north of the sugar region, where, despite large black majorities, black politics came to a definitive halt after 1877. A comparison of the gubernatorial vote in the sugar region and Natchez District from the late 1870s to the early 1890s demonstrates not only that black political power persisted in the sugar region but also that a black majority offers no better explanation for such persistence than does the tariff or planters' political stance.

Whereas the sugar region was home to a substantial black voting majority in the mid-1870s, the Natchez District included an overwhelming one. In 1875, the black voting population in each of the sugar parishes (excluding Orleans Parish) outnumbered the white one; and in the sugar region overall, black voters outnumbered white voters by 26,460 to 12,491 (67.9 percent to 32.1 percent). The black voting population also outnumbered the white one in each of the parishes of the Natchez District, but by much larger majorities than in the sugar region; and in the Natchez District overall, black voters outnumbered white voters by 13,364 to 1,805 (86.1 percent to 13.9 percent) (table 19). The ratio of black to white voters in the sugar region was two to one, but in the Natchez District it was more than seven to one.

25. On the importance of the tariff in accounting for Republican strength in southern Louisiana, see Hair, *Bourbonism and Agrarian Protest*, 246–8; Howard, *Political Tendencies*, 156, 159; and Sitterson, *Sugar Country*, 324–42. On sugar planters' role in the Louisiana Bourbon coalition, see Hair, chaps. 2–4 and 6.

TABLE 19

Number of Potential Voters: Sugar Parishes and Natchez District, 1875

PARISH	White	Black	Total
SUGAR PARISHES			
Ascension	1,098	2,400	3,498
Assumption	1,273	1,902	3,175
Iberville	860	2,355	3,215
Jefferson	992	2,275	3,267
Lafourche	1,953	2,312	4,265
Plaquemines	806	2,232	3,038
St. Bernard	388	765	1,153
St. Charles	321	1,591	1,912
St. James	1,094	2,974	4,068
St. John the Baptist	601	1,614	2,215
St. Mary	1,260	3,194	4,454
Terrebonne	1,484	1,822	3,306
West Baton Rouge	361	1,024	1,385
Totals	12,491	26,460	38,951
NATCHEZ DISTRICT			
Carroll	695	3,010	3,705
Concordia	218	2,839	3,057
Madison	400	3,263	3,663
Tensas	492	4,252	4,744
Totals	1,805	13,364	15,169

Source: 45th Cong., 3rd Sess., Senate Report 855, vol. 1, pp. 565–85.

Despite their black majorities, the two areas' political destinies diverged after Reconstruction. In the sugar region the Democratic vote showed no appreciable increase, while in the Natchez District it increased dramatically (table 20). Throughout the 1880s, Democratic gubernatorial candidates consistently received less than half the vote in the sugar parishes, but in the Natchez District they received clear majorities. Freedmen would not have voluntarily voted Democratic on such a scale; only systematic intimidation and fraud could have caused these results. Redemption's repercussions, if ambiguous in the sugar parishes, were immediate and unmistakable in the cotton parishes. "Election day. Nothing doing on plantation," complained a Terrebonne planter in 1879. "The sight at the polls confirms my belief that a so called republican government is a *farce.*" A Lafourche planter described a similar situation the same year. "This was election day, and there was a very large vote polled. Both races turned

TABLE 20

Parish Percentages for Winning Candidate in Gubernatorial Elections: Sugar Parishes and Natchez District, 1876–1892

	Nicholls	Wiltz	McEnery	Nicholls	Foster*
PARISH	1876	1879	1884	1888	1892
SUGAR PARISHES					
Ascension	37.2	23.5	39.4	67.0	58.4
Assumption	50.1	43.9	36.4	46.8	27.1
Iberville	96.5	21.8	35.3	40.8	38.3
Jefferson	33.7	n/a	23.3	40.0	46.7
Lafourche	50.1	55.6	55.4	63.5	25.3
Plaquemines	29.5	33.6	27.5	36.6	37.8
St. Bernard	48.4	65.5	50.8	69.5	11.4
St. Charles	20.1	9.3	0.4	11.1	5.5
St. James	33.1	35.6	27.6	29.0	26.1
St. John the Baptist	37.0	49.8	21.7	32.7	14.5
St. Mary	37.7	30.5	11.8	63.6	77.1
Terrebonne	41.6	34.2	36.9	45.3	29.7
West Baton Rouge	32.8	37.5	66.0	79.0	23.9
NATCHEZ DISTRICT					
East Carroll	21.0**	11.5	34.7	90.3	6.5
West Carroll	n/a	89.9	99.1	83.8	60.8
Concordia	13.4	55.3	76.5	06.6***	65.4
Madison	1.8	96.8	51.8	100.0	91.4
Tensas	13.2	84.4	99.9	97.6	11.1

Source: Perry H. Howard, *Political Tendencies in Louisiana*, rev. and exp. ed. (Baton Rouge, 1971), 425, 446–7.

* Foster was the Democratic anti-Lottery candidate; Democrats also ran a pro-Lottery candidate, resulting in a split vote.

** Carroll Parish was divided into East Carroll and West Carroll in 1877; this figure represents the total for Carroll Parish.

*** This appears to be an incorrect transcription in the source.

out their fullest strength." Such statements by a Natchez District planter would have been highly unlikely.[26]

The persistence of black and Republican politics owed neither to the tariff nor to the sugar region's black majority but instead to the realities of sugar production. Planters' concerns over the potential demoralization of labor precluded them from bulldozing the black vote. Likewise, sugar plantations' centralized routine enabled freedmen to sustain a unity that their counterparts in the cotton South,

26. Nov. 2, 1879, Plant. Journal 10, Shaffer Papers, SHC; Dec. [Nov.] 2, 1879, AFP Diary, Pugh Papers, UT. See also C. W. Pope to J. H. Gay, Nov. 10, 1879, EJGP.

dispersed as they were throughout the countryside, could not match. Working in gangs and living in centralized quarters allowed freedmen to mobilize collectively for self-defense and to keep potential defectors in line. The cohesion that sugar workers achieved through their labor afforded them a measure of control over their collective destiny. "It is a significant fact that the illegal, brutal methods of electioneering that are now known as bull-dozing have been confined for the most part since 1868 to the cotton-growing regions of the South," stated a U.S. Senate committee report on Louisiana's 1878 elections. Because of the "exigencies of the cane crop," it contended, "there have been no serious or systematic attempts made in the sugar-growing parishes to control by violence the negro vote." "[The] demoralization of agricultural labor," it continued, "occurring at the time of the year when elections are held in Louisiana, would bring ruin to hundreds of wealthy planters in the sugar-growing region." Thus, "bull-dozing is not encouraged either by the concurrence or indifference of the wealthy classes of those sections."[27]

The report understated political terror in the sugar region even as it overstated the significance of "the exigencies of the cane crop." It was not so much the demands of the crop per se as it was the particular labor relations to which sugar production gave rise that explain the persistence of black politics in southern Louisiana after 1877. Nor should the contrasting political conditions to which the report alluded be exaggerated. Despite Republican presence in the sugar region, freedmen there also suffered the travesties of Bourbon rule, as the Louisiana Bourbons systematically dismantled the social-reform agenda that Republicans had initiated during Radical Reconstruction. And with Democrats controlling the state, the larger context within which black political power existed had been fundamentally transformed. Black officeholders no longer served in opposition to but rather with the blessing of local white leaders; their authority rested on an ability to mediate between the white and black communities, and they conveyed a defensive message rather than one of black self-assertion. Finally, Redemption not only ended black influence on public policy but also shifted the balance of power in planters' favor where it mattered most—the use of force. Redemption did not settle the daily contest over labor, as many planters had hoped, but it ensured that the state would intervene unequivocally on their behalf when necessary. The sugar region thus remained a Republican oasis, but only within a Democratic desert.[28]

The significance of Bourbon rule is amply demonstrated by state authorities' response to strikes along the banks of the Mississippi in spring 1880. Despite Redemption's ambiguities, these strikes—the most serious labor disturbances

27. 45th Cong., 3rd Sess., Senate Report 855, vol. 1, xxi.

28. On Bourbon rule in Louisiana, see Hair, *Bourbonism and Agrarian Protest*, esp. chap. 6. On Redemption's larger implications, see Foner, *Reconstruction*, 587–601.

since 1874—made evident several inescapable conclusions about labor in the post-Reconstruction sugar region. The strikes elucidated the inexorable link between political power and labor relations—not just during Reconstruction but also after it. The sugar region survived as a Republican stronghold, but its very political isolation within the state gave planters a decisive advantage over their workers in moments of crisis. Likewise, the strikes exposed the weakness of sugar workers' position, since planters' ability to call upon state power partially neutralized the benefits workers derived from the demands of sugar production and the labor market. Moreover, the strikes underscored the degree to which planters had abandoned their role as former slaveholders and behaved instead as propertied employers in an era marked by tumultuous and even violent labor upheaval. However distasteful they may have found doing so, planters had become accustomed to negotiating with workers in small groups and as individuals, but they responded vigorously to the prospects of organized labor and collective militancy.

Although the strikes' origins are unclear, freedmen were likely responding to price increases by local merchants and planters. The first evidence of labor agitation appeared on March 15, when freedmen on two plantations in St. Charles Parish stopped work and demanded that daily wages be increased from seventy-five cents to one dollar. Over the next several days, strikers reportedly disrupted plantation operations along the river, persuading many workers to join them and bullwhipping those who did not. The disturbances culminated in more than two hundred strikers mounting what was described as an "attack" on three estates. On March 19, Governor Louis A. Wiltz, who had succeeded Francis T. Nicholls in 1879, ordered Louisiana militia troops to St. Charles. The militia quickly dispersed the strikers, arrested the leaders, and returned to New Orleans that evening. The next day, those arrested pleaded guilty to trespassing and were transferred to New Orleans to serve their sentences.[29]

Wiltz's prompt action, however, failed to end labor difficulties in St. Charles. One manager reported in early April that his laborers had returned to work at "the old prices" but that several nearby planters had increased daily wages to eighty-five cents. "[P]ossibly we may do likewise," he added, "but not on compul-

29. Unless otherwise indicated, accounts of the 1880 strike are from Philip S. Foner and Ronald L. Lewis, eds., *The Black Worker: A Documentary History from Colonial Times to the Present*, vol. 3, *The Black Worker during the Era of the Knights of Labor* (Philadelphia, 1978), 52–65, which consists largely of newspaper accounts; *Thibodaux Sentinel*, Apr. 3, 10, 24, 1880; and *NILSB*, Apr. 1, 15, 1880. The caveat on journalistic bias noted in reporting on the 1874 strike (note 5) also applies here. Overviews of the strike can be found in Sitterson, *Sugar Country*, 248–50; Thomas Becnel, *Labor, Church, and the Sugar Establishment: Louisiana, 1887–1976* (Baton Rouge, 1980), 6–7; and Hair, *Bourbonism and Agrarian Protest*, 172–5.

sion." Far from having ended, the strikes spread into neighboring St. John the Baptist Parish, where, on March 22, laborers on several estates struck for one dollar a day. Drawing up a "constitution" and swearing to obey it, they pledged not to work for less than that amount and decreed that any striker who violated his oath would be punished. During the next few days, parish officials were unable to restore order. The sheriff, a black man, declared the strike beyond his control and advised planters to appeal to the governor for assistance. Having dispatched the militia to St. Charles only a week earlier, and aware that a rapid redeployment might attract national notice, Wiltz commissioned Will A. Strong, Louisiana's secretary of state, to investigate the situation in St. John and to determine whether the militia's presence was necessary. Carrying copies of a proclamation by Wiltz ordering "evil doers and mischievous persons" to desist, Strong arrived at the parish seat of Edgard on the afternoon of March 28. There, he found planters preparing for a hastily arranged meeting with freedmen and parish officials at the farm of Henry Demas.[30]

Demas was a major figure in the St. John the Baptist black community. A slave-born Union army veteran, he was elected constable in 1868 and went on to hold parish or state office until the 1890s. In 1880, he was parish state senator. Although a cane farmer whose own dozen workers had joined the strike, Demas was nonetheless sympathetic to the strikers and tried to achieve compromise. He even secured pardons for the St. Charles strikers, penning a petition to the governor on their behalf in which they admitted their guilt and promised to act "in a peaceable manner" in future wage disputes. Again seeking common ground, Demas addressed the three hundred freedmen and planters assembled outside his home. He told the strikers that they had a right to strike but not to compel others to join them, and that they had a right to assemble in public but not to trespass upon private property. Demas read Wiltz's proclamation, adding that he did not want to intercede with the governor again. He insisted that the freedmen's interests were inseparable from planters' and advised freedmen to appoint a committee to meet with planters and settle the dispute amicably.[31]

Following Demas, Secretary of State Strong also appealed for compromise, advising freedmen to select one man from each estate to confer with planters and assuring them that "if you do this the planters will meet you half way." The freedmen, of course, were skeptical, and when the strike leaders were permitted to address the meeting, they proffered a petition explaining that the workers had struck because of "the general advance of the price of provisions, clothing and

30. T. C. Porteous to Heydenreich, Mar. 26, Apr. 2, 1880, Porteous Letterbook, LSU. See also *Thibodaux Sentinel*, Mar. 27 (French edition), Apr. 3, 1880; *NILSB*, Mar. 25, 1880.

31. On Demas, see Vincent, *Black Legislators*, 116, and Foner, *Freedom's Lawmakers*, 61.

food, and everything which constitutes materially the cost of living." Elaborating on this petition, strike leader Andrew Fox denied that the strikers had used violence. A second leader informed the assembly that the strikers had appointed a committee of twenty-seven freedmen to meet with planters over the next two days, March 29 and 30. After some discussion, both sides agreed to abide by the decision of the proposed conference. In the meantime, however, reports circulated that the strikes were gaining momentum and spreading into St. James Parish.

Any hope that the conference might produce compromise was soon dashed. The meeting opened encouragingly when one planter made what the New Orleans reporter present described as a "very sensible speech," but freedmen eschewed compromise and proclaimed their goal to be "a dollar a day or Kansas." Andrew Fox was then said to have made "a most incendiary speech," declaring that the federal government would confiscate lands and distribute them among freedmen. This assertion met with much enthusiasm, causing Fox and his colleagues to make "the wildest declarations." Though such language reveals the reporter's class and racial biases, compromise at this point was clearly out of the question. Armed strikers reportedly prevented freedmen from working, while parish authorities swore out affidavits against and arrested several strikers. Strong traveled throughout the parish and promised protection to freedmen who returned to work, but the strikers countered that Strong was powerless to offer such protection. By the evening of March 29—with the difficulties in St. John one week old and those in St. Charles two, and with no sign of compromise evident—Strong advised Wiltz to send the militia back into the sugar country. Wiltz ordered the famed Washington Artillery, commanded by Captain Frank McElroy, and a detachment of the Crescent City Battalion into St. John. When the troops arrived at the courthouse on the afternoon of March 30, hearings for the strikers arrested the previous day were in progress. The troops encamped without incident.

With many freedmen congregating outside, the courthouse was the center of attention as the hearings continued the next morning. Several freedmen testified to having been assaulted by the defendants, whom the judge remanded and ordered to stand trial in district court. Affidavits were also sworn out against those strike leaders still at large. During the afternoon—with both freedmen and militia troops still at the courthouse—a group of strikers crossed the river bearing a white flag with the inscription "Peace—One Dollar a Day." This addition to their forces emboldened the freedmen and inspired their leaders to hold a mass meeting on the levee. Several freedmen against whom affidavits had just been issued, including Andrew Fox, advocated continuing the strike, but when they finished speaking they were arrested on charges of being accessories to assaults on two freedmen. "This was the critical moment," the reporter noted. "Either the arrests would settle the strike, or else the influence of the leaders would incite a riot." Strong and McElroy brought up the troops "in line ready for instant action."

At this point the strike fizzled. The militia's action had a "desired effect" upon the freedmen, whose leaders surrendered without resistance and were whisked off to jail. To drive the point home, McElroy put the troops "through a series of war-like movements . . . to show the ignorant strikers how hopeless it was to think of rescuing their leaders." The arrests effectively ended the strikes in St. John the Baptist. Addressing freedmen still assembled at the courthouse, Henry Demas urged them to return home and "go to work on the best terms they could." The following day found few freedmen at the courthouse or any other public place. A few strikers held out, but, as one journalist put it, "the backbone of the strike was broken." The troops departed for New Orleans, taking with them the strike's leaders.

The strike's collapse did not end planters' difficulties. Henry Frellsen of St. Charles, for instance, reported sporadic disturbances on his own and on neighboring plantations until well into May. Frellsen's troubles suggest that the fault line among freedmen fell between regular workers, who opposed the strike, and monthly or daily workers, who supported it. The point is speculative, but perhaps regular or yearly workers, who tended to be more sedentary, were less inclined to jeopardize an employer's solvency by striking, whereas the more transient daily or monthly workers may have felt less compunction about threatening a planter's financial security. Whatever the case, isolated strikes flickered up and down the Mississippi. In late April, freedmen in Ascension and St. James Parishes demanded higher wages. Those employed by John Burnside refused to turn out one morning. Instead, according to a witness, "they formed a gang, all mounted on horses, and marched two-by-two" to nearby plantations, where they forced laborers "to suspend work under pain of violence should they refuse to comply with the demand." Officials in both parishes easily suppressed the strikes by arresting the leaders. Strikes also took place downriver in St. Bernard and Plaquemines Parishes in late April but barely attracted notice.[32]

Even after matters appeared to have settled down, planters could not afford to feel secure about their labor situation. "Planters are nervous all along the coast from Bonnet Carre to Iberville," noted an observer who toured the sugar region in May. "They apprehend that the strike will be renewed about the commencement of rolling." Freedmen likewise expressed discontent and were ready, as he put it, to "exode" to Kansas. Although the crop along the river looked promising, most

32. Apr. 4, 11, 18, 25, May 2, 9, 16, 23, 1880, Henry Frellsen Plant. Diary, LSU; *Donaldsonville Chief*, Apr. 24, 1880 (quotation), and *New Orleans Democrat*, Apr. 28, 1880, both reprinted in *New Orleans Weekly Louisianian*, May 1, 1880; *NILSB*, Apr. 8, 29, May 6, 13, 1880.

planters were behind schedule, "owing to strikes and scarcity of labor." On Bayou Lafourche the mood was better, but, the writer believed, "any evil disposed person can easily stir up another riot." He warned planters to "learn who it is that is endeavoring to make mischief." Contrary to such fears, strikes did not disrupt the 1880 harvest, but planters' labor problem was hardly over.[33] The next time sugar planters needed the militia to suppress strikes, the strikers would demonstrate greater resolve and unity than they had displayed in spring 1880—with more tragic results.

33. *NILSB*, May 27, 1880.

⁊⁊

EPILOGUE: THE SUGAR WAR OF 1887

[W]e have had a horrible three days. . . . I am sick with the
horror of it—but I know it had to be. . . . I think this will settle
the question of who is to rule the nigger or the White man? for
the next 50 years. [B]ut it has been *well done* & I hope all trouble is ended. The negroes are as humble as pie today, very different from last week.

    —Mary Pugh to Edward F. Pugh, November 25, 1887

T he shooting began during the early morning hours of November 23, 1887,
and when it finally ended sometime the next day, at least thirty black
sugar workers—and probably many more—had been slain in a hailstorm
of violence in and around Thibodaux. The "Thibodaux Massacre" culminated a
three-week strike that disrupted the rolling season in Lafourche, Terrebonne, St.
Mary, and Iberia Parishes, marking the first time sugar workers had deliberately
attempted to sabotage the crop at this critical period. The strike stemmed from
planters' determination to drive wages downward and workers' demands for better wages and a more desirable method of payment. While it involved issues that
both sides had contested since emancipation, the strike provoked unprecedented
violence, consummating a quarter century of class conflict in Louisiana's sugar
parishes.

Although the massacre's underlying causes can be traced back to 1862, the
events leading up to it began in summer 1887. In August, District Assembly 194 of
the Knights of Labor, the national labor union that had recently begun organizing
sugar workers, requested a meeting with the St. Mary branch of the Louisiana
Sugar Planters Association (LSPA), hoping that planters might agree to raise

rolling-season wages from the standard ninety cents per day and fifty cents per night watch. The LSPA rejected the proposal. During the next several weeks, the Knights continued to organize sugar workers and to devise a new strategy. On October 19, District Assembly delegates announced their demands: wages of one dollar per day plus rations, or $1.25 without rations, and sixty cents per night watch; regular wages to be paid bimonthly and night watch earnings weekly; and abolition of plantation scrip, which planters had substituted for cash during the mid-1880s. The delegates set a strike deadline of November 1 and gave planters until October 29 to demonstrate why they might consider such terms to be "exorbitant." Terrebonne planters, evincing an initial willingness to compromise, offered a dollar a day and sixty cents per watch but refused to meet the other conditions. Workers rejected the offer.[1]

Confronting organized labor for the first time, Lafourche district planters were in no mood to make a case for their opinion that the demands were exorbitant. On October 30, they and other "influential people" met in Thibodaux, with parish judge and sugar planter Taylor Beattie presiding. Adopting a hard line, they refused to recognize the Knights and instead vowed to evict strikers within twenty-four hours of a strike. They also instructed the parish sheriff to request that Governor Samuel D. McEnery deploy the state militia should a strike occur. St. Mary planters followed a similar course. Despite the planters' stance, few workers along Bayous Lafourche and Teche responded to the morning bell on November 1. Between six and ten thousand carried out the threat to strike, displaying "veneration," as W. W. Pugh put it, for the Knights of Labor. Those on one estate insisted that "no power on earth could remove them unless they were removed as corpses," while a strike leader boasted that every member of his local "would die before they would concede one point to the planters." Most estates remained idle, but some planters hired white workers from New Orleans to keep their places running. Planters' spirits were buoyed that afternoon by the arrival in Thibodaux of a detachment of state militia and by the appearance along Bayou Teche of such paramilitary groups as the Iberia Guards and the Attakapas Rangers. Uncowed by

1. Unless otherwise indicated, this account of the strike, including all quotations and statements of fact, relies upon documents, mostly newspaper reports, reprinted in Foner and Lewis, *Black Worker*, 143–242. Although newspapers presented the strike negatively, emphasizing black "lawlessness," they nonetheless provide an indispensable source for reconstructing the events surrounding the strike. Previous accounts of the 1887 strike and massacre include Becnel, *Labor, Church, and the Sugar Establishment*, 7–8; Hair, *Bourbonism and Agrarian Protest*, 178–85; Jeffrey Gould, "Louisiana Sugar War: The Strike of 1887," *Southern Exposure* 12 (November–December 1984): 45–55, and "'Heroic and Vigorous Action': An Analysis of the Sugar Cane Workers' Strike in Lafourche Parish, November, 1887," unpublished manuscript, 1983. I am grateful to Professor Gould for providing me a copy of his unpublished manuscript.

the show of force, striking Lafourche workers met in Thibodaux the evening of November 1 and resolved to stand firm.[2]

Tensions rose as the eviction deadline approached. Hoping to avert violence, strike leaders instructed strikers not to resist evictions on the morning of November 2, precipitating a mass movement into Thibodaux and other towns. Planters in St. Mary extended the deadline another twenty-four hours, thinking the strike might collapse. Instead, it gained momentum. Later that day, the first violent act occurred when Terrebonne strikers reportedly fired upon white men, wounding two, on a plantation near Tigerville. Receiving a request from local authorities for aid, McEnery ordered militia units to the area. Warrants were issued the next day against strikers believed to have been involved in the shooting.

Chances for a peaceful resolution, slim from the start, faded. On November 3, evictions and arrests of strikers who had refused to vacate cabins commenced in Lafourche. Meanwhile, planters again met in Thibodaux. Insisting that they had already lost thousands of dollars and stood to lose more, they nonetheless resolved "not to accede to the demands made upon us by a body of men who have presumed to dictate to us how we shall manage our private and business affairs." A strike that had initially concerned wages and payment—over which compromise might be reached—now seemed to the planters to be a case of black workers telling white owners what to do—a situation the planters would not abide. Yet hope for compromise flickered. The next day, November 4, Terrebonne strike leaders requested a meeting with planters. They were now ready to accept the compromise offer planters had made before the strike, which workers had rejected, of a dollar per day and sixty cents per watch. But, emboldened by some strikers' returning to work rather than face eviction or arrest, and working their plantations on a limited basis with white labor, planters declined the overture. They were willing to increase wages to a dollar a day, but their other terms remained the same—fifty cents per watch, all money paid monthly and in scrip.

Tensions increased. On November 4, a riot was barely averted on a plantation near Lockport, where a posse had formed the previous day in anticipation of trouble. The affair started when a black striker, Moses Pugh, shot and wounded planter Richard Foret. The deputy sheriff and posse tried to arrest Pugh, but strikers prevented them from doing so. The Opelousas Guards were called in and later apprehended Pugh without incident. Elsewhere in Lafourche, strikers were arrested for refusing to vacate cabins, and militiamen drove other strikers off plantations. In St. Mary, several arrested strikers unable to post bond were joined voluntarily by their wives in jail.

[handwritten margin note: moved from a labor issue to a power issue]

2. Pugh quoted in Hair, *Bourbonism and Agrarian Protest*, 180.

Contrary to planters' intentions, evictions and arrests strengthened the strikers' determination, raising the probability of violence. During the morning of November 5, strikers shot at white workers on John Pharr's plantation in St. Mary Parish. Earlier that day parish planters had decided to evict and arrest strikers who were refusing to vacate cabins so as to prevent white workers from replacing them. A sheriff's posse formed and proceeded to the small town of Pattersonville, where many strikers had assembled. After the shootings at the Pharr estate became known, authorities decided to search the town for arms and to arrest several strike leaders. With militia units, a posse, vigilantes, and hundreds of black refugees crowding in, Pattersonville was a powder keg ready to explode. The spark was provided when between fifty and a hundred strikers tried demonstrating that afternoon, to be met by white forces who opened fire and killed several of them. The rest scampered for the woods and swamps. As news of the Pattersonville "riot" spread, passions intensified; they were hardly assuaged by continuing reports of shootings on other plantations.

During the next two weeks—the heart of the rolling season—the situation was volatile. Most plantations remained shut down, though a few operated with white workers. Strikers and planters held frequent meetings, as each side tried to demonstrate its determination to keep up the struggle. In Thibodaux, where strikers and their families gathered, the situation was especially tense. The militia, which could not remain on duty indefinitely, had been withdrawn, but deputized white men stood ready to spring into action. On November 20, some three hundred white people, led by prominent planters, met in Thibodaux to decide upon a response to the continued shootings and prevailing "lawlessness." They established patrols and created a "committee on peace and order" to cooperate with civil authorities. The hundreds of white vigilantes who had descended upon the area, some from as far away as Shreveport, were organized to guard the approaches to Thibodaux. Judge Beattie assumed command of the operation.

By November 21, with black refugees streaming into town and white vigilantes arriving hourly, tension was palpable. White fears that strikers planned to "attack" the town were exacerbated by reports that fighting had broken out. Beattie responded by declaring martial law in Thibodaux and prohibiting the movement to or from town without a pass—actions no doubt also prompted by the first signs that morning of a hard frost. The cane crop was in jeopardy. Urgent measures were needed, yet so long as strikers did nothing to provoke violence, authorities could not act against them. In perhaps what was one such provocation, a group of white men fired into a coffee house frequented by black patrons that evening, killing one and severely wounding another. The night passed without further violence, but as news of these shootings spread the next day, more vigilantes arrived to "preserve order." A peaceful day did not preclude the spreading of further rumors that strikers would attack the town. Pickets were strengthened, but as the night wore on it seemed that Thibodaux had survived the expected assault.[3]

But not quite. At about 5 A.M. on November 23, shots rang out from a corn-field about a hundred yards from a picket post manned by four white deputies at the south end of town. Strikers had evidently fired on them, wounding two. Within moments, armed guards were racing to the scene of the shooting. Another volley came from the same direction, inflicting no injury but betraying the strikers' location. The white guards poured a deadly fusillade into the corn-field, killing six strikers. The "battle," such as it was, ended minutes later with strikers breaking in a *sauve-qui-peut* for the swamps.

"This opened," according to Mary Pugh, "the *Ball.*" Indeed, the initial skirmish commenced what soon became a frenzy of violence against strikers. White guards-men, Pugh noted, began "hunting up the Leaders, & every one that was found or any suspicious character was shot." Especially horrific treatment was meted out to "instigators." "[C]rack shots would take a man they believed a ringleader in the strike to the railroad tracks," a witness reported, "place him ten paces ahead of them, give him a chance to 'run for your life,' and he would be riddled with bullets before he had gone two leaps!" By afternoon, state militia detachments arrived in town, ostensibly to restore order, but they actually did nothing to stop the slaugh-ter. Strikers were killed through the following day, and shots rang out sporadically for several more days. "I am sick with the horror of it," exclaimed Mary Pugh, who nonetheless believed that the violence had been necessary and would "settle the question of who is to rule the nigger or the White man? for the next 50 years." Suppressing the strike had been "*well done,*" she added, "& I hope all trouble is ended. The negroes are as humble as pie today, very different from last week."[4]

Trouble, however, had not ended. Parties continued to comb the woods and swamps for several days in search of strikers. Because many black people fled the area altogether, never to return, it was impossible to determine how many died. Bodies turned up weeks later. One newspaper that minimized the violence nonetheless admitted, "thirty negroes have sacrificed their lives." Lavinia Gay be-lieved "the half has not been published," and Mary Pugh estimated that more than fifty strikers were killed. Covington Hall—the New Orleans labor leader who was raised in the area and spoke to some of the participants—later wrote that the number of victims, according to local legend, was "utterly at variance" with press reports. Casualties, he believed, numbered in the hundreds.[5]

The militia remained in Thibodaux during the week, and pickets challenged

3. Hair, *Bourbonism and Agrarian Protest,* 183; A. Bouchereau, *Statement . . . 1887–88.*
4. M. Pugh to E. F. Pugh, Nov. 25, 1887, Mary W. Pugh Papers, LSU.
5. L. Gay to EJG, Dec. 10, 1887, EJGP; M. Pugh to E. F. Pugh, Nov. 25, 1887, Mary Pugh Papers, LSU.

black people who tried to enter or leave town. Meanwhile, workers trudged back to the plantations—defeated and demoralized, their movement crushed—to resume their lives as best they could. Although reports continued to circulate of shootings into sugar mills and of strikers preparing for "another" attack upon the town, by late November the tumult had died down and plantations were back in operation. The rolling season recommenced, but only with much difficulty, as planters complained of widespread demoralization among their workers, who, having been so brutalized, were hardly motivated to work with the élan necessary to harvest the cane. Some planters estimated that, owing to the strike and subsequent demoralization, they lost a third of the crop. The 1887 crop of more than 200,000 hogsheads was actually good by postbellum standards, but such results must have made planters wonder what might have been had the strike never occurred. In succumbing to violence, sugar workers had exacted a heavy toll.

Although ostensibly a dispute over wages, the 1887 strike involved nothing less than planters' and sugar workers' contrasting visions of free labor, and as such it brought to a head twenty-five years of conflict between the two sides. Capitalizing on the demands of sugar production as well as on the workings of the free-labor market, former slaves and their descendants strove for a form of communal autonomy even as they worked within the sugar plantation's centralized regimen. Planters, by contrast, although having accommodated themselves to the abolition of slavery and the negotiation with labor through the market, nonetheless insisted that they must exercise control over their workers in order to make sugar profitably. Thus it was that a squabble concerning wages could develop into a test of wills with no room for compromise. Planters risked bankruptcy rather than give in to labor; sugar workers pronounced themselves ready to die rather than yield even one concession to their employers.

impossible to compromise

As the strike became a fight to the finish, the massacre provided incontrovertible proof of the importance of political power in deciding the strike's outcome. So long as Reconstruction lasted, and so long as sugar workers enjoyed even a semblance of protection by state or federal government, planters could not necessarily rely upon the coercive power of the state, nor were they at liberty to mobilize vigilante and other forms of extralegal force when confronting labor. The end of Reconstruction, however, while not destroying local black political power in the sugar region, nonetheless placed legitimate, state-sponsored coercion at the planters' service. Of equal importance, Redemption meant that the state government would not only permit but indeed condone any private, extralegal force that planters could bring to bear in suppressing labor unrest. Whatever advantages the demands of sugar production and the labor market conveyed to sugar workers in the economic realm were trumped by planters' political power.

Why did the 1887 strike culminate in such explosive fury when violence had been averted during the strikes of 1874 and 1880? The answer lies in the fact that, while certain conditions remained constant after Reconstruction, 1887 also witnessed several factors not evidenced in previous conflicts. First, the 1887 strike involved not only wage rates but also the payment method—namely, plantation scrip. Most sugar workers by the early 1880s received their wages in full each month, but planters subsequently countered that gain by replacing cash payment with nontransferable tickets that workers must redeem at the plantation store or commissary. It is unclear exactly when planters implemented scrip, but by 1887 it seems still to have been a recent innovation, causing much disaffection among sugar workers. "The 'I owe you' ticket method," noted New Orleans's black newspaper, the *Weekly Pelican*, "has been the largest factor in bringing on the present strike." Scrip did not bind sugar workers involuntarily to particular plantations, nor did it deprive them of full and regular wage payment, but it denied them the benefits—to which they had long been accustomed, and over which they were willing to fight—of cash wages.

If sugar workers were ready to assume a militant stance over scrip or any other issue, the emergence of the Knights of Labor in southern Louisiana provided them the means by which to do so. The Knights began organizing white and black railroad workers in Morgan City, the St. Mary Parish transportation hub, in 1886, the year it attained its peak membership, and it was soon flourishing among plantation workers in St. Mary, Iberia, Terrebonne, and Lafourche Parishes. Home to scores if not hundreds of workers and their families, sugar plantations were ripe for organized labor. The Knights struck a chord with a people familiar with the power of collective action, and who enthusiastically espoused its message of unity among skilled and unskilled, black and white, male and female workers. The Knights' "producerist" ideology also impelled it to invite employers, but the sugar planters were less interested in joining the organization than in eradicating it.[6]

Finally, not only was the Knights of Labor new to the sugar country, but so were its timing and tactics. The labor disturbances of 1874 and 1880 had occurred early in the crop season, either in January, when planters and workers normally negotiated wages and other terms of employment, or during spring planting. The 1887 strike, by contrast, was deliberately scheduled for the beginning of the rolling season—the most critical time of year for planters. Ever since emancipation, freedmen and sugar workers had attempted small-scale, spontaneous work stoppages in order to win better harvest-time wages, but these efforts, lacking coordi-

6. On the Knights of Labor in the sugar region, see Hair, *Bourbonism and Agrarian Protest*, 176–7; Gould, "Louisiana Sugar War," 49–50; and Melton Alonza McLaurin, *The Knights of Labor in the South* (Westport, Conn., 1978), 74–5, 141.

nation or planning, never threatened to became mass movements. The 1887 strike, however, was a coordinated campaign, comprising as many as ten thousand workers. Never before had so many laborers stopped work during the rolling season, deliberately and consciously jeopardizing the sugar crop, in order to force planters to meet their terms. Nor was there any telling how far such a movement might go or where it might lead. Planters responded to the strike not only as southern white men asserting authority over black people, but also as men of property in Gilded Age America confronting labor militancy. They believed they had no choice but to marshal all the legal and extralegal force at their disposal to suppress the strike. The alternative was unthinkable. Thus, the sugar region's history since 1862, combined with the more immediate circumstances of the mid-1880s, made the violence of 1887 all but inevitable.

As an indisputable victory for planters, the strike marked a dramatic turning point in free labor's development. Nonetheless, although the pendulum had swung decisively in planters' favor, their power was still not absolute. Wages continued to fluctuate, indicating the persistence of at least a limited labor market, and planters relentlessly complained about their labor problem well into the twentieth century. In a larger sense, moreover, no matter how much control planters established over their workers, they could never reenslave them, and however limited were black people's options in the late-nineteenth-century South, sugar workers were free citizens. This fact gave rise to a new form of social relations between planters and workers. Despite all of the force, legal and otherwise, that planters could muster, they still had to negotiate with their workers through the medium of the market. The state no longer sanctioned planters' unlimited control, as it once had, over the bodies and labor power of those who lived and worked on their estates.[7]

Although planters' authority over their workers had diminished since the days of slavery, sugar workers' own options were more narrowly circumscribed after 1887. With the Knights of Labor crushed, no attempt was made to organize workers on sugar plantations until the mid-twentieth century. Sugar workers became a rural proletariat, lacking any means of sustenance except the selling of their labor, and living within a larger South characterized by a deplorable lack of educational opportunities, economic underdevelopment, and discrimination in all forms of life. Mary Pugh's pronouncement that the strike would settle the question of "who is to rule the nigger or the White man?" portended what was soon to come. During the 1890s, Redemption finally descended upon the sugar region, not only

7. On wage rates during the late nineteenth century, see Sitterson, *Sugar Country*, 321–2. On the persistence of a labor market after 1887, see Ferleger, "Problem of 'Labor,'" and Reidy, "Mules and Machines and Men."

destroying black political power but also subjecting freedmen and their descendants to the iron hand of legal segregation and disfranchisement. The Thibodaux Massacre was thus an epilogue to the story of emancipation and a prologue to the saga of Jim Crow and the white lynch mob.[8]

For the slaves who were freed during the Civil War and who endeavored to make freedom meaningful in the years that followed, such eventualities could hardly have been foreseen. Freedmen of the sugar region joined their compatriots throughout the South in establishing a new world from the shambles of the old, building upon their experiences under slavery as well as upon the ideals of American citizenship to recast the southern social order. In doing so, they eventually confronted the realization that their vision for the future must inevitably be tempered by the limits of the possible, but they established the foundation from which future generations would continue the crusade to gain access to the benefits of American citizenship and the opportunities of the American economy. This crusade, which traces its origins to the slave era but was precipitated by the arrival of federal troops in 1862, ended neither in 1887 nor after.

8. On the implementation of segregation and disfranchisement in Louisiana, see Hair, *Bourbonism and Agrarian Protest*, 185–92. On lynching in southern Louisiana during the late nineteenth and early twentieth centuries, see Michael J. Pfeifer, "Lynching and Criminal Justice in South Louisiana, 1878–1930," *LH* 40 (spring 1999): 155–77. On sugar workers in the twentieth century, see Becnel, *Labor, Church, and Sugar Establishment*, 197–207; Patsy Sims, *Cleveland Benjamin's Dead: Struggle for Dignity in Louisiana's Cane Country*, exp. ed. (Athens, Ga., 1994); and Debbie Fleming Caffery, *Carry Me Home: Louisiana Sugar Country in Photographs*, text by Pete Daniel and Anne Wilkes Tucker (Washington, D.C., 1990).

§‡

APPENDIX

The Planter Elite and Planter Persistence (Chapter 5)

Because of emancipation, any assessment of the Civil War's impact on the planter elite's economic status must focus on landholding. Doing so, however, presents problems. For measuring antebellum landholding, I defined the planter elite as owners of 500 or more improved acres, based upon the agricultural schedules of the 1860 federal census. Although this source includes improved and unimproved acreage, I calculated only improved acreage in order to ensure that I was dealing exclusively with working plantations. For measuring postbellum landholding, however, the agricultural schedules of the 1870 and 1880 federal censuses are notoriously poor sources, since they do not always distinguish between owners and renters. I therefore relied on parish tax assessment rolls for 1873 and 1880, on microfilm at the Louisiana State Archives in Baton Rouge, to determine postbellum landholding. (Few tax rolls from the antebellum era have survived.) The 1873 tax rolls allow for examination of landholding just before the depression of the 1870s, while those for 1880 provide data for the terminal year of this study. Unfortunately, the tax rolls make no distinction between improved and unimproved land, complicating comparison of landholding before and after the war.

Similar problems arise in measuring planter persistence, which is defined as the percentage of antebellum planters or family members who remained part of the elite in the postbellum era. For calculating planter persistence, I defined antebellum planters as owners of 500 or more improved acres (according to the agricultural schedules of the 1860 federal census) and fifty or more slaves. Doing so enabled me to draw upon Karl Joseph Menn's exhaustive study, *The Large Slaveholders of Louisiana—1860*, for supplemental information. Persistence was determined by whether antebellum planters or family members owned at least 500 acres according to the 1873 and 1880 parish tax assessment rolls. Because the tax rolls do not distinguish between improved and unimproved acreage, however, my postbellum elite undoubtedly includes some individuals who owned less than 500 improved acres.

Several solutions were considered and attempted in order to rectify the problem of making comparisons while using sources not entirely compatible. An initial effort to recalculate 1860 landholding based upon improved and unimproved acreage quickly revealed that a number of landholders owned only small amounts of improved acreage but large tracts of unimproved acreage. Including such individuals as "planters," it seemed, would have significantly compromised my findings. A subsequent attempt to link data from the agricultural schedules of the 1870 and 1880 federal censuses to those from the 1873 and 1880 parish tax rolls proved to be so time-consuming and unrewarding that it was abandoned. I also considered raising the standard for inclusion in the postbellum elite in order to offset the fact that some lands were unimproved. Doing so, however, still would not have guaranteed exclusion of those who owned little improved acreage. Moreover, by changing standards in mid-analysis, I would have introduced an error equal to that for which I was compensating.

In the end, I decided to maintain the 500-acre threshold, realizing that my analyses of both postbellum landholding and planter persistence are somewhat biased. Such bias, however, has certain benefits for examining planter persistence. By lowering the standard for inclusion in the postbellum elite (since it includes those who did not necessarily own 500 improved acres), my analysis indirectly compensates for the overall depressed state of the sugar industry. Many planters, if not all, were compelled to reduce the number of acres they had in production, even if they held onto their estates and in almost all other ways continued to live as planters. In this sense, to have maintained the threshold at 500 improved acres after the war, even were that possible with the surviving evidence, might have been to maintain too high a standard, given general economic conditions. Since my intention has been to measure the percentage of antebellum planters who persisted after the war, as opposed to measuring the percentage of the postbellum elite that had belonged to the antebellum elite, my "liberalizing" of the standard has ensured that antebellum planters who held onto their property, although in somewhat reduced circumstances, have nonetheless been included among the postbellum elite. By using improved acres (as well as slaves) in defining the 1860 elite, moreover, I felt reasonably secure that any surviving landholders were indeed owners of productive plantations rather than land speculators or others not engaged in agricultural pursuits.

I chose to examine Ascension, Assumption, Iberville, and Lafourche Parishes in order to assess postbellum landholding and planter persistence because usable tax rolls have survived, and because, although not in any way statistically representative, these parishes nonetheless provide a cross-section of the sugar region. Ascension and Iberville are Mississippi River parishes, while Assumption and Lafourche make up in large part the Bayou Lafourche district. St. Mary Parish would have been selected to represent Bayou Teche, but the 1868 creation of Iberia Parish from parts of St. Mary and St. Martin meant that reliable data comparisons would be difficult.

BLACK PROPERTY HOLDING (CHAPTER 7)

This analysis is intended not to measure black property holding generally but rather to assess the degree to which plantation laborers acquired property. Unfortunately, the main sources for determining property holding—parish tax assessment rolls—do not identify individuals by race. Thus, a sample of plantation laborers in Ascension Parish was created by selecting every eighth black or mulatto household head (male or female) listed as laborer in the population schedules of the 1880 federal census. (Ascension's third ward, made up largely of the town of Donaldsonville, was excluded.) The resulting cohort of 238 laborers was compared against tax rolls from the early 1880s. (Few tax rolls before then survive, precluding use of the 1870 federal census.) In addition, all forty-three black household heads listed as "farmer" in the federal census—accounting for slightly more than 2 percent of Ascension's approximately two thousand black households—were searched in the tax rolls. Although not statistically representative, Ascension was chosen because it was dominated by large plantations along the Mississippi River, and because it included considerable unimproved land that might have attracted aspiring black property holders. Moreover, only Ascension's tax rolls were organized in a way that made them compatible with the federal census.

The tax assessment rolls distinguished between various forms of personal and real property, but most property fell into three categories. The most frequently mentioned included land—cash value and number of acres—as well as improvements thereto, such as houses and other buildings, fixtures, or machinery. Anything that enhanced the value of land was taxed, even if the resident did not own the property on which such improvements were made. For landholders, a brief indication of the property's location was provided. For those taxed on improvements, the vague phrase "improvements on land of" indicated the plantation or land owner. The second category included cash value of livestock, including horses, mules, cattle, sheep, hogs, and goats, but no specific data were provided on the kinds or numbers of animals owned. The third category included cash value of carriages, wagons, or other vehicles, though again with no specifics.

BIBLIOGRAPHY

Manuscript Collections

Allen J. Ellender Archives, Allen J. Ellender Memorial Library, Nicholls State University, Thibodaux, Louisiana

Martin-Pugh Collection

Freedmen and Southern Society Project, University of Maryland, College Park

Project files (photostatic copies of documents from the National Archives)

George W. Littlefield Southern History Collections, The Center for American History, University of Texas, Austin

James N. Brown Papers (Natchez Trace Collection)
Pugh Family Papers (Southern History Archival Collections)

Louisiana and Lower Mississippi Valley Collections, Hill Memorial Library, Louisiana State University, Baton Rouge

Priscilla "Miltie" Munnikhuysen Bond Diary
Braxton Bragg Letter
Louis Amédée Bringier and Family Papers
Margarett Butler Correspondence
Thomas Butler and Family Papers
Donelson Caffery and Family Papers
Daniel R. Carroll and Family Papers
Consolidated Association of Planters of Louisiana Papers
Edward Cousinard Papers

Alexandre E. DeClouet Papers
Isaac Erwin Diary
Henry Frellsen Plantation Diary
Andrew Hynes Gay and Family Papers
Edward J. Gay and Family Papers
Joseph Kleinpeter and Family Papers
Sévèrin Landry and Family Papers
Gustave Lauve Letter
Louisiana Sugar Planters Association Papers
Henry McCall, "History of Evan Hall Plantation," typescript
Charles L. Mathews and Family Papers
Rebecca A. G. Minor Papers
William J. Minor and Family Papers
John Moore and Family Papers (Michael D. Wynne Collection)
Thomas Overton Moore Papers
William T. Palfrey and Family Papers
Pharr Family Papers
Thomas C. Porteous Letterbook
Alexander Franklin Pugh Papers
Josephine Nicholls Pugh Civil War Account
Mary W. Pugh Papers
Richard L. Pugh Papers
Col. W. W. Pugh and Family Papers
Mrs. W. W. Pugh Civil War Account
Welman F. Pugh Diary
John H. Randolph Papers
Frederick D. Robertson Account Books
Jared Young Sanders and Family Papers
Joseph Savoy and Family Papers
Benjamin F. Tureaud Family Papers
Uncle Sam Plantation Papers
WPA Ex-Slave Narratives
David Weeks and Family Papers (The Weeks Hall Memorial Collection)
Maunsell White Letterbook
Wilton Plantation Sugarhouse Plan (Nelson P. Himel Collection)

National Archives, Washington, D.C.

Records of the Bureau of Refugees, Freedmen, and Abandoned Lands, RG 105

New Jersey Historical Society, Newark

Joseph P. Bradley Papers

Manuscripts Department, Southern Historical Collection, Wilson Library, University of North Carolina, Chapel Hill

Avery Family Papers
Bayside Plantation Records
Taylor Beatty Papers
Brashear and Lawrence Family Papers
James Amédée Gaudet Papers
Gibson and Humphreys Family Papers
Kean-Prescott Family Papers
Andrew McCollam Papers
Robert Campbell Martin Papers
William Porcher Miles Papers
William A. Shaffer Papers
Slack Family Papers
Lewis Thompson Papers
Henry Clay Warmoth Papers (microfilm)
Frank Webb Plantation Diary

MICROFILM EDITIONS OF MANUSCRIPT COLLECTIONS

Records of Ante-Bellum Southern Plantations: From the Revolution through the Civil War. Kenneth M. Stampp, gen. ed.
  Ser. G: Selections from the Barker Texas History Center, University of Texas, Austin. Part 1: *Texas and Louisiana Collections* (Frederick, Md., 1987).
  Ser. I: Selections from Louisiana State University, Baton Rouge. Part 1: *Louisiana Sugar Plantations* (Frederick, Md., 1989).

GOVERNMENT DOCUMENTS AND PUBLICATIONS

Federal Records

39th Congress, 1st Session, House Executive Document 70.
39th Congress, 1st Session, House Report 30.
39th Congress, 2nd Session, House Executive Document 1.
39th Congress, 2nd Session, Senate Executive Document 6.
41st Congress, 1st Session, House Miscellaneous Document 13.
41st Congress, 2nd Session, House Miscellaneous Document 154.
42nd Congress, 3rd Session, Senate Report 457.
43rd Congress, 2nd Session, House Report 101.
43rd Congress, 2nd Session, House Report 261.
44th Congress, 2nd Session, House Miscellaneous Document 34.

45th Congress, 1st Session, House Miscellaneous Document 5.

45th Congress, 3rd Session, Senate Report 855.

Statutes at Large of the United States of America, 1789–1873. 17 vols. Washington, D.C., 1850–1873.

U.S. Army. Department of the Gulf. Bureau of Free Labor. *The Freedmen of Louisiana. Final Report of the Bureau of Free Labor, Department of the Gulf, to Maj. Gen. E. R. S. Canby, Commanding: By Thomas W. Conway.* New Orleans, 1865.

U.S. Bureau of Labor Statistics. *History of Wages in the United States from Colonial Times to 1928.* Washington, D.C., 1929.

U.S. Bureau of the Census. *Agriculture of the United States in 1860; Compiled from the Original Returns of the Eighth Census. . . .* Washington, D.C., 1864.

———. *Eighth Census of the United States.* 4 vols. Washington, D.C., 1864–1866.

———. Manuscript Agricultural and Population Schedules: Federal Census, 1860, 1870, 1880.

———. *Ninth Census of the United States.* 3 vols. Washington, D.C., 1872.

———. *Statistical View of the United States . . . ; Being a Compendium of the Seventh Census.* Washington, D.C., 1854.

———. *Tenth Census of the United States.* 22 vols. Washington, D.C., 1883–1888.

U.S. Department of Agriculture. *Report of the Commissioner for the Year [1867, 1873, 1878].* Washington, D.C., 1868–1879.

———. *Report of the Commissioner for the Year 1877.* "The Cane-Sugar Industry" (Special Report no. 1). Washington, D.C., 1878.

U.S. Department of Commerce. "The Sugar Industry: Sugar Cane and Cane Sugar in Louisiana, Beet Sugar Data, and General Tables." Washington, D.C., 1913.

U.S. Department of War. *The War of the Rebellion: A Compilation of the Official Records of the Union and Confederate Armies.* 128 vols. Washington, D.C., 1880–1901.

State and Parish Records (Louisiana State Archives, Baton Rouge)

Ascension Parish Tax Assessment Rolls, 1873, 1880, 1882

Assumption Parish Tax Assessment Rolls, 1873, 1880

Iberville Parish Tax Assessment Rolls, 1873, 1880

Lafourche Parish Tax Assessment Rolls, 1873, 1880

Pierce, William. *Report of Brig-Gen. William Pierce: Commanding State Troops in the Field in District from Berwick's Bay to New Orleans to General G. T. Beauregard, Adjutant General of the State of Louisiana, November 28th 1887.* Baton Rouge, 1887.

CONTEMPORARY PERIODICALS AND OTHER PUBLICATIONS

Bouchereau, Alcée. *Statement of the Sugar and Rice Crops Made in Louisiana [1878–1890].*

Bouchereau, Louis. *Statement of the Sugar and Rice Crops Made in Louisiana [1868–1877].*

Champomier, P. A. *Statement of the Sugar Crop Made in Louisiana [1859–1862].*

De Bow's Review: After the War Series.

NEWSPAPERS

Franklin (St. Mary) Planters' Banner, 1867–1872
Napoleonville Pioneer of Assumption, 1877–1880
New Iberia Louisiana Sugar-Bowl, 1873–1881
New Orleans Daily Picayune, 1862–1880
New Orleans Tribune, 1864–1869
New Orleans Weekly Louisianian, 1872–1880
Plaquemine Iberville South, 1865–1880
Thibodaux Sentinel, 1865–1880

PUBLISHED PRIMARY SOURCES

Adamoli, Giulio. "New Orleans in 1867." *Louisiana Historical Quarterly* 6 (April 1923): 271–9.

Banks, Nathaniel Prentice. *Emancipated Labor in Louisiana.* New York, 1864.

Barnhart, John D., ed. "Reconstruction on the Lower Mississippi." *Mississippi Valley Historical Review* 21 (December 1934): 387–96.

Berlin, Ira, Barbara Jeanne Fields, Thavolia Glymph, Joseph P. Reidy, and Leslie S. Rowland, eds. *Freedom: A Documentary History of Emancipation, 1861–1867.* Ser. 1, Vol. 1, *The Destruction of Slavery.* Cambridge, U.K., 1985.

Berlin, Ira, Thavolia Glymph, Steven F. Miller, Joseph P. Reidy, Leslie S. Rowland, and Julie Saville, eds. *Freedom: A Documentary History of Emancipation, 1861–1867.* Ser. 1, Vol. 3, *The Wartime Genesis of Free Labor: The Lower South.* Cambridge, U.K., 1990.

Bonham, Milledge L., ed. "Financial and Economic Disturbances in New Orleans on the Eve of Secession." *Louisiana Historical Quarterly* 13 (January 1930): 32–6.

Botkin, B. A. *Lay My Burden Down: A Folk History of Slavery.* Chicago, 1945.

Butler, Benjamin F. *Private and Official Correspondence of Gen. Benjamin F. Butler during the Period of the Civil War.* 5 vols. Norwood, Mass., 1917.

Conway, Thomas W. *Report on the Condition of the Freedmen, of the Department of the Gulf, to Major General N. P. Banks.* New Orleans, 1864.

———. *Annual Report of Thos. W. Conway, Superintendent, Bureau of Free Labor, Department of the Gulf, to Major General Hurlbut, Commanding, for the Year 1864.* New Orleans, 1865.

DeForest, John William. *A Volunteer's Adventures.* New Haven, Conn., 1946.

Dennett, Daniel. *Louisiana As It Is.* New Orleans, 1876.

Dennett, John Richard. *The South As It Is: 1865–1866.* Ed. Henry M. Christman. New York, 1965. Reprint, Baton Rouge, 1995.

Duganne, A. J. H. *Camps and Prisons: Twenty Months in the Department of the Gulf.* New York, 1865.

[Favrot, H. L.] "One Hundred Years of Sugar-Making in Louisiana." *Harper's Weekly* 38 (August 11, 1894): 755–8.

Fearn, Frances (Hewitt), ed. *Diary of a Refugee.* New York, 1910.

Foner, Philip S., and Ronald L. Lewis, eds. *The Black Worker: A Documentary History from*

Colonial Times to the Present. Vol. 3, *The Black Worker during the Era of the Knights of Labor.* Philadelphia, 1978.

Gayarré, Charles. "A Louisiana Sugar Plantation of the Old Régime." *Harper's New Monthly Magazine* 74 (March 1887): 606–21.

Hahn, Steven, Steven F. Miller, Susan E. O'Donovan, John C. Rodrigue, and Leslie S. Rowland, eds. *Freedom: A Documentary History of Emancipation, 1861–1867.* Ser. 3, Vol. 1, *Land and Labor: 1865.* Cambridge, U.K., forthcoming.

Harris, William H. *Louisiana, Her Resources, Advantages, and Attractions: Being a Description of the State and the Inducements Offered to Those Seeking New Homes.* Austin, Tex., 1881.

———. *Louisiana Products, Resources and Attractions, with a Sketch of the Parishes.* New Orleans, 1881.

Hepworth, George Hughes. *The Whip, Hoe, and Sword; or, The Gulf-Department in '63.* Boston, 1864.

Houzeau, Jean-Charles. *My Passage at the New Orleans Tribune: A Memoir of the Civil War Era.* Ed. David C. Rankin, trans. Gerard F. Denault. Baton Rouge, 1984.

Kellar, Herbert Anthony, ed. *Solon Robinson: Pioneer and Agriculturist.* 2 vols. Indianapolis, 1936.

King, Edward. *The Great South: A Record of Journeys in Louisiana, Texas, The Indian Territory, Missouri, Arkansas, Mississippi, Alabama, Georgia, Florida, South Carolina, North Carolina, Kentucky, Tennessee, Virginia, West Virginia, and Maryland.* Ed. W. Magruder Drake and Robert R. Jones. 1879. Reprint, Baton Rouge, 1972.

Latham, Henry. *Black and White: A Journal of a Three Months' Tour in the United States.* Philadelphia, 1867.

McPherson, Edward. *The Political History of the United States of America during the Period of Reconstruction.* 1875. Reprint, New York, 1969.

Marquette, C. L., ed. "Letters of a Yankee Sugar Planter." *Journal of Southern History* 6 (November 1940): 521–46.

Nordhoff, Charles. *The Cotton States in the Spring and Summer of 1875.* New York, 1876.

Northup, Solomon. *Twelve Years a Slave.* Ed. Sue Eakin and Joseph Logsdon. 1853. Reprint, Baton Rouge, 1968.

Olmsted, Frederick Law. *A Journey in the Seaboard Slave States, with Remarks on Their Economy.* 1856. Reprint, New York, 1968.

Parton, James. *General Butler in New Orleans: History of the Administration of the Department of the Gulf in the Year 1862.* New York, 1864.

Reid, Whitelaw. *After the War: A Tour of the Southern States, 1865–1866.* 1866. Reprint, New York, 1965.

Richardson, James D., ed. *A Compilation of the Messages and Papers of the Presidents.* 20 vols. New York, 1897–1917.

Russell, William Howard. *My Diary North and South.* Ed. Eugene H. Berwanger. Philadelphia, 1987.

Shewmaker, Kenneth E., and Andrew K. Prinz, eds. "A Yankee in Louisiana: Selections from the Diary and Correspondence of Henry R. Gardner, 1862–1866." *Louisiana History* 5 (summer 1964): 271–95.

Smalley, Eugene V. "Sugar-Making in Louisiana." *Century Magazine* 35 (November 1887): 100–20.

Somers, Robert. *The Southern States since the War, 1870–71.* Introduction and index by Malcolm C. McMillan. 1871. Reprint, University, Ala., 1965.

Thorpe, T. B. "Sugar and the Sugar Region of Louisiana." *Harper's New Monthly Magazine* 7 (November 1853): 746–67.

Trowbridge, J. T. *A Picture of the Desolated States: And the Work of Restoration, 1865–1868.* Hartford, 1868.

Warmoth, Henry Clay. *War, Politics, and Reconstruction: Stormy Days in Louisiana.* New York, 1930.

SECONDARY SOURCES

Books

Albert, Bill, and Adrian Graves, eds. *Crisis and Change in the International Sugar Economy, 1860–1914.* Norwich, U.K., 1984.

Athearn, Robert G. *In Search of Canaan: Black Migration to Kansas, 1879–80.* Lawrence, Kans., 1978.

Barnes, A. C. *The Sugar Cane.* 2nd ed. New York, 1974.

Becnel, Thomas A. *Labor, Church, and the Sugar Establishment: Louisiana, 1887–1976.* Baton Rouge, 1980.

Bell, Caryn Cossé. *Revolution, Romanticism, and the Afro-Creole Protest Tradition in Louisiana, 1718–1868.* Baton Rouge, 1997.

Bentley, George R. *A History of the Freedmen's Bureau.* Philadelphia, 1955.

Berlin, Ira. *Slaves without Masters: The Free Negro in the Antebellum South.* New York, 1974.

―――. *Many Thousands Gone: The First Two Centuries of Slavery in North America.* Cambridge, Mass., 1998.

Berlin, Ira, and Philip D. Morgan, eds. *Cultivation and Culture: Labor and the Shaping of Slave Life in the Americas.* Charlottesville, 1993.

Billings, Dwight B., Jr. *Planters and the Making of a "New South": Class, Politics, and Development in North Carolina, 1865–1900.* Chapel Hill, N.C., 1979.

Blackburn, Frank. *Sugar-Cane.* London, 1984.

Blackburn, Robin. *The Overthrow of Colonial Slavery, 1776–1848.* London, 1988.

―――. *The Making of New World Slavery: From the Baroque to the Modern, 1492–1800.* London, 1997.

Blassingame, John W. *Black New Orleans, 1860–1880.* Chicago, 1973.

―――. *The Slave Community: Plantation Life in the Antebellum South.* Rev. and enl. ed. New York, 1979.

Bryant, Jonathan M. *How Curious a Land: Conflict and Change in Greene County, Georgia, 1850–1885.* Chapel Hill, N.C., 1996.

Burnham, W. Dean. *Presidential Ballots, 1836–1892.* Baltimore, 1955.

Caffery, Debbie Fleming. *Carry Me Home: Louisiana Sugar Country Photographs.* Text by Pete Daniel and Anne Wilkes Tucker. Washington, D.C., 1990.

Campbell, Randolph B. *A Southern Community in Crisis: Harrison County, Texas, 1850–1880.* Austin, Tex., 1983.

Capers, Gerald M. *Occupied City: New Orleans under the Federals, 1862–1865.* Lexington, Ky., 1965.

Carter, Dan T. *When the War Was Over: The Failure of Self-Reconstruction in the South, 1865–1867.* Baton Rouge, 1985.

Chaplin, Joyce E. *An Anxious Pursuit: Agricultural Innovation and Modernity in the Lower South, 1730–1815.* Chapel Hill, N.C., 1993.

Coclanis, Peter A. *The Shadow of a Dream: Economic Life and Death in the South Carolina Low Country, 1670–1920.* New York, 1989.

Cohen, Lucy M. *Chinese in the Post–Civil War South: A People without a History.* Baton Rouge, 1984.

Cohen, William. *At Freedom's Edge: Black Mobility and the Southern White Quest for Racial Control, 1861–1915.* Baton Rouge, 1991.

Conrad, Alfred H., and John R. Meyer. *The Economics of Slavery: And Other Studies in Econometric History.* Chicago, 1964.

Courtwright, David T. *Violent Land: Single Men and Social Disorder from the Frontier to the Inner City.* Cambridge, Mass., 1996.

Cox, LaWanda. *Lincoln and Black Freedom: A Study in Presidential Leadership.* Columbia, S.C., 1981.

Cox, LaWanda F., and John H. Cox. *Politics, Principle, and Prejudice, 1865–1866: Dilemma of Reconstruction America.* Glencoe, Ill., 1963.

Current, Richard Nelson. *Three Carpetbag Governors.* Baton Rouge, 1967.

———. *Those Terrible Carpetbaggers.* New York, 1988.

Curtin, Philip D. *The Rise and Fall of the Plantation Complex: Essays in Atlantic History.* Cambridge, U.K., 1990.

Daniel, Pete. *The Shadow of Slavery: Peonage in the South, 1901–1969.* Urbana, Ill., 1972.

Davis, David Brion. *The Problem of Slavery in Western Culture.* Ithaca, N.Y., 1966.

———. *The Problem of Slavery in the Age of Revolution, 1770–1823.* Ithaca, N.Y., 1975.

Davis, Ronald L. F. *Good and Faithful Labor: From Slavery to Sharecropping in the Natchez District, 1860–1890.* Westport, Conn., 1982.

Dawson, Joseph G., III. *Army Generals and Reconstruction: Louisiana, 1862–1877.* Baton Rouge, 1982.

DeCanio, Stephen J. *Agriculture in the Postbellum South: The Economics of Production and Supply.* Cambridge, Mass., 1974.

Deerr, Noel. *The History of Sugar.* 2 vols. London, 1949–1950.

Du Bois, W. E. B. *Black Reconstruction in America.* New York, 1935.

Dusinberre, William. *Them Dark Days: Slavery in the American Rice Swamps*. New York, 1996.

Edwards, Laura F. *Gendered Strife and Confusion: The Political Culture of Reconstruction*. Urbana, Ill., 1997.

Ficklen, John Rose. *History of Reconstruction in Louisiana through 1868*. Baltimore, 1910.

Fields, Barbara Jeanne. *Slavery and Freedom on the Middle Ground: Maryland during the Nineteenth Century*. New Haven, Conn., 1985.

Fischer, Roger A. *The Segregation Struggle in Louisiana, 1862–1877*. Urbana, Ill., 1974.

Fitzgerald, Michael W. *The Union League Movement in the Deep South: Politics and Agricultural Change during Reconstruction*. Baton Rouge, 1989.

Flynn, Charles L., Jr. *White Land, Black Labor: Caste and Class in Late Nineteenth-Century Georgia*. Baton Rouge, 1983.

Fogel, Robert William. *Without Consent or Contract: The Rise and Fall of American Slavery*. New York, 1989.

Fogel, Robert William, and Stanley L. Engerman. *Time on the Cross: The Economics of American Negro Slavery*. 2 vols. Boston, 1974.

Foner, Eric. *Free Soil, Free Labor, Free Men: The Ideology of the Republican Party before the Civil War*. 1970. Reprint, with a new introductory essay, New York, 1995.

———. *Politics and Ideology in the Age of the Civil War*. New York, 1980.

———. *Nothing but Freedom: Emancipation and Its Legacy*. Baton Rouge, 1983.

———. *Reconstruction: America's Unfinished Revolution, 1863–1877*. New York, 1988.

———. *Freedom's Lawmakers: A Directory of Black Officeholders during Reconstruction*. Rev. ed. Baton Rouge, 1996.

Fox-Genovese, Elizabeth. *Within the Plantation Household: Black and White Women of the Old South*. Chapel Hill, N.C., 1988.

Fox-Genovese, Elizabeth, and Eugene D. Genovese. *Fruits of Merchant Capital: Slavery and Bourgeois Property in the Rise and Expansion of Capitalism*. New York, 1983.

Fraser, Walter J., and Winfred B. Moore Jr., eds. *From the Old South to the New: Essays on the Transitional South*. Westport, Conn., 1981.

Gay, Edward James, Jr. *The Free Spirit of St. Louis: The Life and Times of Edward James Gay, 1878–1952*. N.p., [1992].

Genovese, Eugene D. *The Political Economy of Slavery: Studies in the Economy and Society of the Slave South*. New York, 1965.

———. *The World the Slaveholders Made: Two Essays in Interpretation*. New York, 1969.

———. *Roll, Jordan, Roll: The World the Slaves Made*. New York, 1974.

———. *In Red and Black: Marxian Explorations in Southern and Afro-American History*. Knoxville, Tenn., 1984.

———. *The Slaveholders' Dilemma: Freedom and Progress in Southern Conservative Thought, 1820–1860*. Columbia, S.C., 1992.

Gerteis, Louis S. *From Contraband to Freedman: Federal Policy toward Southern Blacks, 1861–1865*. Westport, Conn., 1973.

Gillette, William. *Retreat from Reconstruction, 1869–1879*. Baton Rouge, 1979.

Glickman, Lawrence B. *A Living Wage: American Workers and the Making of Consumer Society.* Ithaca, N.Y., 1997.

Glickstein, Jonathan A. *Concepts of Free Labor in Antebellum America.* New Haven, Conn., 1991.

Glymph, Thavolia, and John J. Kushma, eds. *Essays on the Postbellum Southern Economy.* College Station, Tex., 1985.

Gray, Lewis Cecil. *History of Agriculture in the Southern United States to 1860.* 2 vols. Washington, D.C., 1933.

Green, William A. *British Slave Emancipation: The Sugar Colonies and the Great Experiment.* Oxford, U.K., 1976.

Greene, Glen Lee. *House upon a Rock: About Southern Baptists in Louisiana.* Alexandria, La., 1973.

Gutman, Herbert G. *The Black Family in Slavery and Freedom, 1750–1925.* New York, 1976.

Hahn, Steven. *The Roots of Southern Populism: Yeoman Farmers and the Transformation of the Georgia Upcountry, 1850–1890.* New York, 1983.

Hair, William Ivy. *Bourbonism and Agrarian Protest: Louisiana Politics, 1877–1900.* Baton Rouge, 1969.

Hall, Gwendolyn Midlo. *Africans in Colonial Louisiana: The Development of Afro-Creole Culture in the Eighteenth Century.* Baton Rouge, 1992.

Hanger, Kimberly S. *Bounded Lives, Bounded Places: Free Black Society in Colonial New Orleans, 1769–1803.* Durham, N.C., 1997.

Harris, William C. *With Charity for All: Lincoln and the Restoration of the Union.* Lexington, Ky., 1997.

Hearn, Chester G. *The Capture of New Orleans, 1862.* Baton Rouge, 1995.

————. *When the Devil Came Down to Dixie: Ben Butler in New Orleans.* Baton Rouge, 1997.

Heitmann, John Alfred. *The Modernization of the Louisiana Sugar Industry, 1830–1910.* Baton Rouge, 1987.

Hicks, William. *History of Louisiana Negro Baptists from 1804 to 1914.* Nashville, [n.d.].

Higgs, Robert. *Competition and Coercion: Blacks in the American Economy, 1865–1914.* Cambridge, U.K., 1977.

Hobsbawm, Eric J. *The Age of Capital, 1848–1875.* London, 1975. Reprint, New York, 1996.

————. *The Age of Empire, 1875–1914.* New York, 1987.

Hofstadter, Richard. *The American Political Tradition and the Men Who Made It.* 1948. Reprint, New York, 1974.

Hollandsworth, James G., Jr. *Pretense of Glory: The Life of General Nathaniel P. Banks.* Baton Rouge, 1998.

Holt, Sharon Ann. *Making Freedom Pay: North Carolina Freedpeople Working for Themselves, 1865–1900.* Athens, Ga., 2000.

Holt, Thomas. *The Problem of Freedom: Race, Labor, and Politics in Jamaica and Britain, 1832–1938.* Baltimore, 1992.

Howard, Perry H. *Political Tendencies in Louisiana.* Rev. and exp. ed. Baton Rouge, 1971.

Ingersoll, Thomas N. *Mammon and Manon in Early New Orleans: The First Slave Society in the Deep South, 1718–1819.* Knoxville, Tenn., 1999.

Jaynes, Gerald David. *Branches without Roots: Genesis of the Black Working Class in the American South, 1862–1882.* New York, 1986.

Jones, Jacqueline. *Labor of Love, Labor of Sorrow: Black Women, Work, and the Family from Slavery to the Present.* New York, 1985.

———. *The Dispossessed: America's Underclasses from the Civil War to the Present.* New York, 1992.

Kerr-Ritchie, Jeffrey R. *Freedpeople in the Tobacco South: Virginia, 1860–1900.* Chapel Hill, N.C., 1999.

Kilbourne, Richard Holcombe, Jr. *Debt, Investment, Slaves: Credit Relations in East Feliciana Parish, Louisiana, 1825–1885.* Tuscaloosa, Ala., 1995.

Kousser, J. Morgan. *The Shaping of Southern Politics: Suffrage Restriction and the Establishment of the One-Party South, 1880–1910.* New Haven, Conn., 1974.

Kousser, J. Morgan, and James M. McPherson, eds. *Region, Race, and Reconstruction: Essays in Honor of C. Vann Woodward.* New York, 1982.

Lebergott, Stanley. *Manpower in Economic Growth: The American Record since 1800.* New York, 1964.

Litwack, Leon F. *Been in the Storm So Long: The Aftermath of Slavery.* New York, 1979.

Lonn, Ella. *Reconstruction in Louisiana after 1868.* New York, 1918.

McCrary, Peyton. *Abraham Lincoln and Reconstruction: The Louisiana Experiment.* Princeton, N.J., 1978.

McCurry, Stephanie. *Masters of Small Worlds: Yeoman Households, Gender Relations, and the Political Culture of the Antebellum South Carolina Low Country.* New York, 1995.

McDonald, Roderick A. *The Economy and Material Culture of Slaves: Goods and Chattels on the Sugar Plantations of Jamaica and Louisiana.* Baton Rouge, 1993.

McFeely, William S. *Yankee Stepfather: General O. O. Howard and the Freedmen.* New Haven, Conn., 1968.

McKitrick, Eric L. *Andrew Johnson and Reconstruction.* Chicago, 1960.

McLaurin, Melton Alonza. *The Knights of Labor in the South.* Westport, Conn., 1978.

Magdol, Edward. *A Right to the Land: Essays on the Freedmen's Community.* Westport, Conn., 1977.

Malone, Ann Patton. *Sweet Chariot: Slave Family and Household Structure in Nineteenth-Century Louisiana.* Chapel Hill, N.C., 1992.

Mandle, Jay R. *The Roots of Black Poverty: The Southern Plantation Economy after the Civil War.* Durham, N.C., 1978.

Menn, Joseph Karl. *The Large Slaveholders of Louisiana—1860.* New Orleans, 1964.

Messner, William F. *Freedmen and the Ideology of Free Labor: Louisiana 1862–1865.* Lafayette, La., 1978.

Mintz, Sidney W. *Sweetness and Power: The Place of Sugar in Modern History.* New York, 1985.

Montgomery, David. *Beyond Equality: Labor and the Radical Republicans, 1862–1872.* New York, 1967.

————. *Citizen Worker: The Experience of Workers in the United States with Democracy and the Free Market during the Nineteenth Century.* Cambridge, U.K., 1993.

Moore, Barrington, Jr. *Social Origins of Dictatorship and Democracy: Lord and Peasant in the Making of the Modern World.* Boston, 1966.

Moreno Fraginals, Manuel. *The Sugarmill: The Socioeconomic Complex of Sugar in Cuba, 1760–1860.* Trans. Cedric Belfrage. New York, 1976.

Moreno Fraginals, Manuel, Frank Moya Pons, and Stanley L. Engerman, eds. *Between Slavery and Free Labor: The Spanish Speaking Caribbean in the Nineteenth Century.* Baltimore, 1985.

Novak, Daniel A. *The Wheel of Servitude: Black Forced Labor after Slavery.* Lexington, Ky., 1978.

Oakes, James. *The Ruling Race: A History of American Slaveholders.* New York, 1982.

————. *Slavery and Freedom: An Interpretation of the Old South.* New York, 1990.

Osthaus, Carl R. *Freedmen, Philanthropy, and Fraud: A History of the Freedman's Savings Bank.* Urbana, 1976.

Oubre, Claude F. *Forty Acres and a Mule: The Freedmen's Bureau and Black Land Ownership.* Baton Rouge, 1978.

Painter, Nell Irvin. *Exodusters: Black Migration to Kansas after Reconstruction.* New York, 1976.

Paquette, Robert L. *Sugar Is Made with Blood: The Conspiracy of La Escalera and the Conflict between Empires over Slavery in Cuba.* Middletown, Conn., 1988.

Paskoff, Paul F. *Industrial Evolution: Organization, Structure, and Growth of the Pennsylvania Iron Industry, 1750–1860.* Baltimore, 1983.

Perman, Michael. *The Road to Redemption: Southern Politics, 1869–1879.* Chapel Hill, N.C., 1984.

Phillips, Ulrich Bonnell. *American Negro Slavery: A Survey of the Supply, Employment and Control of Negro Labor As Determined by the Plantation Regime.* New York, 1918. Reprint with a new foreword by Eugene D. Genovese, Baton Rouge, 1966.

————. *Life and Labor in the Old South.* Boston, 1929.

Powell, Lawrence N. *New Masters: Northern Planters during the Civil War and Reconstruction.* New Haven, Conn., 1980.

Ransom, Roger L., and Richard Sutch. *One Kind of Freedom: The Economic Consequences of Emancipation.* Cambridge, U.K., 1977.

Rehder, John B. *Delta Sugar: Louisiana's Vanishing Plantation Landscape.* Baltimore, 1999.

Reid, Joseph D. *Agriculture in the Postbellum South.* New Haven, Conn., 1975.

Reidy, Joseph P. *From Slavery to Agrarian Capitalism in the Cotton Plantation South: Central Georgia, 1800–1880.* Chapel Hill, N.C., 1992.

Ripley, C. Peter. *Slaves and Freedmen in Civil War Louisiana.* Baton Rouge, 1976.

Roark, James L. *Masters without Slaves: Southern Planters in the Civil War and Reconstruction.* New York, 1977.

Roland, Charles P. *Louisiana Sugar Plantations during the American Civil War.* 1957. Reprint with a new foreword by John David Smith, Baton Rouge, 1997.

Rose, Willie Lee. *Rehearsal for Reconstruction: The Port Royal Experiment.* Indianapolis, 1964.

Rousey, Dennis C. *Policing the Southern City: New Orleans, 1805–1889.* Baton Rouge, 1996.

Saville, Julie. *The Work of Reconstruction: From Slave to Wage Laborer in South Carolina, 1860–1870.* Cambridge, U.K., 1994.

Scarpaci, Jean A. *Italian Immigrants in Louisiana's Sugar Parishes: Recruitment, Labor Conditions, and Community Relations, 1880–1910.* New York, 1980.

Schafer, Judith Kelleher. *Slavery, the Civil Law, and the Supreme Court of Louisiana.* Baton Rouge, 1994.

Schmidt, James D. *Free to Work: Labor Law, Emancipation, and Reconstruction, 1815–1880.* Athens, Ga., 1998.

Schmitz, Mark. *Economic Analysis of Antebellum Sugar Plantations in Louisiana.* New York, 1977.

Schwartz, Stuart B. *Sugar Plantations in the Formation of Brazilian Society: Bahia, 1550–1835.* Cambridge, U.K., 1985.

Schweninger, Loren. *Black Property Owners in the South, 1790–1915.* Urbana, Ill., 1990.

Scott, Rebecca J. *Slave Emancipation in Cuba: The Transition to Free Labor, 1860–1899.* Princeton, N.J., 1985.

Shifflett, Crandall A. *Patronage and Poverty in the Tobacco South: Louisa County, Virginia, 1860–1900.* Knoxville, Tenn., 1982.

Shugg, Roger W. *Origins of Class Struggle in Louisiana: A Social History of White Farmers and Laborers during Slavery and After, 1840–1875.* 1939. Reprint, Baton Rouge, 1968.

Sims, Patsy. *Cleveland Benjamin's Dead: Struggle for Dignity in Louisiana's Cane Country.* Exp. ed. Athens, Ga., 1994.

Singletary, Otis A. *Negro Militia and Reconstruction.* Austin, Tex., 1957.

Sitterson, J. Carlyle. *Sugar Country: The Cane Sugar Industry in the South, 1753–1950.* Lexington, Ky., 1953.

Smith, Mark M. *Mastered by the Clock: Time, Slavery, and Freedom in the American South.* Chapel Hill, N.C., 1997.

Stanley, Amy Dru. *From Bondage to Contract: Wage Labor, Marriage, and the Market in the Age of Slave Emancipation.* Cambridge, U.K., 1998.

Stewart, Mart A. *"What Nature Suffers to Groe": Life, Labor, and Landscape on the Georgia Coast, 1680–1920.* Athens, Ga., 1996.

Taylor, Joe Gray. *Negro Slavery in Louisiana.* Baton Rouge, 1963.

———. *Louisiana Reconstructed, 1863–1877.* Baton Rouge, 1974.

Thernstrom, Stephan. *Poverty and Progress: Social Mobility in a Nineteenth Century City.* Cambridge, Mass., 1964. Reprint, New York, 1969.

Tregle, Joseph G., Jr. *Louisiana in the Age of Jackson: A Clash of Cultures and Personalities.* Baton Rouge, 1998.

Trelease, Allen W. *White Terror: The Ku Klux Klan Conspiracy and Southern Reconstruction.* New York, 1971.

Tunnell, Ted. *Crucible of Reconstruction: War, Radicalism, and Race in Louisiana, 1862–1877.* Baton Rouge, 1984.

Usner, Daniel H., Jr. *Indians, Settlers, and Slaves in a Frontier Exchange Economy: The Lower Mississippi Valley before 1783.* Chapel Hill, N.C., 1992.

Vandal, Gilles. *The New Orleans Riot of 1866: Anatomy of a Tragedy.* Lafayette, La., 1983.

———. *Rethinking Southern Violence: Homicides in Post–Civil War Louisiana, 1866–1884.* Columbus, Ohio, 2000.

Vernon, Walter N. *Becoming One People: A History of Louisiana Methodism.* N.p., 1987.

Vincent, Charles. *Black Legislators in Louisiana during Reconstruction.* Baton Rouge, 1976.

Wade, Michael G. *Sugar Dynasty: M. A. Patout & Son, Ltd., 1791–1993.* Lafayette, La., 1995.

Wallerstein, Immanuel. *The Modern World-System.* Vol. 1, *Capitalist Agriculture and the Origins of the European World-Economy in the Sixteenth Century.* New York, 1974.

Wayne, Michael. *The Reshaping of Plantation Society: The Natchez District, 1860–1880.* Baton Rouge, 1983.

Wetta, Frank Joseph. *The Louisiana Scalawags.* Ann Arbor, 1980.

White, Howard A. *The Freedmen's Bureau in Louisiana.* Baton Rouge, 1970.

Whitten, David O. *Andrew Durnford: A Black Sugar Planter in Antebellum Louisiana.* 1981. Reprint with a new introduction, New York, 1995.

Wiener, Jonathan M. *Social Origins of the New South: Alabama, 1860–1885.* Baton Rouge, 1978.

Wilkinson, Alec. *Big Sugar: Seasons in the Cane Fields of Florida.* New York, 1989.

Wilson, Theodore Brantner. *The Black Codes of the South.* University, Ala., 1965.

Winters, John D. *The Civil War in Louisiana.* Baton Rouge, 1963.

Woodman, Harold D. *New South—New Law: The Legal Foundations of Credit and Labor Relations in the Postbellum Agricultural South.* Baton Rouge, 1995.

Woodward, C. Vann. *Reunion and Reaction: The Compromise of 1877 and the End of Reconstruction.* Boston, 1951.

———. *Origins of the New South, 1877–1913.* Baton Rouge, 1951.

———. *The Strange Career of Jim Crow.* New York, 1955.

Wright, Gavin. *The Political Economy of the Cotton South: Households, Markets, and Wealth in the Nineteenth Century.* New York, 1978.

———. *Old South, New South: Revolutions in the Southern Economy since the Civil War.* New York, 1986.

Articles

Abbott, Martin. "Free Land, Free Labor, and the Freedmen's Bureau." *Agricultural History* 30 (October 1956): 150–6.

Amundson, Richard J. "Oakley Plantation: A Post–Civil War Venture in Louisiana Sugar." *Louisiana History* 9 (winter 1968): 21–42.

Armstrong, Thomas F. "From Task Labor to Free Labor: The Transition along Georgia's Rice Coast, 1820–1880." *Georgia Historical Quarterly* 64 (winter 1980): 432–47.

Becnel, Thomas A. "The Ellenders: Pioneer Terrebonne Parish Family, 1840–1924." *Louisiana History* 26 (spring 1985): 117–27.

Binning, F. Wayne. "Carpetbaggers' Triumph: The Louisiana State Election of 1868." *Louisiana History* 14 (winter 1973): 21–39.

Burrows, Geoff, and Ralph Shlomowitz. "The Lag in the Mechanization of the Sugarcane Harvest: Some Comparative Perspectives." *Agricultural History* 66 (summer 1992): 61–75.

Byrne, Frank L. "'A Terrible Machine': General Neal Dow's Military Government on the Gulf Coast." *Civil War History* 12 (March 1966): 5–22.

Cohen, William. "Negro Involuntary Servitude in the South, 1865–1940: A Preliminary Analysis." *Journal of Southern History* 42 (February 1976): 31–60.

———. "Black Immobility and Free Labor: The Freedmen's Bureau and the Relocation of Black Labor, 1865–1868." *Civil War History* 30 (September 1984): 221–34.

Connor, William P. "Reconstruction Rebels: The *New Orleans Tribune* in Post–Civil War Louisiana." *Louisiana History* 21 (spring 1980): 159–81.

Coulter, E. Merton. "Effects of Secession upon the Commerce of the Mississippi Valley." *Mississippi Valley Historical Review* 3 (December 1916): 275–300.

Cox, LaWanda F. "The American Agricultural Wage Earner, 1865–1900: The Emergence of a Modern Labor Problem." *Agricultural History* 22 (April 1948): 95–114.

———. "The Promise of Land for the Freedmen." *Mississippi Valley Historical Review* 45 (December 1958): 413–40.

Dabney, Thomas Ewing. "The Butler Regime in Louisiana." *Louisiana Historical Quarterly* 27 (April 1944): 487–526.

Davis, Donald W. "Ratification of the Constitution of 1868—Record of Votes." *Louisiana History* 6 (summer 1965): 301–5.

Delatte, Carolyn E. "The St. Landry Riot: A Forgotten Incident of Reconstruction Violence." *Louisiana History* 17 (winter 1976): 41–9.

Dew, Charles B. "The Long Lost Returns: The Candidates and Their Totals in Louisiana's Secession Election." *Louisiana History* 10 (fall 1969): 353–69.

———. "Who Won the Secession Election in Louisiana?" *Journal of Southern History* 36 (February 1970): 18–32.

Du Bois, W. E. B. "The Freedmen's Bureau." *Atlantic Monthly* 87 (March 1901): 354–65.

Dufour, Charles L. "The Age of Warmoth." *Louisiana History* 6 (fall 1965): 335–64.

Eiss, Paul K. "A Share in the Land: Freedpeople and the Government of Labour in Southern Louisiana, 1862–65." *Slavery and Abolition* 19 (April 1998): 46–89.

Engelsman, John Cornelius. "The Freedmen's Bureau in Louisiana." *Louisiana Historical Quarterly* 32 (January 1949): 145–224.

Engerman, Stanley L. "Contract Labor, Sugar, and Technology in the Nineteenth Century." *Journal of Economic History* 43 (September 1983): 635–59.

———. "Slavery and Emancipation in Comparative Perspective: A Look at Some Recent Debates." *Journal of Economic History* 46 (June 1986): 317–39.

Everett, Donald E. "Demands of the New Orleans Free Colored Population for Political Equality, 1862–1865." *Louisiana Historical Quarterly* 38 (April 1955): 43–64.

Faust, Drew Gilpin. "Culture, Conflict, and Community: The Meaning of Power on an Ante-Bellum Plantation." *Journal of Social History* 14 (fall 1980): 83–97.

Ferleger, Louis. "Productivity Change in the Post-Bellum Louisiana Sugar Industry." In *Time Series Analysis,* ed. O. D. Anderson and M. R. Perryman, 147–61. New York, 1981.

———. "Farm Mechanization in the Southern Sugar Sector after the Civil War." *Louisiana History* 23 (winter 1982): 21–34.

———. "Cutting the Cane: Harvesting in the Louisiana Sugar Industry." *Southern Studies* 23 (spring 1984): 42–59.

———. "The Problem of 'Labor' in the Post-Reconstruction Louisiana Sugar Industry." *Agricultural History* 72 (spring 1998): 140–58.

Fields, Barbara Jeanne. "Ideology and Race in American History." In *Region, Race, and Reconstruction: Essays in Honor of C. Vann Woodward,* ed. J. Morgan Kousser and James M. McPherson, 143–77. New York, 1982.

———. "The Nineteenth-Century American South: History and Theory." *Plantation Society in the Americas* 2 (April 1983): 7–27.

Gonzales, John Edmond. "William Pitt Kellogg, Reconstruction Governor of Louisiana, 1873–1877." *Louisiana Historical Quarterly* 29 (April 1946): 394–495.

Gould, Jeffrey. "Louisiana Sugar War: The Strike of 1887." *Southern Exposure* 12 (November/December 1984): 45–55.

Greer, James Kimmins. "Louisiana Politics, 1845–1861." *Louisiana Historical Quarterly* 12 (July 1929): 381–425; (October 1929): 555–610; 13 (January 1930): 67–116; (April 1930): 257–303; (July 1930): 444–83; (October 1930): 617–54.

Gutman, Herbert G. "The Reality of the Rags-to-Riches 'Myth': The Case of the Paterson, New Jersey, Locomotive, Iron, and Machinery Manufacturers, 1830–1880." In *Work, Culture, and Society in Industrializing America: Essays in American Working-Class and Social History.* New York, 1976.

Hackett, D. L. A. "Slavery, Ethnicity, and Sugar: An Analysis of Voting Behaviour in Louisiana, 1828–1844." *Louisiana Studies* 13 (summer 1974): 73–118.

Hahn, Steven. "Class and State in Postemancipation Societies: Southern Planters in Comparative Perspective." *American Historical Review* 95 (February 1990): 75–98.

Hall, Douglas. "The Flight from the Estates Reconsidered: The British West Indies, 1838–42." *Journal of Caribbean History* 10 and 11 (1978): 7–24.

Heitmann, John A. "Organization As Power: The Louisiana Sugar Planters' Association and the Creation of Scientific and Technical Institutions, 1877–1910." *Louisiana History* 27 (summer 1986): 281–94.

Hennessey, Melinda Meek. "Race and Violence in Reconstruction New Orleans: The 1868 Riot." *Louisiana History* 20 (winter 1979): 77–91.

Hilliard, Sam B. "Site Characteristics and Spatial Stability of the Louisiana Sugarcane Industry." *Agricultural History* 53 (January 1979): 254–69.

Jones, Howard J. "Biographical Sketches of Members of the 1868 Louisiana State Senate." *Louisiana History* 19 (winter 1978): 65–110.

Kendall, Lane Carter. "The Interregnum in Louisiana in 1861." *Louisiana Historical Quarterly* 16 (April 1933): 175–208; (July 1933): 374–408; (October 1933): 639–69; 17 (January 1934): 124–38; (April 1934): 339–48; (July 1934): 524–36.

Lathrop, Barnes F. "The Lafourche District in 1862: Invasion." *Louisiana History* 2 (spring 1961): 175–201.

Leach, Marguerite T. "The Aftermath of Reconstruction in Louisiana." *Louisiana Historical Quarterly* 32 (July 1949): 631–717.

Lerner, Eugene M. "Southern Output and Agricultural Income, 1860–1880." *Agricultural History* 33 (July 1959): 117–25.

Lestage, H. Oscar, Jr. "The White League in Louisiana and Its Participation in Reconstruction Riots." *Louisiana Historical Quarterly* 18 (July 1935): 617–95.

McDaniel, Hilda Mulvey. "Francis Tillou Nicholls and the End of Reconstruction." *Louisiana Historical Quarterly* 32 (April 1949): 357–513.

McDonald, Roderick A. "Independent Economic Production by Slaves on Antebellum Louisiana Sugar Plantations." *Slavery and Abolition* 12 (May 1991): 182–208.

McGinty, G. W. "Changes in Louisiana Agriculture, 1860–1880." *Louisiana Historical Quarterly* 18 (April 1935): 407–29.

McGowan, James T. "Planters without Slaves: Origins of a New World Labor System." *Southern Studies* 16 (spring 1977): 5–26.

McLure, Mary Lilla. "The Elections of 1860 in Louisiana." *Louisiana Historical Quarterly* 9 (October 1926): 601–702.

Marable, Manning. "The Politics of Black Land Tenure, 1877–1915." *Agricultural History* 53 (January 1979): 142–52.

May, J. Thomas. "The Freedmen's Bureau at the Local Level: A Study of a Louisiana Agent." *Louisiana History* 9 (winter 1968): 5–19.

Messner, William F. "Black Violence and White Response: Louisiana, 1862." *Journal of Southern History* 41 (February 1974): 19–38.

Moody, V. Alton. "Slavery on Louisiana Sugar Plantations." *Louisiana Historical Quarterly* 7 (April 1924): 191–301.

Moran, Robert E. "Local Black Elected Officials in Ascension Parish (1868–1878)." *Louisiana History* 27 (summer 1986): 273–80.

Pace, Robert F. " 'It Was Bedlam Let Loose': The Louisiana Sugar Country and the Civil War." *Louisiana History* 39 (fall 1998): 389–409.

Pfeifer, Michael J. "Lynching and Criminal Justice in South Louisiana, 1878–1930." *Louisiana History* 40 (spring 1999): 155–77.

Phillips, Ulrich Bonnell. "Plantations with Slave Labor and Free." *American Historical Review* 30 (July 1925): 738–53.

Pitre, Althea D. "The Collapse of the Warmoth Regime, 1870–1872." *Louisiana History* 6 (spring 1965): 161–87.

Postell, Paul Everett. "John Hampden Randolph, A Louisiana Planter." *Louisiana Historical Quarterly* 25 (January 1942): 149–223.

Prichard, Walter. "Routine on a Louisiana Sugar Plantation under the Slavery Regime." *Mississippi Valley Historical Review* 14 (September 1927): 168–78.

———. "The Effects of the Civil War on the Louisiana Sugar Industry." *Journal of Southern History* 5 (August 1939): 315–32.

Rankin, David C. "The Origins of Black Leadership in New Orleans during Reconstruction." *Journal of Southern History* 40 (August 1974): 417–40.

Razek, Joseph R. "Accounting on the Old Plantation: A Study of the Financial Records on an Ante-Bellum Louisiana Sugar Plantation." *Accounting Historians Journal* 12 (spring 1985): 17–36.

Reid, Joseph D., Jr. "Sharecropping As an Understandable Market Response: The Post-Bellum South." *Journal of Economic History* 33 (March 1973): 106–30.

Reidy, Joseph P. "Mules and Machines and Men: Field Labor on Louisiana Sugar Plantations, 1887–1915." *Agricultural History* 72 (spring 1998): 183–96.

Richter, William L. "James Longstreet: From Rebel to Scalawag." *Louisiana History* 11 (summer 1970): 215–30.

Robinson, Armstead L. "Beyond the Realm of Social Consensus: New Meanings of Reconstruction for American History." *Journal of American History* 68 (September 1981): 276–97.

Rodrigue, John C. " 'The Great Law of Demand and Supply': The Contest over Wages in Louisiana's Sugar Region, 1870–1880." *Agricultural History* 72 (spring 1998): 159–82.

———. "The Freedmen's Bureau and Wage Labor in the Louisiana Sugar Region." In *The Freedmen's Bureau and Reconstruction: Reconsiderations*, ed. Paul A. Cimbala and Randall M. Miller, 198–218. New York, 1999.

———. "Labor Militancy and Black Grassroots Political Mobilization in the Louisiana Sugar Region, 1865–1868." *Journal of Southern History* 67 (February 2001): 115–42.

Roland, Charles P. "Difficulties of Civil War Sugar Planting in Louisiana." *Louisiana Historical Quarterly* 38 (October 1955): 40–62.

———. "Louisiana and Secession." *Louisiana History* 19 (fall 1978): 389–99.

Rusk, Jerrold G., and John J. Stucker, "The Effect of the Southern System of Election Laws on Voting Participation: A Reply to V. O. Key, Jr." In *The History of American Electoral Behavior*, ed. Joel H. Sibley, Allan C. Bogue, and William H. Flanagan, 198–250. Princeton, N.J., 1978.

Russell, Sarah. "Ethnicity, Commerce, and Community on Lower Louisiana's Plantation Frontier, 1803–1828." *Louisiana History* 40 (fall 1999): 389–405.

Saloutos, Theodore. "Southern Agriculture and the Problems of Readjustment: 1865–1877." *Agricultural History* 30 (April 1956): 58–76.

Saville, Julie. "Grassroots Reconstruction: Agricultural Labour and Collective Action in South Carolina, 1860–1868." *Slavery and Abolition* 12 (December 1991): 173–82.

———. "Rites and Power: Reflections on Slavery, Freedom, and Political Ritual." In *From Slavery to Emancipation in the Atlantic World*, ed. Sylvia R. Frey and Betty Wood, 81–102. London, 1999.

Savitt, Todd. "Black Health on the Plantation: Masters, Slaves, and Physicians." *Medical Heritage* 2 (September/October 1986): 368–82.

Scarborough, Thomas A. H. "The Bislands of Natchez: Sugar, Secession, and Strategies for Survival." *Journal of Mississippi History* 58 (spring 1996): 23–62.

Scarpaci, Jean Ann. "Immigrants in the New South: Italians in Louisiana's Sugar Parishes, 1880–1910." *Labor History* 16 (spring 1975): 165–83.

Schmitz, Mark D. "Postbellum Developments in the Louisiana Cane Sugar Industry." *Business and Economic History*, 2nd ser., 5 (1976): 88–101.

——. "Economies of Scale and Farm Size in the Antebellum Sugar Sector." *Journal of Economic History* 37 (December 1977): 959–80.

——. "The Transformation of the Southern Cane Sugar Sector, 1860–1930." *Agricultural History* 53 (January 1979): 270–85.

Scott, Rebecca J. "Comparing Emancipations: A Review Essay." *Journal of Social History* 20 (spring 1987): 565–83.

——. "Exploring the Meaning of Freedom: Postemancipation Societies in Comparative Perspective." *Hispanic American Historical Review* 68 (August 1988): 407–28.

——. "Defining the Boundaries of Freedom in the World of Cane: Cuba, Brazil, and Louisiana after Emancipation." *American Historical Review* 99 (February 1994): 70–102.

——. " 'Stubborn and Disposed to Stand Their Ground': Black Militia, Sugar Workers, and Dynamics of Collective Action in the Louisiana Sugar Bowl, 1863–87." In *From Slavery to Emancipation in the Atlantic World*, ed. Sylvia R. Frey and Betty Wood, 103–26. London, 1999.

Shlomowitz, Ralph. "The Origins of Southern Sharecropping." *Agricultural History* 53 (July 1979): 557–75.

——. "Plantations and Smallholdings: Comparative Perspectives from the World Cotton and Sugar Cane Economies, 1865–1939." *Agricultural History* 58 (January 1984): 1–16.

——. " 'Bound' or 'Free'? Black Labor in Cotton and Sugarcane Farming, 1865–1880." *Journal of Southern History* 50 (November 1984): 569–96.

Shugg, Roger W. "A Suppressed Co-Operationist Protest against Secession." *Louisiana Historical Quarterly* 19 (January 1936): 199–203.

——. "Survival of the Plantation System in Louisiana." *Journal of Southern History* 3 (August 1937): 311–25.

Singletary, Otis A. "The Election of 1878 in Louisiana." *Louisiana Historical Quarterly* 40 (January 1957): 46–53.

Sitterson, J. Carlyle. "Magnolia Plantation, 1852–1862: A Decade of a Louisiana Sugar Estate." *Mississippi Valley Historical Review* 25 (September 1938): 197–210.

——. "The McCollams: A Planter Family of the Old and New South." *Journal of Southern History* 6 (August 1940): 347–67.

——. "The William J. Minor Plantations: A Study in Ante-Bellum Absentee Ownership." *Journal of Southern History* 9 (February 1943): 59–74.

————. "The Transition from Slave to Free Economy on the William J. Minor Plantations." *Agricultural History* 17 (October 1943): 216–24.

————. "Hired Labor on Sugar Plantations of the Ante-Bellum South." *Journal of Southern History* 14 (May 1948): 192–205.

————. "Lewis Thompson, A Carolinian and His Louisiana Plantation, 1848–1888: A Study in Absentee Ownership." In *Essays in Southern History,* ed. Fletcher Green, 16–27. Chapel Hill, N.C., 1949.

Smith, John David. "More Than Slaves, Less Than Freedmen: The 'Share Wages' Labor System during Reconstruction." *Civil War History* 26 (September 1980): 256–66.

Summers, Mark W. "The Moderates' Last Chance: The Louisiana Election of 1865." *Louisiana History* 24 (winter 1983): 49–69.

Taylor, Joe Gray. "Slavery in Louisiana during the Civil War." *Louisiana History* 8 (winter 1967): 27–34.

Toledano, Roulhac B. "Louisiana's Golden Age: Valcour Aime in St. James Parish." *Louisiana History* 10 (summer 1969): 211–24.

Tregle, Joseph G. "Louisiana and the Tariff, 1816–1846." *Louisiana Historical Quarterly* 25 (January 1942): 24–148.

Tunnell, Ted. "The Negro, the Republican Party, and the Election of 1876 in Louisiana." *Louisiana History* 7 (spring 1966): 101–16.

————. "Free Negroes and the Freedmen: Black Politics in New Orleans during the Civil War." *Southern Studies* 19 (spring 1980): 5–28.

Usner, Daniel H., Jr. "From African Captivity to American Slavery: The Introduction of Black Laborers to Colonial Louisiana." *Louisiana History* 20 (winter 1979): 25–48.

Vandal, Gilles. "The Origins of the New Orleans Riot of 1866, Revisited." *Louisiana History* 22 (spring 1981): 135–65.

————. "'Bloody Caddo': White Violence against Blacks in a Louisiana Parish, 1865–1876." *Journal of Social History* 25 (winter 1991): 373–88.

————. "Black Utopia in Early Reconstruction New Orleans: The People's Bakery As a Case-Study." *Louisiana History* 38 (fall 1997): 437–52.

Vincent, Charles. "Negro Leadership and Programs in the Louisiana Constitutional Convention of 1868." *Louisiana History* 10 (fall 1969): 339–51.

Wetta, Frank J. "'Bulldozing the Scalawags': Some Examples of the Persecution of Southern White Republicans in Louisiana during Reconstruction." *Louisiana History* 21 (winter 1980): 43–58.

Whitten, David O. "Tariff and Profit in the Antebellum Louisiana Sugar Industry." *Business History Review* 44 (summer 1970): 226–33.

————. "Sugar Slavery: A Profitability Model for Slave Investment in the Antebellum Louisiana Sugar Industry." *Louisiana Studies* 12 (1973): 423–42.

————. "Medical Care of Slaves: Louisiana Sugar Region and South Carolina Rice District." *Southern Studies* 16 (summer 1977): 153–80.

Wiener, Jonathan M. "Class Structure and Economic Development in the American South, 1865–1955." *American Historical Review* 84 (October 1979): 970–92.

Williams, E. Russ, Jr. "Louisiana's Public and Private Immigration Endeavors: 1866–1893." *Louisiana History* 15 (spring 1974): 153–73.

Wilson, James D., Jr. "The Donaldsonville Incident of 1870: A Study of Local Party Dissension and Republican Infighting in Reconstruction Louisiana." *Louisiana History* 38 (summer 1997): 329–45.

Woodman, Harold D. "New Perspectives on Southern Economic Development: A Comment." *Agricultural History* 49 (April 1975): 374–80.

———. "Sequel to Slavery: The New History Views the Postbellum South." *Journal of Southern History* 43 (November 1977): 523–54.

———. "Post–Civil War Southern Agriculture and the Law." *Agricultural History* 53 (January 1979): 319–37.

———. "The Old South: Global and Local Perspectives on Power, Politics, and Ideology." *Civil War History* 25 (December 1979): 339–51.

———. "Postbellum Social Change and Its Effects on Marketing the South's Cotton Crop." *Agricultural History* 56 (January 1982): 215–30.

———. "The Economic and Social History of the Post-Emancipation South." *Trends in History* 3 (fall 1982): 37–56.

———. "How New Was the New South?" *Agricultural History* 58 (October 1984): 529–45.

Wooster, Ralph. "The Louisiana Secession Convention." *Louisiana Historical Quarterly* 34 (April 1951): 103–33.

Wright, Gavin. "Postbellum Southern Labor Markets." In *Quantity & Quiddity: Essays in U.S. Economic History,* ed. Peter Kilby, 98–134. Middletown, Conn., 1987.

Zeichner, Oscar. "The Transition from Slave to Free Agricultural Labor in the Southern States." *Agricultural History* 13 (January 1939): 22–32.

Dissertations and Unpublished Papers

Binning, Francis Wayne. "Henry Clay Warmoth and Louisiana Reconstruction." Ph.D. diss., University of North Carolina, 1969.

Follett, Richard J. "The Sugar Masters: Slavery, Economic Development, and Modernization on Louisiana Sugar Plantations, 1820–1860." Ph.D. diss., Louisiana State University, 1997.

Gould, Jeffrey. "'Heroic and Vigorous Action': An Analysis of the Sugar Cane Workers' Strike in Lafourche Parish, November, 1887." Unpublished manuscript, 1983.

Lathrop, Barnes Fletcher. "The Pugh Plantations, 1860–1865: A Study of Life in Lower Louisiana." Ph.D. diss., University of Texas, 1945.

McGowan, James Thomas. "Creation of a Slave Society: Louisiana Plantations in the Eighteenth Century." Ph.D. diss., University of Rochester, 1976.

Michot, Stephen Scott. "Society at War: Sectionalism, Secession, and Civil War in Louisiana's Lafourche Region." Ph.D. diss., Mississippi State University, 1994.

Reidy, Joseph P. "Sugar and Freedom: Emancipation in Louisiana's Sugar Parishes." Paper delivered at the annual meeting of the American Historical Association, 1980.

Robinson, Armstead. "Day of Jubilo: Civil War and the Demise of Slavery in the Mississippi Valley, 1861–1865." Ph.D. diss., University of Rochester, 1976.

Russell, Sarah. "Cultural Conflicts or Common Interests: The Making of the Sugar Planter Class in Louisiana, 1795–1853." Ph.D. diss., University of Maryland, 2000.

Sacher, John Michael. "'A Perfect War': Politics and Parties in Louisiana, 1824–1861." Ph.D. diss., Louisiana State University, 1999.

INDEX